An Analysis of Policy Implementation in the Third World

MARCUS POWELL

Ashgate

Aldershot • Brookfield USA • Singapore • Sydney

Published by
Ashgate Publishing Ltd
Gower House
Croft Road
Aldershot
Hants GU11 3HR
England

Ashgate Publishing Company
Old Post Road
Brookfield
Vermont 05036
USA

British Library Cataloguing in Publication Data
Powell, Marcus
    An analysis of policy implementation in the Third World
    1. Vocational education - Jamaica 2 .Vocational education -
    Gambia 3. Technical education - Jamaica 4. Technical
    education - Gambia 5. Education and state - Jamaica
    6. Education and state - Gambia 7. Vocational education -
    Jamaica - Administration 8. Vocational education Gambia -
    Administration 9. Technical education - Jamaica -
    Administration 10. Technical education - Gambia -
    Administration
    I.Title
    379.6'651

Library of Congress Catalog Card Number: 98-74140

ISBN 1 85972 702 6

Printed and bound by Athenaeum Press, Ltd.,
Gateshead, Tyne & Wear.

Contents

List of figures and tables

List of abbreviations

Acronyms used in the case studies of Jamaica and of The Gambia

CGLI: City and Guilds of London Institute.
CID: Canadian International Development Agency
CNC: Computer Numeric Control
EEC: European Economic Commission
ERP: Economic Reform Programme
HOD: Head of Department
HNC: Higher National Certificate
HRD: Human Resource Development
IDB: International Development Bank
ILO: International Labour Organisation
IMF: International Monetary Fund
MOE: Ministry of Education
NGO: Non-governmental Organisation
ODA: Overseas Development Administration
ONC: Ordinary National Certificate
OND: Ordinary National Diploma
PIU: Project Implementation Unit
RSA: Royal Society of Arts
TVET: Technical and Vocational Education and Training
UNDP: United Nations Development Programme
USAID: United States Agency for International Development
VSO: Voluntary Services Overseas

Acronyms used in the case study of Jamaica

ACCC: Association of Canadian Community Colleges
ALA: Approved Lending Agencies
BCS: British Computer Society
BSTP: Basic Skills Training Projects
CAST: College of Arts, Science and Technology
CBI: Caribbean Basin Initiative
CSJ: Computer Society of Jamaica
CXC: Caribbean Examination Certificate
EDP: Electronic Data Processing

EXC:	Entrepreneurial Extension Centre
HEART:	Human Employment and Resource Training
ICL:	International Computers Limited
ITCs:	Industrial Training Centres
JAGAS:	Jamaican and German Automotive School
JIDC:	Jamaican Industrial Development Corporation
JLP:	Jamaican Labour Party
MYCD:	Ministry of Youth and Community Development
NDA:	National Development Agency
NFED:	Non-Formal Education Division
NTA:	National Training Agency
PED:	Planning and Evaluation Division
PNP:	People's National Party
SSF:	Self Start Fund
SDC:	Social Development Commission
SLP:	School Leavers Programme
SRC:	Scientific Research Council
TMI:	Tool Makers Institute
VTDI:	Vocational and Technical, Development Institute
UWI:	University of West Indies

Acronyms used in The Gambian case study

BSC:	Banjul Skills Centre
CAD:	Computer Aided Design
CAPA:	Commonwealth Associations of Polytechnics in Africa
CVEP:	Continuing Village Education Programme
DNVTP:	Directorate for National Vocational Training Programmes
DTEVT:	Directorate of Technical Education and Vocational Training.
ESD:	Entrepreneurial Skill Development
ESDU:	Entrepreneurial skill Development unit
FTC:	Full Technological Certificate
GAMTEL:	Gambia Public Telephone Company
GPTC:	Gambia Public Transport Company
GUC:	Gambia Utilities Co-operation
GTTI:	Gambia, Technical, Training Institute
GTZ:	Gesellschaft fur Technische Zusammenarbeit
HTTC:	Higher Technical Teachers Certificate
IBAS:	Indigenous Business Advisory Service
IVTCs:	In-village Training Centres
NVTB:	National Vocational Training Board
NCTEVT:	National Council for Technical Education and Vocational Training

NVTC: National Vocational Training Centre
MFCs: Mixed Farming Centres
PTQ: Professional Teaching Qualification
RTITSU: Rural Technical Instructor Training and Services Unit
RVTP: Rural Vocational Training Programme
RVTC: Rural Vocational Training Centre
TANGO: The Association of Non-governmental Organisations

Acknowledgements

A number of people have played a vital role in the production of this book. In particular, I would like to express my gratitude to colleagues at the Centre for Labour Market Studies, especially Cheryl Gagin and Richard Errington for their valuable comments on the final draft. Other staff also provided useful suggestions, including Dr. Margaret Black and Dr. Alan Felstead.

Thanks are also due to Dr. Y. Benett at Huddersfield University, for supporting and supervising the original thesis on which this book is based. Special thanks are also due to a number of Jamaicans and Gambians who assisted in the difficult process of collecting data for the present study. Amongst those who played an invaluable role were Mr. K. Christian and Mrs J. Mackenzie in Jamaica; and Mr.A.Bittaye, Mr.E.Dondeh Mr.M.N'jie, Mr.O.N'jie and Mr.B. Sosseh in The Gambia. Finally, I would like to thank Dr.G.Powell, Mr.A. Holt, and Mr. L. Owen for their support and friendship at difficult times during the research

Introduction

This book presents the findings of a study on policy implementation in Jamaica and The Gambia conducted between 1991 and 1996. The aim of the study was to document and analyse the processes involved in implementing Technical and Vocational Education and Training (TVET) policies in these two Third World countries. Before discussing the finer details of the study it is useful to define what is precisely meant by the terms 'Third World' and 'post-secondary TVET'. Although, the author recognises the limitations of the term 'Third World', including its assumptions that development is an evolutionary process and all such countries are a homogeneous group, it still provides a useful means of differentiating low income developing countries of the south from those of the industrialised north. Indeed, the former normally share a colonial past, their economies are often characterised by structural weaknesses, they are dependent on overseas aid, and the majority of employment opportunities are to be found in the informal sector. In contrast, the latter have traditionally had a relatively advanced technological base, a higher GNP per capita and a well developed infrastructure (Clapham, 1990).

In relation to the term 'post-secondary TVET' the study looked at developments in formal and non-formal public TVET institutions. The difference between the two is that formal TVET institutions, such as technical colleges, deliver formalised programmes of study where emphasis is given to theory rather than practice. Whereas non-formal institutions, characterised by skill training centres, normally focus on the practical activities associated with acquiring particular skills rather than the theory behind them (Halliwell, 1986). Besides focusing on developments within the public sector TVET institutions, the study also looked at programmes that supported company or non-governmental forms of provision.

When the research started for this present piece of work at the beginning of the 1990s, not much was known about the process involved in implementing post-secondary TVET policies, or of the roles played by different actors in the process (Carron, 1984). Much of the existing work at the time appeared to focus on two issues. The first of these concerned the issue of manpower planning and the extent to which a country was capable of achieving best fit in terms of the relationship between the supply and demand of its human resources. After decades of experience it is generally recognised that labour markets are more complicated and unpredictable than the former models assumed (Psacharopoulos, 1991; Gray et al, 1993). This has resulted in a shift toward using labour market analysis as a means of informing policy makers (Steele, 1991). Unsurprisingly, numerous studies also started to analyse how labour markets operated in the Third World, with the majority of these arguing that

1

any departure from perfectly competitive labour markets will discourage training, reduce employment and impede economic development (Marshall, 1994; Rama, 1995).

The second most important issue in the literature appeared to be which type of system or approach was most suited to the particular socio-economic or political context of an individual country (see Godwin, 1990, Ishumi, 1988, Oxtoby, 1994 or World Bank, 1991c). This lack of interest in the implementation process until recently appears strange, given the significant role of aid agencies in supporting TVET in the Third World. One of the major players in this field is the International Labour Organisation (ILO) who played an instrumental role in vocationalising Kenya's education system during the 1960s (Sifuna, 1992). However, the greatest influence has come from the World Bank, where TVET was at the cornerstone of the organisation's lending policies during the 1970s, and to a certain extent the 1990s. Indeed, data from the World Bank shows that 40 per cent of the organisation's lending for education during this period went on TVET, with 80 per cent of this supporting pre-employment training (World Bank, 1991b). In this respect, the present study proposed to focus on the complexities involved in implementing TVET initiatives in Jamaica and The Gambia, by looking at developments in the public and private sector.

Implementation within the Public Sector

In dealing with the implementation process at public sector TVET institutions, the study aimed to achieve a number of interrelated objectives. First, it had to document the organisational structures involved in the process of implementation in both countries. This involved an investigation of the various ministerial and TVET institutions operating in each country, and also a study of their relationship to each other vis-à-vis the implementation process. Secondly, the study had to identify the actual initiatives being implemented under each Ministry or at each public TVET institution, including their objectives and sources of funding.

The subject of policy implementation at public institutions has recently begun to attract attention, particularly amongst donor agencies who finance aid projects in the Third World. This interest not only stems from the poor record of past overseas aid projects, but is also due to the increased importance attached to the issues of accountability and efficiency. For example, in an extensive review of 550 of its own educational projects, implemented in the Third World, the World Bank found that no less than half were unsustainable (World Bank, 1990). A similar type of evaluation by the United States Agency for International Development found that 90 per cent of their own educational projects in Third World were also unsustainable (Kean et al, 1988).

The same donor agencies have also financed studies into why these projects were unsustainable in the long-term. One of the most comprehensive of these focused on the implementation experiences of education policies in Sub-Saharan Africa (Craig, 1990). In simplistic terms,

2

the same study found a large number of reasons why policy implementation was so problematic in this part of the world. These ranged from the overambitious aims of such policies, to the way in which they were locally managed. Another consideration in Craig's study was the negative impact of the organisational structures through which the policies passed. The issue of internal structures was a central theme in many World Bank policy documents. For example, in an important publication, outlining the Bank's view on TVET, the organisation suggested how Third World countries could improve their implementation capacity (World Bank, 1991c). According to this study a number of conditions are necessary for successful policy implementation. One of the most important included the participation of employers and employees in the management of the country's TVET system. Another important issue was the provision of adequate funding to ensure a greater commitment from managers and professionals involved in TVET.

The International Labour Organisation has also undertaken research into what are the most important conditions for the successful implementation of aid projects in the Third World (see Herschbach, 1997). Within this work, emphasis is given to the importance of understanding the context in which implementation takes place. Understandably, if a policy or project is not based on a total understanding of the environment or situation then it is very likely to experience implementation difficulties or be unsustainable in the long-term.

However, one of the major limitations of studies conducted or supported by donor agencies is their failure to critically analyse their own influence on the implementation process. For example, what is the nature or role played by a donor agency in the implementation process? Similarly, how are aid-funded projects in the Third World started and what roles do local personnel play in their management and implementation? How do the former issues affect whether a project is successful in achieving its stated objectives? Answers to these issues could help us explain why many aid-funded projects experience difficulties and why so many need the continual support of technical assistance and overseas aid (King, 1992).

Thus, an important issue in the present study was what role did external actors play in the implementation of projects at TVET institutions and what impact did this dependency have? Although the study recognises the usefulness of dependency theory (Larrain, 1989) as a framework of reference, in terms of how development or even implementation could be explained by the unequal relationship between the First World (the core) and the Third World (the periphery), it also recognises its limitations. Indeed, the present study neglected the pessimistic and deterministic nature of dependency theory and instead sought to investigate the extent and influence of dependence on the First World in relation to implementation. In this respect the present study was particularly concerned with how dependence on foreign technical assistance, either in the form of consultants or scholarships, or components obtained from overseas, affected the process of implementation at TVET institutions. By adopting such an approach, the study was also able to link how decision-making processes, either in the

3

initiation or management of a project, could affect whether it was successfully implemented or not. That is to say, to what extent were decisions relating to a project's implementation dominated by aid agencies and what impact did this have?

A variety of different types of projects were analysed in the present study (9 in Jamaica and 10 in The Gambia), ranging from those that supported export-led growth strategies to others that were more concerned with providing basic skills training for those living in rural areas. They also varied in cost, ranging from U$10,000 right up to U$60 million. Nevertheless, the majority of the projects implemented in the two countries were concerned with supporting developments in entrepreneurship or information technology, or with supporting the continuing and professional development of staff working at TVET institutions. The prominence of projects in these areas probably reflects the commitment of donor agencies, and the host governments in the two countries, towards financing initiatives in these areas. Indeed, given that the majority of employment opportunities in the two countries are found in the informal sector it is not surprising that increased emphasis is being given towards entrepreneurship, whether in the form of supporting people to establish their own businesses or encouraging attitudinal changes amongst young people. Some would view the encouragement of entrepreneurs as crucial to the success or failure of a nation's development (Roberts, 1995). At the same time those who graduate from TVET institutions and wish to work in the formal sector, (or even in the informal sector), need to have a good understanding of recent developments in information technology. This is particularly so given the advances which have occurred in personal computers and telecommunications. It has been be argued that the application of information technology could be a means of enabling Third World countries to leap over obstacles to development (Hanna, 1991). Thus, it is not surprising that projects supporting computing and information technology have also been given a high priority in the two countries.

For the final of the initiatives, the continual and professional development of staff at TVET institutions, there is a clear need for staff at institutions in each of the two countries to respond to external pressures, such as those resulting from the need for entrepreneurship training, and also internal pressures, including those resulting from the need to improve the management of resources (in order to reduce dependence on overseas institutions for training and for the validation of its courses). Understandably, it also easy to see why increasing importance is being given to the continual and professional development of staff at TVET institutions in the two countries.

Implementation within the Private Sector

The decision to look at private sector provision was taken because of the increased emphasis being given towards 'rolling back the state' and improving the operation of market forces (World Bank, 1991a). The market approach to development has its origins in neo-classical economics, and as such, is concerned with the role played by the private sector and market forces in a country's development. Since the collapse of Communism, the market has been seen by many Development theorists and overseas aid agencies, as the motor for Third World development. At the end of the 1980s, for example, the World Bank attributed the stagnation and decline of economies in Sub-Saharan Africa to mismanagement of national resources by excessive state intervention and lack of effective market forces. Furthermore, the World Bank (1989d) recommended that African states might reverse their decline through introducing conditions that promote the effectiveness of market forces.

However, in relation to TVET the interest in private sector provision has also stemmed from a general disillusionment with traditional manpower planning models and due to the high cost of institutional-based training, particularly that aimed at technical manpower provision (Gray *et al*, 1993). It is also assumed that employees who receive training within the workplace are more likely to use their skills for the purpose intended than graduates of TVET institutions. Another contributory factor was the high opportunity cost of providing TVET. Indeed, estimates suggest that TVET costs between 10 and 100 times that of primary education (Husen and Postlethwaite, 1988). Understandably, given the high illiteracy levels in some countries, there has been a call for public resources to be diverted from TVET to primary school education (Psacharopoulos, 1991b).

In the light of the these arguments the World Bank (1991c) has suggested ways in which governments in Third World countries could encourage company or non-governmental provision of training. According to the World Bank (1991b) this type of provision is more likely to occur if a country has a liberalised trade regime and a flexible labour market. Under these conditions employers can gauge which skills to invest in, and correspondingly which not to invest in. However, if the opposite conditions exist, such as a high minimum wage and guaranteed employment in the state sector, then both individuals and employers are much less likely to invest in training. Consequently, the study also looked at whether the governments in Jamaica and The Gambia had created favourable conditions for non-governmental forms of training.

A further related aim was to investigate whether the governments in each of the two countries had implemented specific programmes to support companies, or non-governmental organisations, to provide training. In looking at this issue, the study attempted to answer the question of whether these programmes were implemented effectively (in terms of expanding provision) and whether they used resources efficiently, (that is to say, did they encourage the private sector to invest in training?).

The countries of Jamaica and The Gambia were chosen because of both their similarities and differences, and to see what impact these had on the implementation process within each country. Amongst the obvious similarities between the two countries are a small geographical area and a British colonial past. However, more recently each country has experienced International Monetary Fund (IMF) backed structural adjustment or

5

economic reform programmes. In both countries this has had a similar impact, including a reduction in the number of people working in the public sector and an expansion in the number of people having to earn a living in the informal sector. Furthermore, until recently Jamaica and The Gambia both shared a democratic system of politics, with both holding democratic elections. Although in The Gambia this is no longer the case since a military coup occurred at the beginning of the 1990s.

The two countries also share radical differences. The most significant of these concerns contrasts in living standards, with Jamaica being classified as a low to middle income developing country and The Gambia as just a low income developing country. This difference reflects the nature of each country's economy. For example, the economy in The Gambia is predominantly agrarian with the majority of the population engaged in agricultural related activities. However, since the implementation of an economic reform programme at the beginning of the 1990s, tourism and re-exporting have become a vital source of earnings (EIU, 1994b). In contrast, Jamaica has reduced its dependence on agricultural produce both through the use of import substitution industrialisation in the 1960s and more recently by adopting an export-led growth strategy. Thus, in relative terms, with an established bauxite industry and a large number of multinational companies engaged in secondary processing and garment construction, Jamaica could be regarded as having a semi-industrial base. Nevertheless, in both countries the formal sector has been unable to absorb all the new entrants coming onto the labour market and as a consequence unemployment is a major problem, particularly amongst school leavers or college graduates.

Nevertheless, the major reason for choosing the two countries was because of links between the University where the research for the study was being conducted in the UK and TVET institutions in the two countries. The issue of access has been identified as one of the major obstacles to conducting research in the Third World (Halls, 1990). Thus, in the present study, existing links ensured that access was obtained to the appropriate personnel in TVET institutions and ministries in each country.

The overall findings of the present study illustrate the complexities surrounding the implementation process in the Third World. For implementation at public TVET institutions and ministries it argues that dependence on overseas components and foreign technical assistance, in conjunction with the influence of the local physical and political infrastructures, are the major reasons why aid-funded projects fail to achieve their stated objectives and are unsustainable in the long-term. The study also identified the possible existence of a dependency typology, arguing that if policy makers wish to improve the chances of projects being successfully implemented they needed to understand how these different types of dependency operate, and also how they can be generated at different time periods during the cycle of a project's implementation.

However, in relation to the implementation process in the private sector, the study found that the state, and surprisingly international aid organisations, were of critical importance in determining whether this type of provision was effective or efficient. This was an important finding because it illustrated that it was not just TVET institutions and government ministries that were subject to the influence of dependency. The study concludes that a closer study of the observed link between dependency and the stages in the life cycle of a project or programme could provide guidelines (to aid agencies and planners of TVET) on the steps that might be taken to reduce the likelihood of dependency being an influential factor in the implementation process. Only then will it be possible to have independent decision-making within TVET projects or programmes that is based on local labour market needs, rather than those of a donor agencies or host governments.

Outline of the Book

The first chapter turns to the literature underpinning the present study. Within this part of the book we discuss in greater depth many of the issues that were raised in the present section. This includes a review of the existing literature on policy implementation and a consideration of the major debates surrounding TVET in the Third World. Although a large number of the existing studies of policy implementation have been undertaken in the developed world, they still provided the present study with an insight into why certain policies are more successfully implemented than others. The second part of this chapter outlines in further depth some of the more important issues surrounding the provision of TVET in the Third World. This includes a clarification of what is meant by the term TVET, the historical development of TVET systems in the Third World, as well as the roles played by colonialism and international aid organisations. Additional consideration is given to the reasons for investing in TVET, as well as recent criticism of investing in TVET. This chapter also discusses different models of TVET around the globe and the theoretical approaches to interpreting such provision. Finally, the chapter considers the various justifications for looking at the subject of implementation.

Chapter 2 describes the methods and procedures that were used in the present study. In particular the chapter discusses why the methodology of a case study approach was used, as well as a description of how the study's data was collected and analysed. Attention is also given to the issues of reliability and validity.

The subsequent two Chapters, 3 and 4, present the study's findings in relation to policy implementation in Jamaica. The first of these chapters outlines the context in which implementation occurs, including how the TVET system in Jamaica has developed and the different organisational structures through which implementation occurred. This allows the chapter to discuss the three different ministries that are responsible for co-ordinating and planning the country's TVET policies, as well as the various institutions and centres where programmes of study are delivered. Additional consideration is also given to the projects and programmes that were implemented through these structures over the past three decades. By adopting such an approach, the chapter is able to document the aims and

7

objectives of each project implemented at a public TVET institution, their sources of finance and the various personnel, consultants, educational materials and capital developments supported by it.

In the case of government programmes for supporting training within companies and other non-governmental organisations (NGOs); Chapter 3 also outlines their objectives, their target groups and the organisational structures through which they were implemented.

In Chapter 4, the analysis of policy implementation in Jamaica, there are two parts. The first, and major part of Chapter 4, analyses the projects that were implemented at the ministries and public TVET institutions outlined in Chapter 3. In doing so the chapter considers how each project was initiated, managed and implemented; and the extent to which these processes were dependent on overseas technical assistance or foreign components, and the corresponding impact on this dependency. The second, and subsidiary part of this chapter, looks at two related issues. First, it assesses whether or not the Jamaican government has created a favourable macro-economic environment for companies or non-governmental organisations to provide training. Secondly, it evaluates how effectively and efficiently state programmes have supported the provision of TVET by companies and non-governmental organisations.

In the following two Chapters, 5 and 6, a similar approach is used to look at policy implementation in The Gambia. Thus, Chapter 5 outlines how the TVET system in The Gambia developed and the different institutions that were involved in the process of implementation. It also outlines the major organisational structures and the composition of the projects that were implemented in The Gambia over the past thirty years, including their aims and sources of finance. Reference is also made to a number of government owned companies who provide training, as well as the organisations which support training for those who work in the country's informal sector. In analysing these developments Chapter 6 uses a similar approach to the one discussed in Chapter 4.

The last chapter, the conclusion, presents the study's major findings and comments on the observed differences between the two countries by looking at the influence of the political and physical infrastructure on the implementation process. It concludes by pointing to the complexities associated with dependence on overseas aid and suggests a possible framework that could be used by policy makers to avoid the negative impact of dependency, and in doing so help ensure successful implementation in the future.

1 Policy implementation

Introduction

This chapter reviews the literature on the subject of policy implementation and that of TVET in the 'Third World'. It begins by looking at some of the major approaches to interpreting implementation in the developed or 'First World'. Then, we turn to the major debates surrounding TVET in the Third World, including issues such as what is meant by this term and how TVET systems in different countries have developed. In dealing with the former issue, the chapter discusses the role played by aid agencies in supporting TVET initiatives in the Third World, as well as criticisms of TVET based on cost effectiveness and labour market relevance. Additional consideration is also given to recent studies on policy implementation in the Third World. By adopting such an approach, the chapter is able to provide the reader with an overview of some of the major debates which informed the present study.

Policy implementation in the developed world

Until recently the majority of studies on policy implementation were conducted by researchers in the field of social and public policy. This work appeared to interpret the implementation process in one of three ways. The first of these, referred to in the literature as the top-down approach, assumes that policy makers formulate policies at the central government level, and these subsequently pass down through a government hierarchy, and are implemented by the appropriate agencies. The top-down approach to analysing policy implementation was apparent in Pressmen and Wildavsky's (1973) study of the United States of America's federal employment creation plans in Oakwood, California. This piece of work looked at the success of a federal employment creation policy by focusing on the hierarchical structure of the different organisations involved in the implementation process. Pressmen and Wildavsky's study concluded that problems in implementation are more likely to occur if there are disagreements between the different organisations that implemented the same policy.

Other researchers who take the top-down approach view successful implementation as being dependent on a number of factors, including: the availability of resources, the nature of the policy, and the administrative structure. For example, Hogwood *et al* (1984) perceives the success of implementation as being influenced by the availability of resources at critical moments during the implementation process. Furthermore, this approach assumes that if a policy is clearly stipulated, including the specific actions needed for its implementation, then it is less likely to experience problems. Hogwood *et al* (1984) build on the work of Pressmen and Wildavsky (1973) by arguing that if a single administrative structure, rather than multiple structures, is involved in the implementation process, then the policy is more likely to be successfully implemented.

The limitation of the top-down approach is that it is based on technocratic assumptions. In adopting such an approach it assumes that successful implementation is about having the correct procedures and the appropriate organisational structures. If you do not have the former in place then your policy is likely to experience implementation difficulties. By adopting such a narrow perspective, the top-down approach neglects the role that different actors play in the process of policy implementation. However, in contrast to the top-down approach, the bottom-up approach emphasises the importance of actors in the implementation process, particularly those on the ground who are referred to as 'street level bureaucrats'. One of the seminal pieces of work on this subject was Lipsky's (1980) study of government officials and civil servants who had direct contact with the public. Within this study, policy analysts are criticised on the grounds that they generalise about policy implementation without explaining the impact or influence of individuals in this process. According to Lipsky, the influence of 'street level bureaucrats' stems from their discretion in interpreting policies and from their relative autonomy from hierarchical/supervisory control over their day-to-day actions.

There are clear benefits to the bottom-up approach in that it recognises how individuals, through their collective behaviour, can influence the process involved in implementing a policy. However, on the negative side, this approach can be criticised for emphasising the 'street level bureaucrat' at the expense of those who are involved in formulating policy. In response to these limitations the evolutionary approach combines the top-down and bottom-up approaches for analysing implementation. The benefit of this third view is that it recognises implementation as a process of negotiation and interaction between the key decision-makers who formulate policies, and the 'street level bureaucrats' who implement them. Furthermore, in contrast to the former two approaches, the evolutionary one recognises that policy making and implementation are not separate, and that policy making is left to those involved in the planning and in the implementation stages (Ham and Hill, 1993).

Although the three different approaches to interpreting implementation provide a useful framework for interpreting policy implementation, and to a consideration of the actors which influence that process, they also have their limitations for the present study. First, and perhaps the most important, these interpretations of the implementation process are based on the findings of studies conducted in the UK or the USA, rather than those in the developing world where the conditions and circumstances are totally different. Indeed, in the Third World institutional structures and policies have been shaped by totally different historical circumstances. For example, the predominance of external influences, such as colonialism, have had a major impact on the type of bureaucracies which exist in many Third World countries. These 'external influences', whether through overseas aid or foreign investment, still continue to have an influential role in many Third World countries today. Given these limitations there is a need to look at the literature surrounding TVET and policy implementation in the Third World.

Literature on TVET in the 'Third World'

Before the chapter looks at any of the debates surrounding TVET in the Third World there is a need to define what exactly we mean by the term TVET. A review of the literature on the subject reveals a large number of acronyms to describe institutional technical and vocational education and training in the Third World, ranging from TVE (technical and vocational education), to VET (vocational education and training) and more recently TVET (technical and vocational education and training) (see: Grey *et al*, 1993; Middleton and Demsky 1989; World Bank, 1991c). There are also numerous debates over what constitutes TVET or VET. Amongst the many issues discussed in the literature are: what is contained in a TVET programme? What proportion of a particular programme should be devoted to practical work, and what proportion to theoretical studies? What type of institutions are best suited to providing particular forms of TVET? As might be expected, there are numerous answers to these questions and according to Oxtoby (1994) the answers will depend on the developmental needs of an individual country and on its corresponding policy framework.

In an attempt to overcome the complexities associated with defining TVET, Middleton (1988) suggests that TVET can be viewed in terms of three dimensions, including: the mode of delivery, the sector of intended employment and the national level of a country's development. With regard to the first of these dimensions, this encompasses the provision of TVET in universities (through courses of study in subjects such as engineering and computing), post-secondary technical institutions which provide formalised training in specific technical subjects, secondary schools which have diversified their academic curricula to include practical subjects, secondary technical schools which prepare students for direct entry into the labour market, and non-formal organisations which provide TVET outside the formal educational system, such as apprenticeship schemes offered by Ministries of Labour.

The second dimension, the sector of intended employment, refers to the occupational area in which TVET graduates intend to work and encompasses sectors such as agriculture, manufacturing, commerce and the service sector. Whilst the third dimension, the level of a country's development, provides an indication of the country's capacity to absorb TVET graduates.

The above taxonomy has clear policy implications for those involved in planning TVET policies in the Third World. However, one limitation of Middleton's taxonomy is that it neglects the historical circumstances under which TVET systems developed in the Third World, including the influence of colonialism and of International Aid agencies respectively. A second short-coming of this taxonomy is that it fails to consider the political context in which TVET provision occurs. The former has corresponding

11

implications for interpreting the way in which TVET policies are implemented in the Third World.

A number of researchers have looked at the historical development of TVET systems in the Third World and also the influence of colonialism. A brief look at these case studies can help us, in part, to understand some of the constraints and problems facing TVET systems in the Third World to-day. Ishumi (1988) analysed the effect of transferring the English educational system, consisting of an academic stream and a vocational one in parallel, to Third World countries in Africa. The two track system first appeared in Nigeria in 1859, and as in the case of England, the vocational stream was viewed in Africa as comprising a second rate institution for less able students. This attitude towards education was further enforced by the socio-economic conditions which existed, and still exist in some third world countries. Under these conditions African students developed a preference for studying academic subjects (rather than vocational subjects) because they were more likely to obtain a job, with attractive career prospects, in the country's formal sector (Godwin, 1990). According to Watson (1973), as a result of encouraging this 'academic bias' colonialism, unwittingly, destroyed the cultural norms of pre-colonial societies which had a strong technical and vocational bias.

The influence of external factors was also apparent in the post-colonial period when aid agencies helped finance the development of TVET systems in the Third World (Watson, 1994). This influence has been identified by some as a form of neo-colonialism (Altbach and Kelly, 1984). Indeed, Altbach and Kelly regard educational systems in the Third World as being dominated by International Aid networks, which enable Aid Agencies to determine the type of provision that occurs in such countries. Irizarry (1983) focuses on the influence of International Aid networks on post-secondary technical educational systems in the Third World; and in doing so argues that owing to their dependency on First World educational materials, educational institutions in the Third World, are unable to engage in research activities that would be appropriate to their own development needs.

The influence of International Aid agencies was apparent in Kenya where the ILO was instrumental in vocationalising the country's education system (Sifuna, 1992). However, the greatest influence of International Aid agencies, on the development of TVET systems in the Third World, has come from the World Bank. Indeed, Technical and Vocational Education and Training was at the cornerstone of the World Bank's lending during the 1970s and 1980s, and 40 per cent of the Bank's lending for education during this period went on TVET, with 80 per cent of this supporting pre-employment training (World Bank, 1991b).

The decision to introduce vocational subjects into an institution in the Third World, whether by a host government or a donor agency, took many forms. In some countries there was an attempt to introduce universal vocationalisation - that is to say vocational subjects were incorporated into the curriculum at all stages of the educational spectrum. For example, when the government in Tanzania was pursuing a development policy based on the concept of 'Education for Self Reliance' attempts were made to introduce

12

vocational subjects, such as agricultural and basic crafts, into the primary school curriculum. Under this policy it was anticipated that school children would be able to apply their practical skills in the model farms which had been established under 'Education for Self Reliance' (Ishumi, 1988). Also under Tanzania's extensive vocationalisation programme the curriculum within secondary schools underwent extensive diversification, with students spending an estimated 40 per cent of their time studying vocational subjects.

In contrast to Tanzania, the government in neighbouring Kenya, with the support of various funding agencies, introduced a milder form of vocationalisation in the late 1980s called the 8-4-4 education system. This comprised of 8 years of primary schooling in which agricultural and craft subjects became compulsory in the school curriculum, 4 years of secondary and a further 4 years of post-secondary education. Under this approach emphasis was given towards pre-vocational subjects at the primary level and technical subjects at the post-primary level. A large number of the schools at the secondary level, called the Harambee Institutes of Technology, were private institutions owned by the community (Esemon *et al*, 1988). The responsibility for curriculum development within the former rested with the Ministry of Technical Training and Applied Technology. However, although the Ministry paid teachers' salaries it only contributed towards part of the schools recurrent operating costs - the remainder having to be financed by the communities themselves.

In other parts of the world, VET systems have been shaped by their own unique historical circumstances. However, in Latin America it is possible to speak of a generic approach, or as it is referred to in the literature as the 'Latin American Model'. Although, the 'Latin American Model' originated in Brazil in the late 1940s, the Brazilians borrowed the approach from Germany and Austria. Thus, the Brazilian National Industrial Learning Service, SENAI, resembles in some aspects BBIB in Germany. For example, SENAI uses an industrial levy-type system to finance the provision of the country's vocational training system. This system consists of pre-service training for 14 to 18 year old apprentices which is delivered in SENAI vocational schools. These schools are also responsible for providing training to technicians at the post-secondary level and those employees who need skill-upgrading or retraining. The curricula within the SENAI schools is based on task analysis. Thus, rather than focus on the technical knowledge and procedures associated with doing a job, it is more concerned with the information and actions required to perform a job (Wilson, 1993). The relative success of this approach can be judged by the fact that the SENAI approach, is now operational in 19 other countries in Latin America and two in the Caribbean.

The countries discussed above will have numerous reasons or justifications for investing in TVET, although the most well known of these has its roots in human capital theory. Put simply, this assumes that a better trained workforce would be more productive, and that this in turn would contribute towards a country's economic development (Blaug, 1985). However, the simple causality between investment in training and economic development is not without its critics (see Ashton and Green, 1996). Other well known reasons for investing in TVET include: increasing the relevance of schooling to occupational futures and easing the transition from school to work.

Besides economic justifications for investing in TVET there are also political reasons. Within Tanzania, for example, vocationalisation had ideological goals in that it attempted to re-orientate attitudes away from academic book learning and more towards vocational skills which could benefit the wider community. Furthermore, the provision of TVET, can be viewed in many Third World countries as a response to the harsh labour conditions in which school leavers and graduates are unable to find paid employment. The political motives for vocationalising schools were particularly apparent in the Third World during the 1970s, when vocationalisation was seen as a response to the rising incidence of unemployment amongst school leavers (Bacchis, 1988). Even more recently, the vocationalisation of the curriculum was also being used during the 1980s and 1990s, by governments in the First and Third Worlds, as a response to the continual problem arising of unemployment amongst school leavers (Lauglo and Lillis, 1988). Although, in contrast to the 1960s and 1970s, the emphasis was on encouraging school leavers to become entrepreneurs by incorporating entrepreneurial development skills in to the curriculum (Godwin, 1990). However, by using the curriculum as a response to the problem of rising unemployment, the state is only responding to the aspirations of those who are leaving the education system, rather than meeting specific skills shortages in the economy; and at the same time, the state is placing sole responsibility on the school leaver to find paid employment.

Within the Third World there are also debates about what constitutes entrepreneurship training and what form it should take. For example, should entrepreneurial programmes be concerned with training TVET graduates so that they can establish their own businesses? Alternatively, should such programmes focus upon attitudinal developments, thereby encouraging TVET graduates to work for small enterprises in the informal sector? The point remains that the content of an entrepreneurship programme depends on its objectives. If, for example, a programme is designed to encourage graduates to become self-employed, then it will need to provide support services, such as finance and advice to ease the transition from school to productive employment (Godwin, 1990). The cost of providing such additional support services for TVET graduates is high; some academics have argued that governments should be more concerned with providing suitable economic conditions for entrepreneurial development, than with 'wasting resources' on entrepreneurial development programmes (Marsden, 1990); the assumption being that entrepreneurs are born and not made.

Despite economic and political justifications for vocationalising the curricula in the Third World, it has been subject to much criticism from both academics and international funding agencies. The apparent mismatch between the technical manpower a country's TVET system produces, and what is actually needed, has led to a variety of criticisms. According to Psacharopoulos (1991b) the matching of supply to demand in education is a

14

utopia which will never be achieved owing to the distorted nature of labour markets in the Third World. The major distortions include a sizeable public sector and a rigid labour market (with fixed wage rates), all of which prevent a downward movement of wages if there is an excess supply of trained personnel. The demand for trained personnel in the Third World is also unpredictable due to factors such as advances in technology and emigration. In order to mitigate this mismatching, and thereby reduce the problem of the 'trained unemployed', Psacharapoulos (1991a) suggests a number of measures which include: the relaxation of minimum wage laws, the abolition of manpower forecasting and the introduction of student fees to enable post-secondary TVET institutions to recover some of their recurrent costs.

Criticisms have also been levelled at the education and training of TVET staff. In order to deliver TVET programmes, lecturers/instructors need to receive continuous training and development. This is particularly so with the introduction of new subjects such as entrepreneurship. Formerly, a high proportion of training for TVET lecturers who work in the Third World was undertaken in institutions overseas, through aid-funded scholarships. Gray (1993) has questioned the effectiveness of such overseas training because on completing their courses, and returning to their home countries, TVET lecturers are normally promoted to positions where they can no longer use their technical skills. Furthermore, there is the issue of the efficient use of resources, since in-house training can be provided in organisations in the Third World at a fraction of the costs of overseas scholarships (Baker *et al*, 1984).

However, the World Bank argues that given the rapid pace of technological change, Third World countries are better able to expand their cognitive and theoretical knowledge base through investing resources in primary and secondary general education. This they argue is a more cost effective means of developing a labour force that can enter traditional craft type occupations, as well as those in the modern dynamic modern sector. The World Bank also criticises governments who attempt to vocationalise their primary and secondary school curricula, arguing that the rate of return from vocationalising the curriculum is much lower than from traditional primary and secondary general education. For example, Misha (1994) analysed the effectiveness of attempts to vocationalise the curriculum in Malawi. The government anticipated that this would provide school leavers with the skills to enter particular occupations and thereby ease their transition to the labour market. Overall, the study highlighted that vocational education costs twice as much as general education. At the same time Misha (1994) argued that owing to the rapid technological changes which were occurring in Malawi, vocational education can only have a limited impact in facilitating a young person's access to the labour market. This issue of rates of return is a very important one in the Third World, particularly when illiteracy levels are high and when the opportunity costs of resource allocation need to be carefully considered. Psacharopoulos *et al* (1995) look at education provision in Latin America, and on the economic and social returns from secondary education, from the point of view of academic versus vocational schooling. One of the central conclusions of his research was that

15

the returns are much higher in academic education than in vocational education. Whilst even the World Bank itself has shown that the social rates of return to vocational schooling in Bangladesh are negative.

On an equity issue, the World Bank (1991b) has found that public sector vocational education is not one of the most effective ways of reaching the poor. For example, from research based in Thailand, the World Bank showed that although farmers and labourers comprise 88 per cent of the country's labour force, their children occupied less than 20 per cent of places in secondary schools, with the remaining 80 per cent of places being held by the children of businessmen and government officials.

It is surprising that the World Bank has taken so many decades to recognise the importance of primary and secondary education, relative to TVET; indeed as long ago as the early 1970s, Sklair (1973) commented that further increases in the numbers of scientists, technicians and others with tertiary level education, without broadening the base of those acceding primary and secondary education, would have little point and would result in less than optimum progress.

The Bank also suggested that if governments wish to support the expansion of training within their country they should encourage provision within the private sector. The assumption underlying this principle is that employers are the best regulators of the skills that an economy requires. Furthermore, the Bank argues that in-plant company training costs a fraction of the costs of institutional or school based training and at the same time individuals are in jobs where they are most likely to use their skills. In their 1993 annual report the World Bank states,'that the Bank stands ready to support countries that want to move their training policies in (their) suggested direction'. They also point towards a number of conditions that are necessary to achieve such an objective, including what they call a 'favourable policy environment'. Essentially this includes the creation of a liberalised trade regime and a flexible labour market. Under such a scenario employers are likely to receive signals about which skills to invest in. Conversely, if a country has a high minimum wage rate, a policy of guaranteed public sector employment and a narrow skill differential between wage levels in the public sector, then it is likely to send the wrong signals, and employers and individuals are likely to invest in the wrong skills.

However, the World Bank (1991b) recognises that in some countries it may not be politically acceptable to remove minimum wages and so it has suggested that compensatory measures, such as exempting apprentices from minimum wage scales, should be taken. Additionally, the World Bank also suggests means of supporting this market-based provision. This includes more collaborative arrangements to deliver training between public TVET institutions and private companies.

Nevertheless, the move towards company training is not without its critics. For example, in Africa there are few countries which have a modern sector large enough to support in-house training on any scale (King, 1986). Also, the relatively weak position of trade unions, particularly in Africa, means that there is relatively little pressure for apprenticeship schemes or other forms of industry-based training (King, 1988). Moreover, even if in a

Third World country there are a large number of multinational companies, and a developed modern sector, the opportunities for in-house training could be minimal. This is true, for example, in the screwdriver factories of Sri-Lanka where training is limited to repetitive tasks associated with the production line (Sklair, 1991). There are also potential dangers if a country becomes dependent on the private companies for the majority of its training and skill formation. This scenario can be seen in Mexico where the majority of companies with the capacity to provide training are foreign owned multinationals (MNCs). This could present a worrying situation since if the MNCs were offered more favourable conditions over the border in Guatemala, then MNCs could suddenly relocate, leaving Mexico without the capacity for skill development in certain sectors (Powell, 1997).

This disillusionment with traditional manpower planning models, and the escalating costs of institutional and school-based training, particularly that aimed at technical manpower provision, has emphasised the need for a system that is efficient and more sensitive to the fluctuations in the labour market. This has resulted in a shift towards using Labour Market Analysis (LMA) as a means of informing policy makers (Steele, 1991). The increasing importance given towards LMA has also seen a proliferation of studies analysing how labour markets operate in developing countries. The majority of these rest on neo-classical assumptions, arguing that any departure from a purely competitive labour market will discourage training, reduce employment and impede economic development (Marshall, 1994). The movement towards LMA and market-based provision has become widespread or common in many Third World or First World countries. An example of this trend is particularly apparent in Chile where the training system has undergone extensive privatisation during the past decade-and-a-half. The National Training Institute (INCAD), the former government body responsible for initial training and upgrading, has become a private training institute directed by business leaders. However, the jewel in the crown in the Chilean system was the implementation of the 1976 Vocational Training Act (Vasquez *et al*, 1994). As a result of this Act, private companies, rather than public institutions, became responsible for delivering the country's training. The government's role, via the National Training and Employment Service (SENCE), became limited to one of monitoring quality, financing and co-ordination. Under this new arrangement private training providers had to register with one of the 156 SENCE employment offices scattered throughout the country. Once the provider has been accepted for registration they are invited to bid for training contracts from the government. It is envisaged that this competition between the private training providers will help ensure an efficient quality of training services is provided. Whilst the localised delivery mechanism is supposed to help ensure that local labour market demands are met effectively.

However, the dominance of the market as a mechanism for delivering training is not universal. For example, some of the recent studies on Newly Industrialising Countries (NICs) in South-East Asia have emphasised the role played by the 'developmental state' in creating the conditions for high skill development, and subsequent rapid economic growth (Ashton and

Green, 1996). Within this body of work the state is seen as providing a series of mechanisms which link the skill requirements of the country's trade and industry policy with the outcomes from the education and training system and thereby enhance economic growth. In light of this framework Ashton and Green (1996) identified a number of conditions as responsible for the high skill routes adopted in South-East Asia, and these included: (i) the ability of the ruling elite to establish a strong, efficient state bureaucracy, relatively independent of the immediate interests of capital and labour, (ii) the commitment of these elites to an integrated policy of development and high skill development, and also the support of employers and workers to these goals. Once in place these conditions are reinforcing in that the state, employers and employees all become committed to a country's longer term economic goals.

The interest in training in the Newly Industrialising Countries of South-East Asia has resulted in researchers asking whether similar conditions are present in other countries (see Goodwin, 1997). Using such an approach Tzannatos *et al* (1997) look at what lessons can be learnt from the development of VET systems in Korea, Malaysia, Singapore, Taiwan and China. Overall their findings show that one approach is no more effective than another. However, they do suggest that certain characteristics are more important than others. Although, this piece of work may provide some useful guidelines for countries embarking on policy reform, they do not help us to understand the actual process of implementation, or what conditions are necessary to ensure that a policy achieves its stated objectives. Only recently have commentators started to focus on the issue of implementation in the Third World. In part this has been a response to the poor record of overseas aid and to a consideration of why aid-funded projects continually fail to achieve their stated objectives or are unsustainable in the long-term. The majority of the initial research in this area, particularly with regard to education and different aspects of training, has been conducted by the international aid agencies themselves. In an internal review of 212 educational projects implemented in the developing world, the United States Agency for International Development (USAID) revealed that nearly 90 per cent were unsustainable (Kean *et al*, 1988). Furthermore, a similar study of 550 World Bank educational projects in the developing world found that only half were sustainable (World Bank, 1990a). These organisations have also investigated why aid-funded projects experienced implementation difficulties or failed to achieve their intended impact. Amongst the reasons identified for projects experiencing implementation difficulties were: the overambitious aims of the project; the way in which they were managed; and the influence of the organisational structures through which they pass (Craig, 1990).

Once again the World Bank (1991b) suggests ways in which Third World countries can improve their implementation capacity. This centres on the need for employer/worker participation on the boards of training bodies. In addition it points out that such bodies should be autonomous - presumably this means that the decision-making process should be free of state interference. Other conditions include the provision of adequate training funds to encourage private and public training institutions to adjust to changing patterns of labour market needs. The Bank further comments that successful implementation is dependent on well paid training managers and professionals. Some might wonder how some of the former conditions could be present in TVET system without considerable state support and investment.

More recently, an added dimension to the debate on implementation has been provided in Herchbach's (1997) model of project implementation. Besides emphasising what can be regarded as the technical complexities associated with a project's implementation, such as those that focus on procedures, Herchbach emphasises the importance of understanding the context in which these processes take place. Undoubtedly, if the design of a project fails to take into account specific cultural or contextual particularities of the country in which implementation is taking place, then it is likely to experience difficulties in meeting its intended aims. The practice of exporting western-based models or policies to developing countries is increasingly attracting criticism from academics and policy makers alike (Middleton and Ziderman, 1997).

However, this begs the question of what role do overseas aid agencies play in implementing TVET projects in the developing world, and what impact does this have on their sustainability? For example, how are aid-funded TVET projects in the developing world started and what roles do local TVET personnel play in their management and implementation? The relationship between the involvement of local personnel, and their commitment to aid-funded projects is increasingly being recognised by donors. The importance of local involvement in the construction of a project proposal, and in the management of its subsequent implementation, is also being recognised by both academics and aid agencies. King (1992, p.260) has referred to this as a new paradigm and cites evidence from a World Bank report:

> ... close national involvement in analytical work related to, for example, project preparation is the key to helping ensure country ownership of the analyses and their translation into viable reforms. Such ownership is crucial to the implementation of most reforms, and to create it is an important reason why project preparation must largely be done by the borrower. Indeed, as project preparation generally includes elaboration of policy options to address sensitive sector issues, it is very difficult to create ownership if the work is done by donors or external consultants.

However, despite the recognition of the possible conditions necessary for improving the chances of successful implementation, few studies have actually documented the process involved in implementation, or addressed the issue of why so many projects experience difficulties. Even project-based research, sponsored by aid agencies has been termed 'unimpressionable' (Verspoor, 1990). Furthermore, the methodology adopted in such studies is not of the type which is suitable for publication in refereed journals. The present study attempts to deal with some of these issues and provide a more comprehensive understanding, both empirically and conceptually, of the implementation process in the Third World. The methods and procedures which were used to achieve these objectives are discussed in the following chapter.

2 Methodology

Introduction

The present study has drawn heavily on qualitative as opposed to quantitative research methods in order to elicit primary evidence. The distinction between both approaches has been extensively discussed in the literature (see for example: Bryman, 1988, 1989; Babbie, 1990; Lewins, 1992). By using a qualitative case study approach, the research was able to study human behaviour in its natural cultural environment, rather than create an artificial environment in which variables can be manipulated to alter behaviour. Furthermore, the process of conducting qualitative research allowed the present study to concentrate on processes, such as the implementation of TVET policies, rather than on outcomes (Vulliamy, 1990). This chapter begins by documenting why a case study approach was chosen as opposed to other methods of inquiry. This is followed by a discussion of the research design used to guide the present study, including how a research problem was identified, what methods and procedures were used for collecting data and how the subsequent data was analysed. Additional consideration is also given to the issues of validity and reliability.

The case studies of TVET in Jamaica, and TVET in The Gambia, can be regarded as explanatory (Yin, 1989), in that the present research is attempting to explain the relationship between the implementation process and the factors that influence it. The methodology of case study also provided the means of 'getting close' to the implementation process for TVET, enabling the study to cast its net widely for evidence and to document the context in which implementation occurred in each country. The issue of context is very important and pivotal to explaining the unique circumstances surrounding the implementation process in each country. Other research methods, such as experiments and surveys would have proved impractical for the present study. For example, experimental methods aim to measure the influence which one variable (independent) has on another (dependent), but in the present study it would have been impossible to manipulate the variables that influenced the implantation process and to measure the corresponding effects. Survey research tends to concentrate on a small number of variables across a large number of instances, often attempting to make generalisations (Cohen and Manion, 1994). However, a survey of implementation processes would have proved impossible for the present research, given the large number of possible instances of implementing TVET policies in the Third World. With the resources (human, material and financial) available for the present study, it was also impossible to contemplate undertaking a study of the implementation process in more than two countries.

Case study research design

A research design is a sequence of events which connects the procedures for collecting the empirical data to the initial research questions on the one hand, and to the subsequent data collection, analysis and conclusions on the other. At present there is no consensus amongst researchers as to the stages involved in designing a research project. However, the design for the present research drew on the work of Yin (1984), Majchrzak (1984), Robson (1993) and Merriam (1989), and is shown in Table 2.1.

Table 2.1 The research design for the present study

1. Identification of the problem to be studied.

2. Review of the appropriate literature.

3. Development of a conceptual approach and general proposition.

4. Construction of a research methodology, including identification of, and approval for, the case to be studied.

5. The field work in Jamaica.

6. The field work in The Gambia.

7. Analysis of collected data using a conceptual framework.

8. Conclusion.

In doing so, the present study viewed the research design as consisting of a number of interconnected stages, although it is important to keep in mind that the majority of activities were undertaken simultaneously.

The first stage, or activity, to any piece of research must involve identifying a problem to be investigated or a possible area for investigation. In the present study, the literature review revealed that little attention has been directed towards the process of policy implementation, or to a consideration of the factors which influence this process. Indeed, when the present study started, little was known about how the planners of TVET in Third World countries decide on what to do or how they go about doing it (Carron, 1984). Thus, one of the central aims was to trace, analyse and document the strategies for implementing TVET policies in Jamaica and in The Gambia. In this respect, the research planned to identify how various factors influenced the implementation process, particularly resourcing. It has long been recognised that the implementation of government plans in the Third World are highly dependent on overseas aid for their implementation (Webster, 1989). Therefore, the present study was particularly concerned with how reliance on overseas aid influenced the process of implementing TVET policies in Jamaica, and in The Gambia. Aside from dependence on overseas aid, Third World countries are increasingly looking at how local resources could be used to implement TVET policies, and in particular how the state could encourage the provision of training by private companies and NGOs. Thus, another consideration was how effective and efficient programmes for supporting non-governmental forms of training could be implemented.

The third stage to the study consisted of developing a conceptual approach and a general proposition. The importance of a conceptual approach cannot be underestimated since this played a vital role in guiding the data collection and data analyses processes. Within the present study the conceptual approach had to initially identify what exactly was meant by the term 'implementation', where it occurred and what factors could influence this process. In relation to the first issue, the study had to identify *strategies for implementation*. In other words how do planners of TVET decide on what to do and how do they go about doing it? When the study started to investigate this first issue it was naively assumed that civil servants within planning units, or government ministries, formulate implementation strategies, and that these are passed down through the appropriate organisational hierarchy and were subsequently implemented at TVET institutions or companies. Although this process was true in some instances, in the majority of cases it was found that donor agencies played an influential role in this process via their funding of projects at TVET institutions. As a consequence, the study decided to focus not only on initiatives developed within government planning units, but also on projects that were implemented at TVET institutions.

Having identified what exactly was meant by the term 'implementation' the study had to consider what factors could influence this process. According to Robson (1993) the best way to develop a conceptual approach is to have a general proposition. Thus, within the present study the general proposition was that: *strategies adopted for implementing TVET policies are influenced by the same internal and external factors that influence development generally in the Third World.* For example, a country's state apparatus can influence development and indeed the implementation process, both directly and indirectly. It is able to influence implementation directly through the policies which are formulated at central government by institutions such as the legislature and the judiciary. Whilst indirectly, the state is able to influence the process via the administrative system (the planning units and institutions) through which centralised policies are implemented (Abercrombie *et al*, 1984). In looking at the former issue, there has recently been a revitalisation of the Weberian approach which assumed that owing to the values (such as patronage) held by those who work in the state sector, a certain proportion of the resources in a Third World country are either misappropriated or mismanaged (Ayittey, 1993). Besides the

23

provision of TVET in the public sector there is also the issue of whether the state has provided an economic climate that is conducive to non-governmental forms of training. All of these issues were a consideration of the present study.

Besides what could be termed 'internal' influences there are also 'external' influences. The external influence on the Third World started during colonialism and has continued during the post-colonial period, in what some have called 'post-colonialism'. The latter term is generally used to explain an exploitative relationship in which the First World continues to dominate the Third World through its representative transitional organisations, namely multinational companies and aid agencies (Cardoso and Faletto, 1979). The former paradigm is normally used by dependency theorists, all of whom share a common interest in studying peripheral capitalist countries from the point of view of the conditioning effects which external forces and structures produce on these countries (Bernstein, 1973). Central to dependency theory is Frank's (1967) thesis of *underdevelopment*. Frank rejected the evolutionary view of development, arguing that development would be explained by the historical relationship between the First World (the core) and the Third World (the periphery). Within this paradigm, underdevelopment was seen as a result of the metropolitan country syphoning economic surplus out of a Third World country.

However, dependency theorists have to a certain extent been discredited by the successful development of the East Asian and Latin American Newly Industrialising Countries. In response to the latter developments, dependency theorists have simply argued that although development may have occurred in these countries this is only 'dependent development'. Moreover, although the 'dependency' paradigm can be criticised for being too deterministic, and for focusing on external factors at the expense of internal ones, there is no doubt that overseas aid and foreign technical assistance continue to have an important influence on developments in what has been traditionally called the 'Third World'. This issue was highlighted in the previous chapter where it was shown that external influences, in the form of international aid agencies, continue to play an important and influential role in supporting TVET initiatives in the Third World. In this respect, when looking at the implementation of aid projects at public institutions, the present study analysed the role played by donor agencies in initiating projects and also in their management and subsequent implementation.

A further consideration in the conceptual approach was the provision of TVET by private companies and NGOs. Much of the initial work in this area, in relation to provision in the Third World, has been dominated by World Bank studies (see World Bank, 1991c). Thus, in drawing on this work the present study addressed whether the governments in each of the two countries had created a macro-economic environment, and also implemented programmes, to encourage company and NGO provision of TVET.

In addition to the issue of internal and external influences on the process of implementation, another consideration of the present study was the actual

24

programme or project itself. Indeed, as we have seen in the previous chapter the nature of a programme or project, including its aims and the methods stipulated for implementation, can have an influence on whether a project or programme is likely to be successfully implemented.

After developing a conceptual approach the study could engage on stages four, five and six of the research process, namely the identification of cases to be studied and collection of the study's data. With regard to stage four, the decision to conduct the research in Jamaica and The Gambia, was primarily taken because of links between the university where this study was being conducted, and TVET institutions in the two countries. This close relationship has been built up over a period of ten years and provided important access to the appropriate personnel in each of the two countries. The issue of access in these circumstances has been identified as one of the major constraints facing researchers in the developing world (Hall, 1990). At the same time it also enabled the study to compare and contrast the implementation experiences of Jamaica and The Gambia, and also to analyse the role and impact of the overseas aid agencies in each of the two countries.

Numerous methods were used to collect the relevant data for stage five and six of the research process, consisting of a desk study and also field work. The first data collection method was used in Jamaica, in The Gambia and in England. The advantage of using documentation, as a source of collecting data, is that it was an efficient means of obtaining condensed information in a short period of time. The present study used a variety of documents, including student dissertations, project proposals, evaluations from aid agencies and unofficial and official reports produced by TVET institutions (including development plans and statistics from relevant ministries and planning units in each of the two countries). The first of these sources, students' dissertations, provided the research with a realistic description of the process of implementing TVET policies and an insight into that process prior to the study's field work in Jamaica and in The Gambia. Whilst the government plans collected during the field work in both countries enabled the research to identify what questions needed to be asked in the interviews.

Merriam (1989) has likened this process of data collection to a paper chase, and as expected, the 'chase' was different in each country. There were more documents detailing the development of the TVET system in Jamaica than in The Gambia, probably because the TVET system in Jamaica has been delivering training courses for over five decades. However, the lack of published documents in The Gambia was compensated for by obtaining access to relevant filing systems at the country's TVET planning unit and major TVET institutions. The desk study also played a vital role in identifying the organisational structures for implementing TVET projects, and for each project finding out its objectives, its sources of funding, the components (both physical and human) that it provided, and the collaborative relationship between the donor agency and the recipients of aid for the project in each of the countries.

The field study was based on the strategies of both respondent and informant interviewing (Powney and Watts, 1987). The respondent interviews normally lasted between thirty and fifty minutes and took place at the interviewee's place of work. Moreover, the interviews in Jamaica and The Gambia took place in the capital cities of Kingston (in Jamaica) and Banjul (in The Gambia). This provided an ideal means of networking and accessing TVET institutions and officials in Jamaica and The Gambia, and also managers of companies where training took place. Nevertheless, the process of obtaining interviews was different in each of the two countries visited. For example, in Jamaica it was possible to arrange interview appointments with government officials of a particular Ministry without difficulty, to arrive at the government Ministry and conduct the interview. In The Gambia the circumstances for arranging an interview were more complex. Telecommunication difficulties made it difficult to contact government officials, and even when an appointment had been made, other factors, such as petrol shortages, made keeping the appointment problematic. Furthermore, sometimes interviewees would arrive late causing subsequent appointments to be missed.

At the start of the field work the author had intended to record all the interviews on audio tapes. However, owing to the political nature of TVET in Jamaica, and in The Gambia, interviewees often refused to be recorded. As a consequence, the author had to record the interviews either manually on paper, or mentally (to be written-up directly after the interview had taken place). On reflection there are many disadvantages to not using a tape recorder, including the failure to record precisely what the interviewee said. Despite such disadvantages, the research found that interviewees were much more willing to talk about the politics of TVET in their country, including the relationship between a government ministry and an aid agency, when a tape recorder was absent. Nevertheless, when interviewing it was found that some government officials were still reluctant to answer questions, particularly those relating to the problems experienced during the implementation of a TVET project, or questions associated with the political issues surrounding TVET. Within Jamaica a total of 63 respondent interviews took place and within The Gambia 36 interviews were completed. The positions of the interviewees included civil servants who worked within government ministries or TVET planning units, consultants from international aid agencies, instructors or lecturers working at TVET institutions, representatives from non-government agencies and managers who worked in private or state-owned companies.

As far as the informal interviews were concerned, it was a matter of tactical opportunism and of not knowing what line of questioning to pursue until there was a chance to see what kind of information was available. The informal interviews were used to question senior government TVET officials with whom daily contact was made during field work visits, both at work and outside working hours, and also with senior government TVET officials who were on study leave in the UK.

Finally, the analysis, the last part of the research process consisted of two interconnected phases. In some senses, the first phase could be regarded as descriptive in that it was concerned with outlining the context against which implementation took place. This included the organisational structures through which implementation took place, the institutions and organisations involved in this process, as well the aims and objectives of the projects or programmes being implemented. The findings from this part of the analysis are documented in Chapter 3 and Chapter 5 of the present book. As regards the second phase, which is also documented in Chapters 4 and 6 of the present book, this drew heavily on the conceptual approach outlined earlier. For example, in relation to the use of dependency, the analysis concentrated on the relationship between the aid agencies and the TVET institutions in each country. Thus, for each of the projects analysed, evidence of the influence of the donor agency was sought by examining each stage in the implementation process and considering:

- whether a project was initiated by an overseas aid agency,

- whether the project was managed by foreign consultants,

- the effect of using foreign consultants and educational materials
  obtained from the First World,

- the effect of the TVET project on the institution where it
  was implemented.

This enabled the study to also address issues such as democratisation and the extent to which local personnel are involved in the implementation process and/or whether the donor agencies dominated the decision-making process. Furthermore, if donors do dominate the decision-making process, does this generate dependency and what effect does this have on the institution where it was implemented?

The second part of the analysis was also concerned with those policies or programmes for supporting or encouraging non-governmental forms of training. As can be recalled from the previous chapter, these latter programmes provided the state with an alternative means of resourcing training. Furthermore, the move towards the provision of training by private companies is becoming increasingly common in many low income or Third World countries. Thus, in adopting what could be regarded as a 'market approach', the analysis considered whether the government had created an economic environment to facilitate this type of provision, and also how efficient and effective have government programmes been in expanding provision within companies or NGOs. In looking at this issue the study needed to address the state's role in this process, and whether it facilitated or impeded the implementation of such programmes/policies.

Although the study intended to focus on projects implemented at public TVET institutions and programmes for supporting private sector provision, it did not assume that overseas aid only affected the implementation process within public institutions. Nor did it assume that programmes which support provision within the private sector were only influenced by the state. Indeed,

27

in undertaking research the dichotomy between *hypothetico-deductive* and *inductive* reasoning is far too simplistic and in reality the process of conducting research involves an oscillation between deductive and inductive modes of thinking (see Chalmers, 1994). In this respect the present study also considers how the state influenced the implementation process at public TVET institutions; and whether donor agencies influenced or even encouraged support for training within companies or Non-governmental Agencies.

Another important issue in conducting research is that of reliability and validity. Much of the criticism of case study research has centred on the reliability and validity of the research findings. In essence, the issue of reliability is concerned with whether the same piece of research if replicated, using the same procedures, would arrive at the same research findings and conclusions. One of the ways to achieve reliability in case study research is to make as explicit as possible the many steps taken operationally when conducting the research so that the research can be replicated (Yin, 1989). In the present study this was demonstrated by the stages shown in Table 2.1. Reliability is increased by minimising errors and in the present study, possible biases in respondents' statements were checked through the informal interviews of senior officials that were conducted in Jamaica, in The Gambia and in England, over prolonged periods. The senior officials were able to refute or confirm the earlier findings that were obtained from the respondent interviews. This procedure served at the same time the purpose of establishing the 'internal validity' of the findings by ensuring that events were causally related, that is, for example, that the use of foreign components did or did not result in the implementation process being impeded (Merriam, 1989).

Another important consideration in case study research is the extent to which a study's findings are generalisable (Yin, 1989). However, generalisability in this context does not refer to statistical generalisation (that is the generalisation of the statistics obtained in a sample to the population from which the sample is derived) but to the extension of knowledge in the same way that a scientist generalises from experimental results to existing knowledge. Arguably, the present study has contributed to the extension of existing knowledge by clarifying how donor agencies and the state influence the implementation of TVET projects and TVET programmes, in the particular circumstances of two Third World countries. In this sense the findings of the present study are generalisable.

Quite apart from the issue of generalisability (or external validity) there is the issue of content validity. In data collection for case studies, the operational starting point for the field work is often the development of interview schedules. However, prior to this is the conceptual approach or the theoretical starting point, because interview schedules are not produced in a theoretical vacuum. Here, the approach was one of looking at how dependency on overseas aid and the behaviour of the state influenced the implementation process and deriving appropriate questions for interviews.

In summary, this chapter has looked at the rationale behind the choice of research methods and methodology used to generate our primary data. The intention has been to justify the choices made whilst at the same time recognising some of the potential pitfalls. This has been done in order to subject our methodology to close scrutiny so that its suitability for the intended purposes of this research become apparent. To this end, we have spend time critically assessing some of the assumptions that underpin quantitative and qualitative research paradigms - especially with regard to the use of the case study approach in social research.

3 An outline of the Jamaican TVET system

Introduction

A variety of different organisations and institutions provide TVET in Jamaica. Some of these offer formalised programmes of study, targeted at young people wishing to become qualified technicians. Others are more concerned with providing basic skills to enable trainees to enter the labour market as quickly as possible. The origins of TVET provision in this country can be traced to the Apprenticeship Board and the Kingston Technical Institute. The former of these was set-up under the 1955 Apprenticeship Act to provide on-the-job training for the state-owned utilities and the country's expanding bauxite sector (Apprenticeship Board, 1973). Whilst the Kingston Technical Institute, the forerunner of the College of Arts, Science and Technology, was established in the 1930s to give school leavers the opportunity to study technical subjects (CAST, 1989b).

However, when Jamaica achieved independence in 1962, and the country was given control over its own affairs, a greater emphasis was given to TVET. One of the first training organisations to be established, by the elected Jamaican Labour Party (JLP) in 1969, was a company called *Things Jamaica Ltd*. This company was set-up to improve the employment opportunities of people living in rural areas through providing them with basic craft skills. Then at the beginning of the 1970s when the PNP came to power, eighty Industrial Training Centres (ITCs) were constructed to enable students to study for their City and Guilds of London Institute (CGLI) Certificates in engineering. During their first period in office the PNP also set up the Vocational and Technical Development Institute (VTDI) to provide training for the ITC instructors. Other training institutes to be established during this period included the Jamaican and German Automotive School (JAGAS), and the Tool Makers Institute (TMI). Students at JAGAS also studied for the CGLI in Automotive engineering and the TMI designed specific training programmes to meet the needs of industrialists. Furthermore, as a results of major capital developments during the 1980s, financed by the Jamaican government and the World Bank, the College of Arts Science and Technology became the largest post-secondary technical institute in the Caribbean.

When the JLP returned to power in the early 1980s, attempts were made to co-ordinate the country's TVET system by establishing the Human Employment and Resource Training Trust (HEART). The Trust was established under the 1982 Human Employment and Resource Training Act and later it became directly involved in training through the construction of four HEART Academies (USAID, 1992). These Academies provide school leavers, and later displaced workers, with basic skills training for employment in specific occupations. Another programme, implemented by the HEART Trust during the late 1980s, called the school leavers programme, was also concerned with assisting young people in their transition from school to the labour market.

Other major developments to occur during the mid to late 1980s included attempts by TVET institutions in Jamaica to respond to the country's rising unemployment problem. At CAST this resulted in the setting-up of an entrepreneurial extension centre to provide entrepreneurship training for the College's full-time students. It was hoped that this measure would orientate its graduates towards the possibility of working for small business or event starting their own enterprise. The HEART academies have also recently introduced entrepreneurship training for students who wished to set up their own businesses.

In looking at these developments, the chapter begins by outlining the three major organisational structures responsible for co-ordinating, planning and implementing TVET policies in Jamaica. This enables us to discuss in greater depth the type of TVET institutions that operate in Jamaica, the courses they provide and the initiatives responsible for their formation and subsequent development.

Provision under the Ministry of Education

Besides being responsible for the provision of primary and secondary education in Jamaica, the Ministry of Education oversees the activities of the College of Arts Science and Technology. This is the largest post-secondary technical institution in the English speaking Caribbean and at the beginning of the 1990s had an annual intake of 2000 full-time and 3000 part-time students. The full-time students are normally recruited from high school and are expected to have passed four or more CXC (Caribbean Examination Certificate) examinations. These examinations are taken by the majority of secondary school students in the English-speaking Caribbean countries, and have generally replaced the British GCE O-Level examinations in Jamaica.

The organisational structure of CAST is shown in Figure 3.1. At the top of this organisational structure is the Academic Board and the College Council, who are responsible for academic standards and policy respectively. The departments offer a variety of courses ranging from Certificate to Degree level programmes. There are two categories of awards for CAST graduates. Students who study for a diploma or degree receive a qualification accredited by the College's Academic Board. A small minority of students receive their awards from external bodies such as the Association of Certified Accountants in London.

The direction of the College has been influenced by a series of five-year development programmes. These specify broad objectives for the College, and outline the various strategies to be used during the five years. The most recent of these, entitled 'CAST the way forward', had two major objectives

31

for the 1990 to 1995 period. The first of these was to improve the status of award-bearing courses, in preparation for the elevation of the College to Polytechnic or University Status. This was given momentum by the 1986 Education Act. Under the rules and regulations of this Act, the College became responsible for awarding degrees or diplomas to its students who passed the examinations in programmes approved by its academic board. Since the College has now been given official approval to grant its own degrees, various departments have developed their own degree programmes. Also the building and construction department has introduced its own Master's degree programme and the Technical Education department is developing a degree programme at Master's level. In addition, the College has expanded the programmes that are delivered at its extra-mural outreach centres. The largest of these is located in Spanish Town. There are also plans to join other technical Colleges in the English speaking Caribbean in order to deliver programmes that are validated by CAST (CAST, 1991). The combination of these measures will enhance the corporate image of CAST and the expectation is that this will confirm its perception as an institution complementary to, and parallel with, the University of the West Indies.

The second objective of the latest development plan is to make the College more responsive to developing local labour market needs, and anticipated changes in the economy. As a response to labour market needs, the College has modularised its diploma and degree programmes in order to accommodate response to the move towards work-based learning (CAST, 1988b). To facilitate access to these modules, the College introduced a number of evening courses and has started to develop open learning packages for many of its diploma programmes (CAST, 1991). In addition, the computer and engineering departments have delivered their own modules as part of an in-house programme for private sector companies in Jamaica.

Furthermore, in order to equip students with the technical skills which are required by the changing labour market, the CAST Development Plan stated that 'courses should continue to be work-related, scientifically based and technologically relevant' (CAST, 1991). In this respect the College recognises the problem of high unemployment, and of the need to equip students with the necessary skills to work for small businesses, including their own. This led to the introduction of 'entrepreneurship training' as an option for all full-time students on the diploma award bearing courses.

The CAST plan (1990-1995) also commented on how much the success of these five years would depend on the quality of the teaching staff and the support staff. The programme also recognised the problem of high staff turn-over and suggested measures for improvement. These included a better remuneration package and the improvement of in-house staff development. The remuneration package would attempt to attract and retain staff of the desired quality, whilst staff development would assist other individuals to develop specific skills within the context of the institutional setting (CAST, 1991).

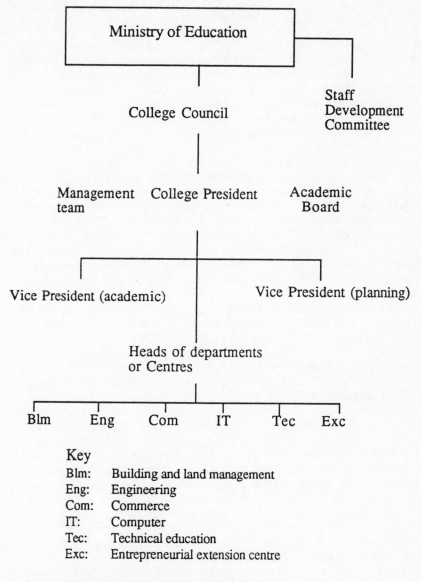

Ministry of Education

College Council

Staff
Development
Committee

Management
team

College President

Academic
Board

Vice President (academic)

Vice President (planning)

Heads of departments
or Centres

Blm   Eng   Com   IT   Tec   Exc

Key
Blm: Building and land management
Eng: Engineering
Com: Commerce
IT: Computer
Tec: Technical education
Exc: Entrepreneurial extension centre

(*source*: interviews with officials at CAST)

Figure 3.1 Organisational structure of CAST

Not surprisingly, the institution plays a central role in supplying skilled manpower at a variety of levels in order to meet the growing needs of the Jamaican economy. The College has trained the majority of secondary technical teachers in Jamaica and the majority of middle-managers and technicians in Jamaica's manufacturing and service industries (World Bank, 1991a). Prior to the establishment of CAST the education system in Jamaica provided little in the field of post-secondary technical education (Halliwell, 1986). Until the late 1980s, the College was totally dependent on central government for its recurrent expenditure. Since then, the College has adopted a more market-orientated philosophy, including the introduction of higher course fees (Hendrikson and Associate Consultants, 1991).

As mentioned previously, the College has its origins in the former Kingston Technical School, which was established in 1935. The initiative for upgrading the school came from a British Advisory committee set-up in 1940 to look at technical education in Jamaica (CAST, 1989b). The Committee recommended that the proposed institution should be comprehensive in nature, providing training for students in building, commerce and engineering as well as teacher training. They also indicated that the content of all courses should reflect the practical, industrial and commercial skills needed within Jamaican society (CAST, 1991). In response to the Advisory Committee's recommendations, the Jamaican House of Representatives introduced an Education Bill in the early 1950s (CAST, 1991) which subsequently became an Act. This provided the framework and guidelines for the Kingston Technical Institute and its successor, when the latter became known as the College of Arts, Science and Technology in 1958, under the recommendations of the then Minister of Education (CAST, 1989b). The College was subsequently given its operating schedule under an Act of Parliament in 1964 (CAST, 1991).

The College began to take recognisable shape in the late 1950s, when it received a capital grant from the British government to construct a new engineering and science department. A year later, the British government provided an additional grant for the development of a commerce department (CAST, 1989b). In the decades that followed (1960-1990), there was considerable expansion in the physical infrastructure, including the technical equipment and facilities for the students. This expansion was achieved through a combination of central government funding and assistance from overseas aid. As a result, seven departments have been established at the College during the last four and a half decades (from 1950 to 1995). In addition, the College has an entrepreneurial extension centre which services other departments by offering modules in entrepreneurship. From discussion with department heads, and through the collection of policy documents, the projects that have been most influential at CAST appear to be those funded by CIDA and the World Bank. The departments most affected have been the entrepreneurial extension centre and the computer department. Besides projects funded by overseas aid agencies, the College has also supported a number of local initiatives, particularly in relation to staff development. Each of these are now discussed in turn.

The entrepreneurial extension centre (EXC) was established at the College of Arts, Science and Technology in 1986. The Centre's primary role is to provide entrepreneurship training for students who are studying at the College (Community Secretariat, 1988). However, since 1991 the Centre has extended its activities to include the provision of support services for small entrepreneurial businesses operating in Jamaica (CAST, 1989b). Overseas aid has played an important part in developments at the Centre. Effectively, the EXC was started in order to co-ordinate the Canadian International Development Agency (CIDA) project entitled 'Education and Entrepreneurship' (Glasgow, 1989). CIDA provided the College with a grant to implement the project over a three-year period. This project aimed to assist the College departments to develop students' projects that were commercially viable. The departments that were affected included commerce, building and construction, engineering and the computer department. The students' projects involved each of the departments setting up a small business. For example, the engineering department used a CNC machine to manufacture specialised fastening devices which were marketed and sold to local companies in Jamaica. Allegedly, these student projects were supposed to simulate the process involved in becoming an entrepreneur, by equipping students with the practical skills that were necessary to become one (Hamilton and Glasgow, 1990). As already indicated, the entrepreneurship training was offered as an optional extra to students studying for the full-time three-year diploma. A number of components were funded under the CIDA project including equipment for the EXC, funding for five Canadian consultants and staff development. The five consultants were based at the College for the duration of the project. One of the consultants had the role of co-ordinating the project and was based at the EXC. The other four consultants were based in the other departments and assisted them to develop their students' projects (Browns College, 1986).

The staff development provided under the CIDA project aimed to familiarise the Jamaican lecturers at the College, with the concept of 'entrepreneurship'. The consultants hoped to achieve this by providing a single afternoon seminar on entrepreneurial development. The function of the seminar was to discuss the different stages in developing student-based projects, and in becoming an entrepreneur (CAST, 1991). The other main form of in-house staff development was based on an approach commonly used in Canada, called 'Counter-parting'. This involved a consultant working closely with a Jamaican lecturer, who was a member of the College staff, for the duration of the CIDA project. The aim of 'Counter-parting' was to enable the Jamaican counterparts to become familiar with developing entrepreneurial projects, and to perform the duties of the consultants once the project was completed (Browns College, 1986). The CIDA project also included overseas study tours (to Canada) for the Jamaican counterparts who were involved in developing student projects and for the Deputy

Director of the EXC. During these study tours, the counterparts visited numerous Community Colleges in Canada to examine student project work. The Jamaicans were also given tours of a number of small businesses that operated in Canada (Association of Canadian Community Colleges, 1989).

When the project 'Education and Entrepreneurship' was completed in 1989, CIDA provided the resources to finance a second project, entitled 'Education and Productivity'. Although, this project was in part a continuation of the first CIDA project, it was also concerned with developing entrepreneurial attitudes and values amongst the College's students. It also financed software developments at the College's computer department. But, in relation to the EXC the second CIDA project aimed to develop entrepreneurial values amongst students through a course entitled *'How to start a small business and succeed'* (CAST, 1991). The course contained ten modules, and provided an introduction to all the major aspects of starting a small business. The course culminated in requiring students to identify a business opportunity, and to write a development plan (Glasgow, 1992). Other components provided under the second CIDA project consisted of funding for two more consultants and equipment to establish the first 'business incubators' in the Caribbean. In total, eight business incubators were established. They provided self-help facilities for entrepreneurs (such as the use of personal computers and printing facilities), and access to facsimile services. The project also enabled the EXC to have a small but specialised library in entrepreneurship (Glasgow, 1989). The two new Canadian consultants assisted the EXC in setting up and implementing the course on entrepreneurship. The consultants were specifically concerned with incorporating case studies of small business development in Jamaica. These case studies were designed to simulate the 'realistic assumptions of how a small business operates in Jamaica' (ACCC, 1989). The course was established by the end of 1989 and, as already indicated, is now offered as an optional module to all students who are studying at the College. Since the course began, a total of 1,549 full-time students have completed the course (Glasgow, 1989). This second CIDA project was completed in April, 1993.

A third project to be implemented at the EXC was the Micro-Enterprise project. This commenced in 1991 and was jointly funded by the Jamaican and Dutch governments. In conjunction with this third project, the ILO funded overseas scholarships for the director of the EXC and for its training co-ordinator. These scholarships consisted of one month study tours to entrepreneurial institutes in India. The aim of the project was to increase the number of micro-enterprises operating in Jamaica (Glasgow, 1992), whilst at the same time expanding its technological base. In order to achieve these objectives, the project provided various support services such as access to short-term and medium-term credit on a favourable basis and advice on business planning. In addition, a training programme was established for small business counsellors which facilitated access to appropriate technology for small businesses.

Under this third project, the Office of the Prime Minister was identified as the executive agent. Whilst other Jamaican organisations (that is, the EXC, the Self Start Fund Ltd (SSF) and the Scientific Research Council

(SRC), were allocated responsibility for implementing different parts of the project. The SRC at the University of the West Indies was responsible for developing appropriate technology and also for providing the institutional mechanisms for getting the technology into the hands of small entrepreneurs (Glasgow, 1992). The SSF was in charge of dispersing loans to micro-entrepreneurs. At the EXC itself, the Micro-Enterprise project provided funding for two areas of development. The first was the establishment of a Counselling course at the EXC. The course lasted for a period of ten days, and aimed to equip small business advisers with the necessary skills to develop small businesses in their local communities (Glasgow, 1992). The course provided seminars on the conditions attached to obtaining a loan, basic record keeping, how to construct balance sheets, profit and loss accounts, how to prepare applications for a loan and how to deal with applicants who were having problems in meeting payments.

The second area of development was the production of an 'enterprise package' which was intended as a starter package for people who wished to become entrepreneurs. The package contained a business plan, recently developed appropriate technology, and the resources necessary to buy raw materials. The technology used in the package was designed by the Scientific Research Council, and the business plan was developed by the EXC staff. In practice, the EXC invites potential entrepreneurs to take a personality test if they wish to be considered for a package. The test attempts to identify whether an individual has the personality traits associated with entrepreneurship.

Information Technology (IT) at CAST

The computer department was established at CAST in 1976 and its primary function is to teach information technology to students at the College. In addition it provides administrative support for the management of the College (CAST, 1991). The computer department delivers a wide variety of study programmes, and services the other departments at the College with a module entitled 'Information Processing'. Its own programmes of study allows students to study for qualifications at Certificate, Diploma and Degree levels. The Certificate is validated internally by CAST's Curriculum Development Council. Students who pursue the Certificate programme are also offered the opportunity of taking Stage One of the British Computer Society examination (BCS), which is marked and validated in London.

The origins of the computer department can be traced to the mid-1970s when the British government, in collaboration with a former British company, International Computers Limited, installed a single mainframe computer at the College (CAST, 1989b). Discussions with the computer department staff indicated that the British government had also provided technical assistance. This comprised the appointment of two short-term ODA consultants, whose function was to establish a course at the department entitled 'Electronic Data Processing'. Further developments at the computer department were influenced by the World Bank III Education

Project, the CIDA Education and Entrepreneurship Project and the CIDA Education and Productivity Project.

The World Bank Education III Project was a multi-million dollar one, jointly financed by the World Bank and the Jamaican government, each of which provided equal contributions (World Bank, 1990). It was anticipated by the World Bank that implementation of the project would start in 1980. However, the computer department was only one of the minor components financed under the World Bank Education III Project and its overall aims were to address the inadequate output of trained technicians and middle-level managers and the weak management of the country's TVET system. Under the World Bank Education project, the computer department received new equipment, an overseas scholarship, and funds for capital developments. The scholarship allowed the Head of department to study for the MSc Degree in computer science at the University of Minnesota, and to also undertake study tours of other technical institutions involved in training computer technicians. The scholarship was intended to provide the knowledge necessary to improve the quality of the programmes delivered at the department. The capital funds provided by the project also enabled the College to use a larger building to house the computer department, together with its new equipment (USAID, 1991).

The second and third projects implemented at the computer department were those funded by the CIDA. As mentioned earlier in this chapter the objective of the first CIDA project was to develop student projects that were commercially viable. Under this project, the computer department was provided with long-term technical assistance and an overseas scholarship. However, the CIDA Phase II project was concerned with improving the delivery of department's programmes and in helping the department to support IT developments, both within other departments and in the College's administration system. In order to achieve this, CIDA provided the computer department with three different software packages, short-term technical assistance and a further 16 IBM compatible computers (ACCC, 1989). In connection with each of the software packages the project provided short-term technical assistance. According to a senior lecturer interviewed, this technical assistance consisted of an ACCC consultant installing each of the software packages and providing the department with corresponding instruction manuals.

Staff Development at CAST

At the beginning of the 1990s the College had nearly 150 full-time members of staff. However, one of the major problems facing the College was retaining teaching staff. For example, in the computer department the retention rate was only 20 per cent. Although, in part this problem could be solved through relying on part-time staff, the College is attempting to reduce turn over by providing existing teaching staff with improved training opportunities. In this respect the goals of the College staff development policy at the beginning of the 1990s were to ensure that all teaching staff without a First Degree were given the opportunity to obtain one.

Furthermore, those who already had obtained this qualification were given the opportunity to engage in at least one professional development activity. It was envisaged this would help to alleviate the high turn-over rate. Thus, with regard to the first of these goals it was required that all teaching staff without a degree should study for the B.Ed in-service degree course, delivered by the College's Technical Education department (CAST, 1989).

Whilst in relation to the second goal, participation in a professional development activity, attempts were made to find the appropriate members of staff overseas scholarships. Indeed, the College's recently established Human Resource Development Unit acted as a clearing house for overseas scholarships and also helped departments with their applications. Over the past 10 to 15 years a large number of staff had been able to benefit from overseas scholarships attached to aid-funded projects. Thus, at the computer department, the World Bank project enabled the head of department to study for an MSc in computer Studies, and the CIDA project financed familiarisation tours to Canadian institutions involved in entrepreneurship training. Whilst at the science department the Kellogg's project financed three senior lecturers to study at American universities for Degrees at Master's level. Other departments, including engineering, building and construction and technical education benefited from similar type scholarships. From conversations with department heads it was revealed that the basis for selecting candidates for overseas scholarship was the lecturer's number of years of service.

This short discussion of CAST has attempted to illustrate how the College has become the largest post-secondary technical institution in the English speaking Caribbean. A variety of initiatives and projects were shown to be responsible for this development. However, all of these must be seen in the light of the College's commitment to strategic planning. Not only his this ensured that CAST is responsive to the dynamics of the country's labour market, but also to the changing needs of students and employees. This is reflected in the type of courses which are developed at CAST, including the innovative ways in which they are delivered. Other TVET institutions in different countries could learn some important lessons from the practices that are occurring at CAST.

Provision under the HEART Trust

The second of the structures in Jamaica responsible for the implementation of TVET policies is the HEART trust (see Figure 3.2) There are a number of different organisations operating under the umbrella of the HEART Trust. These include the Vocational, Technical and Development Institute which provides pedagogical and vocational skill upgrading for instructors in Jamaica; the HEART academics which provide basic skills training for those who work in the country's growing export sector; and the school leavers programme (SLP) which facilitates the movement of school leavers into the workplace. The HEART Trust also co-ordinates the activities of the other TVET structures in Jamaica, including Jampro. This latter body plays an important role in supporting the country's drive for exports and is responsible for the Tool Makers Institute (an organisation which provides short-term training courses for the private sector).

The Trust itself was established by a Parliamentary mandate in 1982 to co-ordinate the country's skills training and enhance employment opportunities in Jamaica (USAID, 1992). The HEART Trust, and the various institutions that operate under it, have benefited from numerous aid-funded projects and local initiatives. For example, the HEART Trust received funding from the United States Agency for International Development, under the Basic Skills Training Project (BSTP). This project had two overriding goals, the first of which was to support the institutional development of the Trust, whilst the second was to upgrade and expand the skills training programmes at the Ministry of Youth and Community Development (USAID, 1989a). Both of these objectives must be seen in the light of the government's recent commitment to an export-led growth strategy and of the need to make TVET provision more responsive to private sector needs. Thus, in relation to the institutional development of the HEART Trust, the BSTP proposed to achieve this by developing a number of inter-agency agreements between the institutions involved in skill training, and also by setting-up a Management Information System to aid the process of labour market analysis (USAID, 1986). Whilst the second objective was to be achieved by establishing a Non-Formal Education Division within the Ministry of Youth and Community Development. The purpose of this division was to update the curricula of skills training institutions in Jamaica, particularly the Industrial Training Centres. Other developments financed under the BSTP included the upgrading of the country's Apprenticeship Programme, together with the capital developments and the introduction of new courses at the Vocational and Technical Development Institute (VTDI).

However, in the mid-1980s the direction of the BSTP changed and rather than focusing on the institutional development of the HEART Trust, the BSTP became more concerned with the construction and equipping of the four HEART Academies. The decision to establish the former occurred at the same time the government decided to close 80 per cent of the country's Industrial Training Centres. Other changes included the replacement of support for the Apprenticeship Programme with the establishment of the School Leaver's Programme. By looking at the process involved in constructing one of the HEART academies it is possible to comment on how some of the project resources were spent. For example, the BSTP financed the construction of the Garmex Academy, the largest institution in the Caribbean, to provide training in garment construction skills. At Garmex, the BSTP financed the construction of a teaching auditorium with a 1,000 seat capacity, a 16,000 square foot training factory, a dexterity and vision testing room, and a library. The equipment purchased for the Garmex academy consisted of 250 sewing machines and training books, all of which were obtained from the United States (HEART, 1990). The USAID officials who were interviewed said that the workbooks enabled the students to study at their own pace, and according to their own ability.

Under the project, a number of overseas scholarships were provided for the Jamaican staff at the academy. This allowed one manager to study for a BA in Business Management in the United States. Three other managers travelled on two months familiarisation tours to garment training academies in the USA. These tours enabled the managers to observe how American students were taught garment construction skills. The American academies also familiarised managers with the occupational culture of a garment factory which consisted of conducting training in a regimented manner and through operating a strict system of security. When the managers returned to Jamaica these techniques were applied to the training process at Garmex.

Other components provided by the BSTP at Garmex consisted of technical assistance. This involved a number of USAID consultants developing a curriculum for the machine operators and the machine mechanics courses. The USAID officials interviewed explained that the curriculum for the Garmex Academy were derived from a specific job analysis of the skills required under the 807 programme (this related to a component within the North American Free Trade Agreement). Factories operating under this programme have a very strict division of labour in which four types of machinery are used in the construction of a garment. Industries require that workers have a degree of specialisation in operating one of these machines. Consequently, trainees at Garmex received 'hands-on experience' in operating one of these machines and so become familiar with constructing one part of a garment.

Before dealing with the other components provided under the BSTP it is useful to briefly discuss another project which was implemented at Garmex Academy in the late 1980s. This project, funded by the Jamaican government, enabled the Garmex Academy to upgrade its courses and to introduce new courses at the beginning of the 1990s. The process of upgrading was performed by the Academy's own staff and supported with technical assistance from the HEART Trust. As a consequence of these developments the Academy's courses now offer supporting studies in English and Maths, to improve the level of literacy and numeracy of the trainees. A new course in tailoring was also developed for trainees who wished to become self-employed and produce garments for the domestic market. The tailoring course also offered students six afternoon seminars on the subject of self-employment, which looked at where to obtain loans, how to develop a business plan, and how to market the final garment. The managers at the Garmex Academy also removed what could be regarded as the Academy's 'authoritarian management techniques', including the searching of trainees as they left the premises. Other components provided under the BSTP included the school leavers programme and support for upgrading the Vocational Technical and Development Institute.

The School Leavers Programme

The school leavers programme was set-up by the HEART Trust in 1983 to provide on-the-job training for young school leavers. As already indicated, the purpose of the SLP was to bridge the gap between school and work, and

41

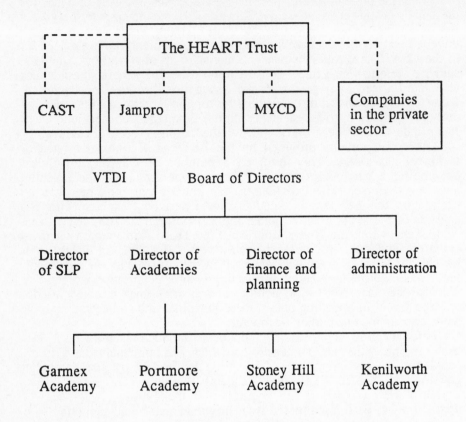

Key

HEART: Human Employment and Resource Training

--------- : Direct responsibility of the HEART Trust

- - - - - : Co-ordinating responsibility of the HEART Trust

SLP : School leavers programme

MYCD: Ministry of Youth and Community Development

(*source*: interviews with officials at HEART)

Figure 3.2 Organisational structure of the HEART Trust

to provide school leavers with the necessary skills to obtain future employment. The programme varies in length from two to three years, depending on the type of placement school leavers receive. If school-leavers are interested in obtaining a placement, they have to register with HEART, indicating their employment preference. There are seven HEART offices scattered throughout Jamaica where school leavers can register. HEART officials attempt to find each registered school-leaver a suitable vacancy in his/her locality. On finding such a vacancy, the school leaver is interviewed by HEART officials and if successful, is placed in a company where he/she will follow a training programme. The programme is prepared by the HEART officials and company representatives jointly, and contains different competencies which trainees are expected to achieve during their placements. An official from HEART commented that companies participating in the school leavers programme are regularly monitored by one of the organisation's placement officers to ensure that training is taking place. The trainees on the school leavers programme receive an allowance each week from their employers. The government encourages companies to employ trainees on the school leavers programme by reducing the amount of training tax they are required to pay each year. According to one of the HEART administrators, companies are also entitled to a larger tax deduction if they employ female trainees on the school leavers programme.

Instructor development at the Vocational and Technical Development Institute

The Vocational and Technical Development Institute is responsible for the training and development of instructors in Jamaica. The VTDI was set up in the mid 1970s to provide training for instructors who worked in the country's Industrial Training Centres (Ministry of Youth and Community Development, 1984). Since 80 per cent of the country's ITCs closed in the mid 1980s, the VTDI plays a major role in the training and development of instructors from other TVET institutions, particularly those from the recently established HEART Academies. However, one of the major problems faced by the VTDI in the past is obtaining the quantity of instructors with the right qualifications to deliver the organisation's programmes (World Bank, 1990). As a consequence, officials at the VTDI and at HEART have commented that owing to the lack of suitably qualified instructors they are forced to recruit candidates with lower qualifications than they would like.

The VTDI has developed out of a number of different aid projects and programmes. The first of which, supported by the United Nations Development Programme and the Jamaican government, involved a team of ILO consultants who helped supervise the construction of the VTDI workshops and the development of the institution's original courses. Thus, by the mid 1970s the VTDI was able to deliver a basic instructors training course and two in-services courses.

The second major project to be implemented by the VTDI was financed by the World Bank and proposed to improve the Institution's capability

43

through an upgrading of the physical facilities and by providing technical assistance. With regard to the first of these objectives the project was supposed to construct a number of new workshops in areas of growing demand, including industrial electronics and information technology (World Bank, 1989b). Whilst technical assistance included three overseas consultants, each to be based at the VTDI for four months, and overseas fellowships for four of the institution's instructors. The overseas consultants were to oversee the physical developments discussed previously and also develop new syllabuses to help upgrade the VTDI's courses (World Bank, 1990b).

The final aid-funded project to be implemented at the VTDI was a component provided under the USAID's Basic Skills Training Project. This proposed to establish a new diploma course in Human Resource Development (HRD) for the instructors who worked at the VTDI. Furthermore, overseas fellowships provided under the USAID project also enabled four of the VTDI instructors to study at overseas institutions for their B.Eds. Another twenty man-months of overseas study programmes were provided to upgrade the technical skills of VTDI instructors. The VTDI staff interviewed revealed that a number of USAID consultants were based at the VTDI for the first two years of the project, and provided short-term seminars on the testing and monitoring of students and the development of curriculum and teaching materials (USAID, 1990). In order to support curricular development at the VTDI and at the HEART Academies, and to provide these institutions with instructional technology, the USAID consultants also proposed to establish a Non-Formal Education Division (NFED) within the Ministry of Youth and Community Development.

In addition to the foreign aid-funded projects discussed above, the Jamaican government financed the development of two new courses at the VTDI, the first of which was entitled the Cadet Training Programme, and the second a diploma in HRD. The former was supposed to have been developed under USAID's BSTP, and was instead developed jointly by the VTDI and the HEART Trust. The HEART Trust also developed guidelines for a two-year, in-service diploma in Human Resource Development which provided further development for the HEART instructors. The diploma's proposed structure will be based on a modular system to encourage flexibility of learning and achievement, permitting different routes or combinations of learning to take place in order to meet the needs of instructors (Oliver, 1992).

The Tool Makers Institute at Jampro

The final training organisation directly under the HEART Trust is the Tool Makers Institute. When the TMI was established at the beginning of the 1970s its objective was to meet the training needs in the tool and dye industry. Since 1980, the TMI has extended its training activities to include electrical engineering and new areas such as Production Management and Garment Construction (Jampro, 1992). The TMI attempts to meet the training needs of industry through delivering diploma courses, in mechanical, electrical and maintenance engineering, which are delivered on a full-time and part-time basis. In addition it offers a number of short-term courses which are non-award bearing. There are a number of procedures involved in constructing these courses. First, the TMI attempts to identify the needs of private industry by conducting a training needs analysis survey. The Institute is then able to decide on the content of its short courses. When designing the courses, TMI instructors always liaise with representatives from industry. When a draft has been constructed it is presented to industrialists to see if it will meet their training objectives. The course is then advertised in the local press, stating its content, costs and venue. The Tool Makers Institute then has to find qualified instructors to deliver the courses.

Provision under the Ministry of Youth and Community Development

The final of the organisational structures in Jamaica for planning and implementing the country's TVET policies is the Ministry of Youth and Community Development. This structure is shown in Figure 3.3. The major distinction between the programme delivered under the MYCD, and that of the MOE, is that the former delivers training outside of formal institutions and the emphasis is on practice rather than theory.

Things Jamaica Ltd

One of the major organisations to provide non-formal training is *Things Jamaica Ltd* which is owned by the Jamaican government. Essentially this company is run as a profit-making organisation manufacturing craft items for sale in both Jamaica and overseas, acting as a marketing agent and provider of training services for independent craft producers in Jamaica.

The origins of the company can be traced back to the late 1960s when the Jamaican Labour Party (JLP) funded the construction of a craft factory. In 1973, the factory employed 950 persons (Seaga, 1988). The designs for the factory's products originated from crafts produced locally such as ceramic pots and cane baskets. During the 1970s, the PNP administration further assisted the company with the sale of its crafts through establishing a number of marketing outlets. A total of three shops were constructed, one at each of the country's airports and one at Kingston's craft market. A shopping complex was also developed called Devon House. This contained several shops, each selling items produced at *Things Jamaica Ltd* and two restaurants. It was hoped the complex would attract tourists and so expand the company's sales.

In 1981, when the JLP returned to power, the function of *Things Jamaica Ltd* changed radically. The company closed down its manufacturing activities and instead became a marketing agent for independent craft producers in Jamaica. The JLP administration planned to re-introduce the Social Development Commission's (SDC) former Village

45

Programme and make *Things Jamaica Ltd* responsible for the collection and marketing of crafts produced there. This programme was originally implemented in the 1960s and consisted of 100 organised community groups who produced craft items such as cane baskets and wood carvings. Under these proposals, crafts produced by village community groups would be marketed through outlets such as Devon House. There were further plans by the JLP administration to expand the number of community-based projects to 200. The government estimated that by the time the crafts had reached the company's outlets, national employment would have increased by 25,000 people (MYCD, 1984).

According to officials at *Things Jamaica Ltd*, the structure and function of the organisation further changed in the late 1980s when it became the responsibility of the HEART Trust. The organisation was now accountable to the HEART Trust as opposed to the Ministry of Youth and Community Development; and its activities reverted to the manufacturing of its own craft items and the collection and marketing of crafts produced by local communities.

Furthermore, under the direction of HEART, attempts were made to improve the efficiency of collecting craft items through re-organising the SDC's community projects into 14 larger production groups. Officials at *Things Jamaica Ltd* said this provided craftsmen with access to cheaper raw materials and also enabled community leaders to access training programmes at *Things Jamaica Ltd*. HEART also attempted to improve the quality of crafts manufactured by independent producers through establishing a Craft Bank. The purposes of the craft bank were two fold. First it would provide *Things Jamaica Ltd* with the opportunity to determine the type and quality of craft items manufactured by each of the 14 production groups. Second, it would enable HEART to design an appropriate curriculum on how to manufacture items contained in the craft-bank.

There were several items contained in the bank including baskets, wicker crafts, wood carvings, ceramic pots and clothes. A quality control unit at *Things Jamaica Ltd* set the standards for judging crafts and the criteria for determining whether they become part of the organisation's Craft Bank. The craft items must be manufactured from indigenous materials and the production costs must be low. Furthermore, the items must be simple to produce, require minimum tools and be of a certain quality and appeal to the public. The crafts are then compared by the quality control unit using the above criteria and are assigned a star rating from 0 to 3, the latter being the optimal. If the product is approved then it goes to a management committee at Things Jamaica Limited where the final decision is made to accept or reject the crafts and where necessary, make the modifications (Things Jamaica Ltd, 1992)

The HEART Trust assists *Things Jamaica Ltd* with its training activities through designing its curricula. The courses are intended to provide students with the skills required to construct items contained in Things Jamaica's craft bank. The training courses last between 3 and 6 weeks and are delivered by one of the 20 full-time instructors who work at *Things Jamaica*

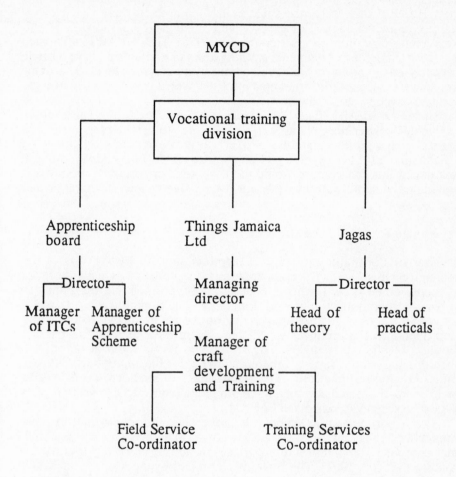

Key
MYCD: Ministry of Youth and Community Development
ITCs : Industrial Training Centres

(*Source*: Interviews with officials at MYCD)

Figure 3.3   Organisational structure of the Ministry of Youth and Community Development

Ltd. The persons attending the courses are NGO employees, or community leaders from one of the organisation's producer groups. Senior officials from HEART said that once students had completed their courses they returned to their communities and provided training to other individuals who were interested in craft production (Seaga, 1988). Thus HEART anticipated that these short courses delivered at *Things Jamaica Ltd* would have a ripple effect by encouraging skills development at community level. The items which were successfully marketed in 1991 were: small wood carvings, costume jewellery and straw items.

Under the HEART Trust, the factory at *Things Jamaica Ltd* also started producing 'pewter mugs' and 'period furniture' to commemorate the 300 years since the former capital Port Royal was destroyed. This venture was a collaborative effort between a private company and *Things Jamaica Ltd.* It was hoped that the venture would earn the country foreign currency and provide training and full-time jobs for twenty five people (*Things Jamaica Ltd*, 1992).

The Apprenticeship Scheme

Another of the major programmes administered by the MYCD is the apprenticeship scheme. The apprenticeship scheme was originally designed to supply domestic industries including public utilities and the Jamaican railway corporation with skilled craftsmen. The apprenticeship lasts for between three and five years, depending on the nature of the trade. During their apprenticeship, trainees spend four days a week learning their trades through 'on-the-job training'. The remaining day is spent at one of the country's Industrial Training Centres, studying for the appropriate City and Guilds London Institute certificate. To become an apprentice, a person must be 15 years of age and educated up to 9th grade (equivalent to year 10 - key stage 4, in secondary schools in England).

The Apprenticeship scheme is governed and controlled by the Apprenticeship law of 1955. Under this law a Board was set up to establish and supervise standards of non-formal, in-house, company training in Jamaica (MYCD, 1991). The Board is controlled by the Ministry of Youth and Community Development, and the Minister is responsible for selecting its members. On becoming an apprentice a person enters into a contract with the Apprenticeship Board. Under this contract the trainee is paid a fixed wage by his or her company and is required to abide by the terms of his contract to the end of his training. In effect this means they must: attend work and College regularly, perform diligently at work, protect the employer's property and develop what is referred to as 'safe working habits'. The employers, in turn, are obliged to send the apprentice to an institution providing theoretical training relating to his trade and also submit progress reports to the Board on the performance of the apprentice. To ensure that standards of training are maintained, trainees are trade tested at the end of their apprenticeship. The test is administered by MYCD officials at one of the country's Industrial Training Centres.

4 An analysis of the implementation process in Jamaica

Introduction

The present chapter analyses the process involved in implementing projects and programmes in Jamaica. As can be recalled from the methodology chapter, two approaches were used to analyse these implementation processes. The first of these focuses on projects that were implemented at public TVET institutions, including how they were initiated, managed, and implemented. Consideration is also given to the effect these projects had on the institution where they were implemented. This enables us to address the role played by donor agencies in the implementation process and to the corresponding impact of depending on foreign technical and components obtained from the First World. The first projects analysed are those that were implemented at the College of Arts, Science and Technology. The subsequent part of the chapter turns to those projects that were implemented at public TVET institutions operating under the HEART Trust and the Ministry of Youth and Community Development (MYCD).

However, in using the market approach, the second part of the chapter examines the provision of TVET by companies and non-governmental organisations. In doing so, particular attention is paid to whether the government has created a favourable policy environment for companies and non-governmental organisations to provide TVET, and also how effectively and efficiently the government has supported this type of provision.

Analysis of developments at CAST

CAST in the only post-secondary TVET institution in Jamaica operating under the Ministry of Education. In dealing with CAST, this chapter initially focuses on projects implemented at the entrepreneurial extension centre (EXC), then those that were implemented at its computer department and finally the programme that was used to support the continuing and professional development of the College's staff.

49

Projects implemented at the EXC

The entrepreneurial extension centre (EXC) was established at the College of Arts, Science and Technology in 1986 under the CIDA phase I project (CAST, 1989b). Under this project the Centre's primary role was to encourage students to become entrepreneurs through establishing their own businesses. However, as a result of the CIDA phase II project the EXC became more concerned with developing entrepreneurial values amongst its students. Further changes occurred in the 1990s as a result of the Micro-Enterprise project, which enabled the EXC to extend its activities to include the provision of support services for small businesses which operate in Jamaica. Each of these projects are analysed in turn below.

The CIDA phase I project

The initiative for this project came from the Association of Canadian Community Colleges (ACCC). One of the roles of the ACCC is to establish and strengthen links between institutions in Canada and institutions in the Third World (Browns College, 1986). In 1985, the ACCC consultants had just completed a project at CAST, and were concerned with strengthening the existing links by establishing a further project at the College. The consultants had to identify an area which would be beneficial for both the Community Colleges in Canada, and CAST. At the time entrepreneurship training was expanding in Canada, and it was felt by the Canadian consultants, and the president of CAST that such training would benefit the employment prospects of students (Hamilton and Glasgow, 1990). Further justification for entrepreneurship training came through a survey conducted by the ACCC in Jamaica. The survey aimed to identify the contributions that small businesses made to the Jamaican economy. The results indicated that 41 per cent of the workforce in Jamaica could be classified as self-employed, or as working in small businesses (Hamilton and Associates, 1986).

Having identified the area of entrepreneurship training as one for closer links with CAST, the ACCC consultants in Jamaica sent a project proposal to the funding agency CIDA for further funds (Browns College, 1986). The project was approved and CIDA provided the necessary resources for implementing the 'Education and Entrepreneurship' project. The dependency of CAST on overseas aid meant that the Canadian representatives were able to determine the components provided under the project. From interviews conducted at the College none of the academic members of CAST staff were involved in identifying areas for project funding, or in constructing the project proposal. It appears that the assumption underpinning CIDA's control was that CIDA had a superior knowledge of entrepreneurship training, and that through dominating all aspects of the project's operation they could ensure its successful implementation.

The extent of CIDA's control was also apparent in the early management stages of the project. Under an agreement with CIDA, the ACCC consultants were given full responsibility for the project's management and implementation in Jamaica (Browns College, 1986). Once the project was initiated, the ACCC consultants were totally responsible for formulating its strategy and determining the components provided. In formulating the strategy the ACCC consultants were influenced by the entrepreneurship training which was occurring at the Community Colleges in Canada. These Colleges were attempting to develop entrepreneurs by encouraging their students to undertake projects that were commercially viable. As a consequence, students' projects became the main vehicle for entrepreneurial development at CAST (CAST, 1991). Furthermore, prior to developing the actual students' projects, the ACCC consultants had identified the departments in the College where the projects could be based. The departments were those of computing, commerce, building and construction, and engineering (CAST, 1989b). The ACCC consultants had also identified the Jamaican lecturers who would act as their counterparts for the duration of the project. According to the Director of the EXC, the Jamaicans were chosen because of their 'successful business experience'.

The guidelines for implementing the project were outlined in a project document designed by the ACCC consultants and specified the amount and type of equipment, personnel and materials that would be supplied under the project. The guidelines also stated that all components of the project, including personnel, would be obtained from Canada (Browns College, 1986). Under these conditions, the ACCC ensured that an additional five Canadian consultants were appointed to provide technical assistance to the different departments of the College. As well as controlling all aspects of the project's implementation, CIDA ensured that the majority of resources were invested in Canadian personnel and materials, and in overseas scholarships to institutions in Canada. Interestingly, out of the total project expenditure, over 70 per cent of the resources were spent on staff costs for the Canadian consultants (Hamilton and Glasgow, 1990). Thus the College's dependency on overseas aid and the tied nature of this aid, ensured that the majority of the resources used in the project flowed indirectly back to Canada, rather than to the development of the educational infrastructure in Jamaica. The cumulative effect of the CAST's dependency on CIDA was an attempt to replicate the 'Canadian Entrepreneurial Model' within the confines of selected departments at CAST. There was no attempt by CIDA or by the ACCC consultants to consider how the 'Canadian Entrepreneurial Model' would operate in the context of a different environment, or what changes needed to be incorporated into this Model.

Despite the good intentions of the project, by the end of the second year none of the College departments had developed projects for students (ACCC, 1989). The research could identify a number of reasons why the project failed to achieve the former objectives. Basically, nearly all of these related to CIDA's control of the implementation process and to the attempt to replicate the 'Canadian Entrepreneurial Model' in Jamaica. Indeed, from discussions with CAST staff it transpired that although the five consultants from the Community Colleges in Canada were experts in their respective subject areas such as engineering and computing, they had limited experience or knowledge of entrepreneurship. Even the ACCC's (1989) appraisal report commented that the Canadian consultants spent less than 50 per cent of their time on activities related to entrepreneurship and instead spent the majority of their time teaching (ACCC, 1989). As a result, they were unable to function as co-operants in each of the selected departments. Consequently, their Jamaican counterparts were unable to gain the knowledge of entrepreneurship which the project had been designed to impart to them.

There were also limitations to the other forms of staff development provided under CIDA's Phase 1 project. The College staff interviewed commented that the single seminar on Entrepreneurial Development was too short. It did not fully explain what was meant by the term 'entrepreneurship', and what was expected of them under the CIDA project. The relevance of the overseas scholarships for Jamaicans could also be questioned. The context and circumstances under which a small business operates in Canada are very different from those in Jamaica. Indeed, the Director of the EXC explained that in a First World country such as Canada, a small business has the support of a well-developed government infrastructure, including access to support services and government loans on a favourable basis. In contrast, the infrastructure in Jamaica is not so advanced, and the government lacks the necessary resources to support the development of small businesses. Also, a small business in Canada is normally much larger both in physical size and turnover. Given the differences between the two countries, the EXC Director argued that Jamaicans can gain little from studying small businesses in Canada or attending seminars at the Canadian Community Colleges. The Jamaicans in question would have benefited more from the project if they had visited a developing country, such as Kenya or India, which has experience of developing entrepreneurial training programmes. Another point to consider was that the ACCC consultants' choice of Jamaican counterparts was made without an adequate consideration of their availability or suitability. Many amongst the Jamaican teaching staff at CAST were unable devote the necessary time to entrepreneurship because of their large teaching loads (Hamilton and Glasgow, 1990). Also, from the staff's answers to questions about their qualifications and experience, it emerged that whilst some of the CAST staff had industrial experience, none had been previously self-employed or had worked for a small business.

In relation to the second of the issues, the attempt to replicate the 'Canadian Entrepreneurial Model' in Jamaica', the six ACCC consultants also seemed to have ignored the cultural context within which the project would operate. The Director of the EXC commented that in contrast to students in Canadian Community colleges the concept of 'entrepreneurship' was culturally alien to the majority of the Jamaican students who studied at CAST. According to the Director, these differences stem from the structure of the secondary school system within each country. In Canada, the secondary education system is structured towards encouraging independent learning through project-based assignments. Whilst, in Jamaica, secondary school education is based on the former British system, under which full-time students have large amounts of contact time with their teachers. Consequently, unlike their colleagues in Canada, secondary school students in Jamaica have little experience of combining study with periods of part-time paid employment. For that matter, they are unfamiliar with paid employment and do not have the same opportunities for entrepreneurial activities.

Another explanation (albeit a minimum one), for the project failing to achieve its stated objective, relates to the students' perceptions of 'entrepreneurship training'. According to the manager of the EXC, students' perceptions had an important influence on the project's implementation. As already indicated the entrepreneurial projects were offered as an optional extra to all students studying on CAST's diploma programmes. However, the students received no recognisable reward for developing their projects. Given this lack of incentive the students would probably have preferred to spend time working for their award-bearing courses, rather than for projects which offered no paper qualifications.

In summary, the evidence shows that the problems experienced during project implementation originated from a variety of factors, including CAST's total dependency on CIDA for both technical assistance and the overall management of the project. Arguably, if the project had involved Jamaican staff instead of depending on CIDA's 'alleged expertise', and incorporated the award of a qualification, then many of the 'problems' experienced during implementation might not have occurred.

The CIDA phase II project

The initiative for the CIDA phase II project came from a report which was commissioned at the end of the 1980s. The report was concerned with assessing the effectiveness of the first CIDA project, and with offering guidance for a second (CAST, 1989b). The report was produced by two other consultants (as evaluation specialists). One was a Canadian representative from CIDA, and the other a Jamaican member of CAST staff (ACCC, 1989). Thus, a Jamaican national was involved in constructing the guidelines for the second CIDA project. The decision to involve Jamaicans represents a change in CIDA's procedures, and a recognition of the possible benefits this involvement could bring. This change in procedures was also evident in the management of the project. The responsibility for managing the implementation of the second project was given to an Advisory Team at the EXC, headed by the former Deputy Director of the EXC and a new Jamaican Training Co-ordinator. The team included the Heads of departments of CAST whose students had participated in the Entrepreneurship Project, and who were responsible for determining how the resources of the project were used in Jamaica (Hamilton and Glasgow, 1990). The change in the management of projects at the EXC was a direct result of the report produced by the two evaluators who had recommended that the ACCC should question its ability to manage 'entrepreneurship programmes' in future (Hamilton and Glasgow, 1990).

However, despite the EXC's relative autonomy in managing the resources of the project, CIDA was still able to have a major influence on the project's implementation. For although the Advisory Team was responsible for managing the project's implementation in Jamaica, they could not determine the components that were provided under the project. The point was that as a result of an agreement specified by CIDA, the ACCC was still responsible for the management of the project at CIDA's Head Office in Canada (ACCC, 1989). This resulted in the project securing a course on entrepreneurship which was provided by the Federal Business Development Bank in Canada (Hamilton and Glasgow, 1990). Nevertheless, attempts were also made to ensure that the course was adjusted to local conditions. For example, two ACCC consultants provided under Phase II of the CIDA project had to introduce nomenclature into the entrepreneurship Course, such as changing the Canadian city names to Jamaican ones and also adapt to Jamaican local government regulations and income tax requirements.

The second CIDA project also resulted in a change in the function of the EXC and instead of aiming to produce 'entrepreneurs', the EXC became more concerned with developing the attitudes and values which are required to become an entrepreneur (CAST, 1991). This change in strategy was a result of the recommendation made by the two evaluation specialists, whose report had commented that:

> Entrepreneurship training is only one small aspect of small enterprise development; and it is advisable that an educational institution such as CAST concentrates on introducing new skills and attitudes towards enterprise development rather than on encouraging the establishment of small businesses themselves (ACCC, 1989).

It was difficult to identify who was actually responsible for determining the new strategy. The EXC Director commented that she had complained to CIDA during the first project about the failure of the ACCC consultants to play their specified roles and had also suggested to CIDA that there was a need for the first project to be reoriented towards developing entrepreneurial values amongst CAST students. The involvement of the Jamaican evaluation specialist from CAST in constructing the project report, and the contribution of the EXC Director, suggests that representatives from CIDA were not totally responsible for determining the new strategy.

As a result of the second project being managed by an Advisory Team at the EXC, there was greater Jamaican involvement in the implementation of the project. This was particularly evident in the technical assistance provided. Thus, instead of depending on the two ACCC Canadian consultants for technical assistance, the advisory team identified a senior member of staff in the College's Technical Education department to act as a third consultant. Their role was to introduce cultural changes into the course on entrepreneurship (ACCC, 1989). The nature of technical assistance in the second CIDA project was also different. The consultants were employed for only the first two months of the project in order to assist the EXC to set up the course on entrepreneurship (Hamilton and Glasgow, 1990) (in contrast to the first CIDA project when consultants were employed for the project's three year life span (Browns College, 1986). The decision not to use long-term, overseas consultancies under the second project meant that more resources were available for the other areas of project expenditure. Thus, in addition to providing computers, business incubators and the course on entrepreneurship, the advisory team was able to use the resources of the project to assist the EXC to upgrade the position of the Deputy Director to that of Director and to also employ a new Training Co-ordinator (both were Jamaicans and members of CAST's staff). In addition, it also provided additional financial resources to supplement the income of the Jamaican department Heads who were involved with the CIDA project.

As a consequence, the EXC Director and the Training Co-ordinator were employed full-time at the EXC, and were relieved of regular teaching duties. In addition, the other project staff did not have to supplement their income through undertaking work outside college hours (ACCC, 1989). The introduction of financial incentives clearly improved the remuneration of the Jamaican lecturing staff, and at the same time probably increased their commitment to the implementation of the project. Performing additional jobs was identified by the evaluators as one of the factors that prevented Jamaican lecturing staff from participating fully in the first CIDA project.

The entrepreneurship course was implemented at the EXC by the end of 1988 and offered as an option to all full-time students (CAST, 1991). At the end of 1989, the Director of the EXC carried out a short appraisal of the new entrepreneurship course. The appraisal involved sending out course evaluation questionnaires to students who had just completed the course. The survey found that participation on the course had resulted in changes in attitudes amongst the course participants and that many of the students now recognised the possibility of working for a small business (Hamilton and Glasgow, 1990). However, the survey also found that the case studies in each of the modules had failed to reflect the reality of the conditions in Jamaica and that as a consequence, students had difficulty in relating to them (Hamilton and Glasgow, 1990). This latter issue appears strange given that the project was meant to ensure that the course was adjusted to local conditions. However, interviews with the Director of the EXC revealed that although the two ACCC Canadian consultants had introduced the necessary nomenclature changes, the Jamaican representative in the Advisory Team had failed to introduce the necessary cultural changes. As a result, the Entrepreneurial course was delivered to students without the modifications required to its cultural content. Discussions with the Training Co-ordinator at the EXC further revealed that the consequence of incorporating technical changes in the module, but foregoing the relevant cultural modifications, resulted in serious problems in delivering the course. For example, one of the staff members at the EXC reported that although town names had been changed in the modules, students were perplexed and had difficulty in understanding why a person would establish a tourist business in May-Pen, one of the poorest rural areas in Jamaica, where the market for tourism is non-existent. The consultants who incorporated 'May-Pen' into the module's first case study were clearly unaware of the adverse effects it would have. The Advisory Team at the EXC should have ensured that problems such as these were limited, through the employment of a local consultant to replace the example of 'May-Pen' by that of Montego-Bay or another area which had a developed market for tourism.

There were further problems associated with the case studies contained in each of the modules. For example, the first case study in module 1, attempted to show the dilemma that a young Jamaican faced in moving from salaried employment to self-employment. The case study assumed that the transition in work patterns from paid employment to self employment occurred in one move. However, a recent survey on the extent of self employment in Jamaica found that the transition is not as straightforward (Hamilton and Associates, 1989). According to the survey, the transition to self employment normally occurs through an intermediate phase, of being employed in the formal sector and being self-employed at the same time. This intermediate phase is identified as one of working in the 'middle informal sector'.

Thus, the problems experienced during the project's implementation were partly a reflection of the project's dependency on the ACCC consultants, and partly on the use of the Canadian programme entitled 'How to Start a Small Business and Succeed'. The ACCC consultants assumed that the Jamaican students would relate to the case studies contained in the Canadian programme if nomenclature changes were introduced. However, the changes introduced by the ACCC consultants resulted in confusion rather than in clarity. Arguably, students at CAST would have been better served by a programme specifically designed by Jamaicans for conditions in the Caribbean. Nevertheless, the effects of dependency were not the total responsibility of the donor agency. Indeed, in this second phase of the CIDA project, CIDA had provided funds for the case studies to be further adapted to the Jamaican culture. Despite the availability of these funds, the Advisory Team failed to introduce the changes. Thus the problems associated with the case study were as much the responsibility of the Advisory Team, as that of the ACCC consultants on whom the project depended.

The Micro-enterprise project

In the previous two aid projects the emphasis was on providing 'entrepreneurship training' to students at CAST. The third project was concerned with diversifying the activities of the EXC to include the provision of support services for micro-entrepreneurs. The initiative for the Micro-Enterprise project came when the People's National Party (PNP) replaced the Jamaican Labour Party as the ruling Party in 1989 (EIU, 1994d). The former was more interventionist than the latter and was concerned with implementing what could be regarded as active labour market policies. In this respect the PNP financed 51 per cent of the costs for the Micro-Enterprise project, with the remainder being provided by the government of the Netherlands. Thus, the initiative for the project was dependent on the political ideology of the Jamaican government of the day and on the activities of CAST, rather than on donor agencies.

As described in Chapter 3, the entrepreneurial extension centre (EXC), the Scientific Research Council (SRC) and the Self Start Fund Ltd (SSF) were each responsible for managing specific aspects of the Micro-Enterprise project. In spite of the project's dependency on overseas financial aid from the Netherlands and the ILO, it was not dependent on international organisations for determining the components, or the personnel used in the project. The Jamaican organisations that managed the project were responsible for these. Thus, the Micro-Enterprise project contrasts with the two CIDA projects in which representatives from Canada determined how resources were invested in TVET.

The strategy for managing the project was formulated by representatives from the EXC, the SSF and the SRC, and involved each of these organisations taking responsibility for the different support services which were financed under the project. Under this strategy of decentralisation the EXC was responsible for training Investment Counsellors, and for constructing 'enterprise packages'. The SRC had the role of developing the technology for these 'enterprise packages'. The SSF was responsible for the distribution of loans through Approved Lending Agencies (ALAs). The ALAs were in turn responsible for disbursing and collecting loans from the micro-entrepreneurs. According to EXC staff, this strategy ensured that the EXC and the SRC had closer control over the project resources through providing the entrepreneurs with ready-made packages. Furthermore, it enabled the SSF to disburse loans through non-governmental organisations, on a commercial basis. When the strategy was initially formulated, it was presented to two overseas agencies for funding. The first of these agencies, CIDA, refused to fund the project because it was concerned with developing entrepreneurs. According to CIDA, the EXC should be concentrating on providing courses on entrepreneurship, rather than on giving advice and support to people who wished to become entrepreneurs (ACCC, 1989).

Further interviews with EXC staff revealed that the proposed strategy was then subsequently submitted to consultants from the International Development Bank (IDB). The IDB sent a project mission to Jamaica in order to meet representatives from the EXC, the SRC and the SSF. The IDB also refused to fund the proposed Micro-Enterprise project but on different grounds. It would fund the project only if the resources were managed and controlled by a single government agency, rather than by non-governmental agencies such as the People's Co-operative Bank or the Worker's Bank. However, adhering to the terms of the IDB would have involved a reversal of the original proposal, which stated that resources would be managed by a number of different organisations (government of the Netherlands/Jamaica, 1990). As a result of these differences, the relationship with the IDB ended, and alternative sources of assistance were sought. Assistance was ultimately obtained through a combination of funding from the Dutch and Jamaican governments (CAST, 1991). This suggested that Jamaican organisations were not always influenced by the conditions attached to project funding by international organisations such as the IDB.

The lack of involvement by international organisations in managing the project enabled the three Jamaican organisations themselves to determine how the resources for the project were used in the implementation process. Thus, at the EXC, a Jamaican consultant was employed to develop a programme for Investment Counsellors. The programme was established at the EXC in January, 1992, and during the first six months of its operation, 35 people successfully completed it. At the time of writing there were plans to use the EXC as a Caribbean regional centre for Investment Counsellors (CAST, 1991). The relative success of the programme suggests that any problems which were experienced during the development of the programme did not have a negative effect on its implementation.

The SRC used the financial resources from the project to develop the appropriate technology. In developing this technology the SRC relied totally on indigenous materials (in this case the government of the Netherlands, 1990). The major technological development was a solar dehydration machine for fruits. The aim of this technology was to enable micro-entrepreneurs to sell dried tropical fruits wholesale to bakeries and hotels in Jamaica. The solar fruit drier was targeted at minority groups who had difficulty in getting access to the finance which is necessary to set-up a micro-enterprise; particularly young women living in rural areas. The SRC's technological developments were incorporated into the 'enterprise packages' which were being developed at the EXC. The reasoning was that if the enterprise packages proved to be a success then the EXC would have contributed towards expanding the technological base of Jamaica and helping to reduce the country's technological dependence on the First World. The SSF also determined the interest rate on loans which were available to micro entrepreneurs. In Jamaica, interest rates in the informal sector were between 60 and 200 per cent. These high interest rates often acted as a serious barrier for people wishing to become entrepreneurs (Glasgow, 1992). From interviews with SSF officials it was revealed that they were attempting to overcome this barrier by offering loans on a much lower rate of interest.

Thus, the non-involvement of the international agencies in the implementation process reduced the dependency of the Micro-Enterprise project on the First World for technology and technical assistance. In turn, the lack of dependency enabled each of the organisations involved in the project to make decisions independently of international aid agencies and to invest financial resources in Jamaican materials and personnel. As a consequence, the resources for the project helped to develop an infrastructure in Jamaica which was likely to promote entrepreneurship rather than developments in the 'First World'.

Overseas aid played an important role in supporting developments in entrepreneurship at the EXC. In particular, both the CIDA phase II project and the Micro-enterprise project appear to have had positive impacts on the College. However, the CIDA phase I project illustrates the problem of transferring models developed in one country and using them in another.

Other implementation difficulties stemmed from the way in which a project was managed locally. We now turn to the provision of information technology at CAST, with a view to identifying whether the implementation experiences of the computer department were similar to those of the EXC.

An analysis of project implementation at the computer department

The various activities of the computer department were spelt out in Chapter 3 and these included the provision of Certificate and diploma courses, as well as support for the College's administrative activities. In this part of the chapter we assess at the extent to which dependence on foreign technical assistance and overseas aid has influenced developments at CAST's computer department. This is achieved by analysing the process involved in establishing the department, and the role played by the World Bank III project, and the two CIDA projects, in its subsequent development.

The establishment of the computer department

The research found no written documentation relating to how the computer department was established in 1976. A member of the senior management team at CAST said that the multinational company, ICL provided the Centre's initial mainframe computer and the ODA was responsible for establishing a course entitled 'Electronic Data Processing' which enabled students to take the British Computer Society's (BCS) examination. However, a member of staff at the Computer department questioned the usefulness of the BCS examination for students who wished to work for local companies. The BCS examination tests students' knowledge of computer programming, rather than the use they make of computer business packages. At the time of writing, the computer department, in conjunction with the Computer Society of Jamaica (CSJ), was attempting to replace the BCS qualification with a CSJ qualification (CAST, 1989b). The proposed CSJ examination will be validated by CAST's Curriculum Development Committee, and will attempt to test students' ability to use business computer packages, rather than their capacity to write computer programmes.

Nevertheless, the failure to develop a comparable qualification sooner, and the dependence of the computer department on the British Computer Society for nearly 20 years, would at first suggest that either students in Jamaica wish to obtain a qualification that is validated by an overseas institution, or Jamaican Institutions are unable to develop a comparable qualification. The first of these suggestions appears more probable, as the department had the capability to establish a comparable qualification and the time to do so, as indicated by the courses which it offers and which are validated by the Curriculum Development Committee and the University Council of Jamaica. Thus, in terms of dependence it appears that CAST students, through their choice of course, had ensured that for 16 years, the computer department remained dependent on the BCS for the validation of the course.

The initiative for the World Bank III Education Project came from the People's National Party in 1978. The project was designed to provide skilled manpower to support the government's policy of expanding under-utilised sectors of the economy including, agriculture, manufacturing, tourism, mining and the service sectors (World Bank, 1990c). The World Bank provided over 60 per cent of the total costs in the form of a loan and the influence of this dependency was seen in 1979 when the World Bank (1991a) refused to process the project loan, because of what it regarded as 'the country's mounting economic and political difficulties'. These 'difficulties' stemmed from the austerity programme which the PNP was attempting to implement, with the assistance of the IMF, in the late 1970s. Under this austerity programme, the PNP government was required to reduce the country's budget deficit through exchange rate devaluations, and by increasing the price of everyday commodities such as food (Killick, 1984). Clearly, the austerity measures were required if the PNP government wished to receive further loans from the International Monetary Fund through its extended loan facility (EIU, 1990). However, the PNP government was unable to introduce the austerity programme because of the pressures it faced from the trade unions and from the radicals within its own party. In February 1980, the PNP government rejected the economic austerity programme, and introduced a socialist style of planning involving closer links with its neighbour, Cuba (Europa Publications, 1992). In rejecting the austerity programme, the PNP government severed links with the IMF and the World Bank, and in doing so prevented the country from obtaining the loan for the Education III Project.

However, the conditions for processing the Education III loan were facilitated by a general election which was called by the PNP government in October 1980 (EIU, 1994d). The election was won by the opposition party, the Jamaican Labour Party. The policies of the JLP were concerned with promoting closer economic links with the USA, and the establishment of a more market-orientated economy. Under the country's new economic policies, austerity measures were reintroduced, and relations with international organisations, including the IMF, were resumed (Europa Publications, 1992). In 1982 the World Bank processed the loan needed to start the Education III Project. Nevertheless, further delays were experienced because the Jamaican government was unable to raise the remaining contribution needed to start the project. The shortage of government resources was a result of the new austerity measures which required a cut back in public expenditure to reduce the public sector deficit. As a consequence of the additional delays, the completion date for the project was subsequently extended to June 1988.

The question at issue is whether the World Bank was justified in not processing the loan in the late 1970s. If the loan had been processed during the country's period of instability, the benefits of the project would have been minimal. At best, the earlier start of the project would have simply produced skilled labour to fill the places of those who continued to migrate. Under this assumption the project would have done little to improve the reservoir of skilled labour in Jamaica, or to support the government's policy of expanding under-utilised sectors of the economy. Taking these views into account, it is not difficult to see why the World Bank did not process the loan until there were more favourable economic and political conditions. It would seem logical that international organisations, rather than the government of Jamaica, should be blamed for the further delays in starting the project (those which occurred between 1982 and 1988). Under the auspices of the IMF, the Jamaican government was required to reduce the country's budget deficit. At the same time, the Jamaican government was required, by the World Bank, to provide the remaining funds which were needed to finance the World Bank Education III project. The Jamaican government, given its lack of financial resources, was understandably unable to respond to these competing demands. The government of Jamaica chose to respond to the requirements of the IMF because of the importance of the extended loan facility; as a consequence, it was late in providing finance for the World Bank Education III project. It is difficult to place full responsibility on the IMF, although it is possible to suggest that if there had been improved co-ordination between the IMF and the World Bank, further delays might not have occurred - but then again, competing terms of reference could not be co-ordinated! Thus, the influence of the government's policy in Jamaica, and the activities of international organisations, resulted in the project being implemented towards the end of the 1980s rather than at the beginning of the 1980s as originally planned.

In order to co-ordinate the overall management of the World Bank project, the Jamaican government created a National Development Agency (NDA). The Agency operated under the jurisdiction of the Ministry of Finance, and was responsible for civil works and equipment procurement. The Ministry of Education and the Ministry of Youth and Community Development were jointly responsible for the respective education and training aspects of the project, including their evaluation of tenders for furniture and equipment, and the selection of education specialists and candidates for fellowships (World Bank, 1990c). Staff at the computer department said that the College Council collaborated with the NDA on matters relating to the capital developments which occurred at CAST and for the procurement of equipment for departments at CAST. Furthermore, the same staff said that they themselves, were responsible for identifying the computers provided under the World Bank Education III project, and for the upgrading of the department's course in 'Electronic Data Processing'.The above evidence shows that despite being financially dependent on the World Bank for 60 per cent of the project's costs, the World Bank had minimal involvement with the management of the project in Jamaica.

The NDA was responsible for formulating the project's strategy. The strategy proposed to expand the number of computer technicians trained in Jamaica through upgrading the physical facilities and equipment at CAST's computer department and also by upgrading the department's EDP course. Interviews conducted with lecturers at CAST and evidence from the World

Bank's (1990b) appraisal report suggested that there were no noticeable problems with the project's implementation until the government of Jamaica disbanded the NDA in 1985, and decided to decentralise the process of implementation. As a consequence of this decentralisation no co-ordination occurred between the Ministry of Education who were responsible for equipment procurement and the releasing of funds, and the institutions affected by the project's initiatives (World Bank, 1991a). The CAST staff, when interviewed, said that they had no idea what project funds were available, or when they were likely to receive such funds and the corresponding equipment. Individual institutions such as CAST were left to implement their respective project initiatives without technical and financial support from the NDA. The lack of co-ordination during the project's implementation resulted in a poor synchronisation of equipment procurement with the completion of capital developments (World Bank, 1991a). This was evident at the computer department, where the physical expansion of the department was completed a long time before the arrival of the equipment.

However, the Jamaican government was not totally responsible for the lack of co-ordination. The World Bank must also take its share of the blame for failing to provide technical assistance during the project's most critical period, when capital developments at CAST were near completion and when the NDA was being disbanded. The World Bank had planned to send a consultancy mission during this period, but the mission failed to materialise, possibly because a general election was being held in Jamaica during this period.

As a result of the World Bank project, the department was able to reduce its dependence on overseas institutions, such as the British Computer Society, for validating its Courses. The number of computer technicians who were trained at CAST had also increased as a consequence of the project. In the three years (1983-1986) prior to the Centre's upgrading, a total of 56 students graduated. In the following three years (1986-1989) the figure was 113. Also, as a consequence of reducing the department's dependency on the British Computer Society for validation, there has also been a reduction in examination fees for Jamaican students. Interviews with senior management at CAST revealed that students were finding it increasingly difficult to meet the cost of overseas examinations owing to the continual devaluation of the Jamaican dollar. In real terms the cost for taking Part One of the British Computer Society's Examination had increased by 400 per cent during the period 1983 to 1988.

Developments at the computer department through the CIDA phase I project

Interviews with the computer department staff revealed that they were not involved in either managing the project, or in identifying the consultant who was based at the department for its duration. Furthermore, the implementation of initiatives at the computer department were totally dependent on technical assistance and on a grant provided by CIDA. The ACCC consultant who arrived at the computer department in 1986 had limited knowledge of entrepreneurship training, and was unaware of how the project intended to develop entrepreneurs (ACCC, 1989). As a consequence, the computer department was unable to implement the CIDA project in its intended form.

Nevertheless, a lecturer remarked that the ACCC consultant supported the computer department with other initiatives, particularly those which were financed under the World Bank Education III project. As no technical assistance was provided for the computer department under the World Bank Education III project, the ACCC consultant helped with the installation of the computers at the department's new premises. The ACCC consultant also developed an additional option for the diploma programme on graphic design and data programming. According the department's staff, the assistance of the consultant was invaluable (because they themselves lacked the necessary time to perform such tasks, owing to a heavy teaching load). The implementation of the CIDA phase I project at the computer department also illustrated the unintended external benefits which can be derived from depending on overseas aid. Because, although the computer department did not participate in identifying the project's technical assistance, they were nevertheless able to determine how it was used.

Developments through the CIDA phase II project

As mentioned earlier in this chapter, the initiative for the CIDA Phase II project came from two Evaluation Consultants, (a Canadian and a Jamaican) who designed the proposal for the second project. They had asked the computer department staff what initiatives they would like to see financed under this second CIDA project. A member of staff commented that they had wanted to establish a networking system since 1986 but had lacked the necessary financial resources. These views were taken into account when the proposal for the second CIDA project was formulated. The decision to involve the staff at CAST enabled the identification of a project which would be of benefit to themselves, rather than one which CIDA thought would benefit the department.

The control of the project's operation in Jamaica was given to an Advisory Team at the EXC. However, staff at the computer department and one of the College's administrators were responsible for managing the information technology components of the CIDA project. The project proposed to improve the delivery of the department's programmes and services through installing three software packages on the department's existing computer system and by producing a number of instruction manuals. Despite involving Jamaican staff in the construction and management of the project, CIDA was responsible for identifying the different software packages which would be provided under the CIDA project, as well as the short-term ACCC consultants who would be responsible for installing the computer packages, and producing the instruction manuals. Thus, although staff at CAST were allowed to participate in the project's implementation they were still dependent on decisions made by CIDA. There was a disagreement between CIDA and the computer department staff over the type of components which had been identified for the project. Under the original project proposal, CIDA intended to supply the computer department with additional software packages for word processing and data processing. However, a senior lecturer interviewed commented that these software packages were widely used by the students, and that the department would benefit from more recent developments in software, such as 'Windows'.

CIDA had also identified a network package for the computer department. However, the copyright protection on the proposed network package limited the number of computers which could be linked up at the College. The College administrator who was involved with the project pointed out that CAST would be better served by a particular network package (entitled Network 3.11) which would enable a greater number of machines to be connected up at the College and also provider users to access programs through a file server. Subsequently, the views of staff at CAST were taken into account, and the CIDA project provided the packages which the senior lecturer and the senior administrator had requested.

The project experienced problems in synchronising the arrival of the computer software with the arrival of the first ACCC consultant. Thus, although the consultant arrived on time to install this software, he was unable to fulfil his role since the Canadian company who supplied the package had gone bankrupt. Moreover, eventually when a new supplier was found the consultant had returned to Canada. Nevertheless, this did not create difficulties for the computer department due to the fact that one of the College's Administrators had more computing experience than the previous ACCC consultant, and was therefore able to install the network package.

The experience of the computer department illustrate how a variety of different factors can influence the implementation process, ranging from a country's broad macro-economic policy, to the relationship between donor agencies, such as the IMF and the World Bank. It was also interesting to note how students at CAST regarded courses validated by the British Computer Society as more preferable to locally validated ones, suggesting the existence of some form of *ideological dependency*. The next part of the chapter deals with the issue of staffing and how dependence on First World institutions and overseas aid has influenced provision within this area.

Analysis of staff development at CAST

The aim of CAST's staff development programme was to ensure that all teaching staff had the opportunity to gain a B.Ed degree, and that those who already held this qualification were given the opportunity to engage in at least one type of professional development activity. Thus, the first part of the analysis looks at the process involved in developing the B.Ed degree and the second turns to the various other initiatives provided by the Human Resource Development Unit.

The development of the B.Ed courses

The initiative for the B.Ed courses resulted from the findings of a questionnaire circulated by the College's Technical Education department in 1978. The questionnaire was concerned with obtaining information for evaluating the qualifications of all the lecturing staff at CAST. According to the department head, the survey indicated that although the majority of full-time lecturers were graduates in their subject areas, they lacked pedagogical training. Given these findings the Ministry of Education had agreed to finance the development a B.Ed degree, but due to budgetary constraints imposed by Central government, no resources were available for this purpose. As a consequence, the Technical Education department decided in 1981 to use its own funds to develop the B.Ed courses. The funds were used to hire three consultants from the University of Minnesota for a period of three months to develop the syllabus. The funds were subsequently supplemented by a loan from the World Bank Education III project under which the department received funding to upgrade its courses and its physical facilities. The support for these developments was provided by a number of World Bank consultants. The decision to use these foreign consultants was probably justified given that no members of staff at the Technical Education department were qualified in curriculum design prior to the World Bank Education III project.

The first of the B.Eds in Business Education was developed by the Technical Education department in 1982, but as a result of their successful experience they developed three more B.Ed's in Home Economics, Industrial Technology and information technology, over the next five years (CAST, 1991). Despite the initial dependency on overseas consultants, no major problems were experienced in developing the courses. The only noticeable problem related to the duration between the department identifying the shortage of pedagogical skills in 1978, and the development of the latest B.Ed course in 1988. The delay in developing this B.Ed course can be attributed to the fact that the Ministry of Education had failed to provide the funds which were initially expected, and also because of further delays experienced in processing the loan for the project. However, despite this delay, 15 lecturers graduated with B.Eds in the late 1980s (CAST, 1991).

The role of the Human Resource Development Unit

During the field work there was no evidence to suggest that the HRD unit had conducted an assessment of the College's staff development needs. According to staff working at the Unit, the lack of support from the majority of the College departments had prevented any co-ordinated form of in-house staff development. Indeed, when interviewed, representatives from these departments commented that they were unable to provide support owing to the high turn-over of staff in their departments and due to their reliance on part-time staff. With regard to the former issue, the computer and science departments had staff turn-over rates of 80 per cent and 71 per cent respectively. As a consequence, the College's staff development programme was dependent on overseas aid, predominantly comprising overseas scholarships for study at institutions in the First World. The only exception was an initiative developed by staff at the Technical Education department using its own funds. Indeed, in 1991, the department introduced a project to upgrade its three-year diploma Course, and staff development through staff participation in curriculum change played a vital role in this process. An afternoon seminar was held at the department to identify what changes needed to be incorporated into the diploma programme. The seminar identified two areas for change. The first of these centred on the need to change the content of the diploma for the first year, so that the students could take three subjects rather than one. Thus, instead of studying electrical engineering, in depth, the students would study electrical, mechanical and civil engineering. Secondly, the seminar identified the need to incorporate an information technology component into the third year of the diploma Course which depended on the subject specialism. For example, in business education, the emphasis was on personal computers, and in engineering on robotics and aspects of CNC machines.

These changes were being implemented at the time of the present research by members of staff of the Technical Education department. Furthermore, this department was the only one at CAST to fund scholarships for its own staff to study at the University of the West Indies. According to a senior lecturer in the department, there was an attempt to ensure that all internally funded initiatives for staff development are in line with the needs of the department. The findings suggest that the Technical Education department was the only department which was not totally financially dependent on the First World for staff development. This enabled it to make decisions independently of international aid agencies, and to identify its own initiatives, and the evidence suggests that these have been relatively successful in meeting the department's needs and those of the College.

The financial dependency of other departments on the First World scholarships enabled aid organisations such as the World Bank and CIDA to have a major influence on the type of staff development provided at CAST. As a consequence, a high proportion of the initiatives for staff development were connected to aid projects, and involved senior members of staff attending post-graduate courses at institutions in the First World. This is not to say that international organisations such as CIDA and the World Bank are totally responsible for the College's dependency on institutions in the First World. Indeed, the College must share some of that responsibility since it probably has the capability and the facilities to formulate a programme of staff development for its own academic staff. The development of initiatives at the Technical Education department, and the establishment of a Human Resource Unit, would indicate that certain aspects of staff development are possible at CAST. Nevertheless, the majority of departments chose to rely on overseas scholarships, rather than to develop their own in-house initiatives.

The analysis also found that many of the departments used overseas scholarships as a means of rewarding or retaining senior members of staff. Thus, the way in which departments use overseas scholarships as a reward, helps to explain in part why the College is dependent on institutions in the First World. Seemingly, the nature of the department's dependency on overseas institutions may be regarded as a 'self-imposed' form of dependency. It is questionable whether overseas scholarships as such are necessarily an effective means of retaining staff. The international aid organisations appear to have recognised this problem and are providing short-term overseas scholarships to develop specific skills, (as have occurred at the EXC under the Micro-Enterprise project, and at the computer and health food and science departments under the CIDA Phase II project). However, the decision of international aid organisations to base aid-funded staff development on short-term, identified needs, could have a detrimental effect on departments at CAST. The use of such short-term scholarships will prevent lecturers from obtaining the skills and knowledge associated with post-graduate studies, and could also lead to other possible losses for the College. For example, interviews with lecturers at the computer, engineering and science departments revealed that the majority of staff who leave after the completion of their post-graduate studies are still an important resource because they often provide part-time teaching services.

However, the dependency of departments on First World institutions has done little to meet the developmental needs of all the staff at CAST. Only the senior members of staff received scholarships, despite the fact that 73 per cent of teaching staff are junior members (Christian, 1990). The usefulness of the overseas scholarships for senior staff is also be questioned. In the case of the EXC, for instance, the scholarships financed by the first CIDA project were clearly not relevant to the work at the Centre. Similarly, the World Bank funded scholarship in environmental engineering did not meet the anticipated needs of the engineering department since there was no student demand for this subject.

The development of staff at CAST clearly shows some of the management problems faced by a TVET institution operating in the Third World. Although, the failure to develop a coherent programme of staff development could be blamed on the department heads or even the HRD unit, it is important to understand the constraints faced by department heads working at CAST. Indeed, not only do they have large teaching loads to manage, they also have the problem of retaining experienced staff who could earn four to five times their existing salary in the private sector. Given these circumstances it is difficult to see what other options are available, apart from using scholarships as a means of rewarding and retaining senior teaching staff.

Having analysed the implementation processes within selected departments at CAST, we now turn to provision under the HEART Trust. Once again we are concerned with the role played by donor agencies in project implementation, but this time we focus on developments at the Garmex Academy and the Vocational and Technical Development Institute.

Analysis of developments at Garmex

As we saw in Chapter 3, the Basic Skills Training Project was responsible for the construction of the Garmex Academy. However, originally the BSTP was concerned with the institutional development of the HEART Trust. Thus, in looking at this project the chapter needs to consider why these changes occurred in the BSTP's objectives. Only then will it be possible to analyse the actual process of implementation and to comment on its longer term impact.

The initiative for the BSTP came from the government's attempts to restructure the country's economy and reduce the budget deficit (USAID, 1992). The BSTP played a vital role in this process, by supplying the skilled labour needed by foreign investment. In the initial proposal, there was no trade union representation on the Project Steering Committee, as USAID believed that such representation might cloud the basic team concept and so prevent the public and private sectors working together (USAID, 1991). Consequently, the views of working people were not represented on the Steering Committee. However, the ultimate influence of USAID on the project's direction was more questionable. In Chapter 3 we saw how the original components of the BSTP were primarily concerned with the institutional development of the HEART Trust. The representatives of USAID believed that this development would improve the co-ordination of the country's training system, and make it more responsive to public and private sector training needs (Tomlin, 1991).

However, apparently unknown to the Steering Committee and to USAID, the Jamaican government had begun to build four HEART Academies. It appears that the Jamaican government believed that the country's training needs would be better met through what they called a 'supply side approach to human resource development' (USAID, 1989a). Under this strategy, the Jamaican government wanted to construct and equip four HEART Academies, so that Jamaica could produce the skilled labour necessary to attract foreign investment, thus earning the country foreign currency (USAID, 1989b). Despite their differences, USAID elected to support the Jamaican government's wishes and provided technical assistance and equipment to support the construction and development of four HEART Academies. After the agreement to construct four HEART Academies, the Steering Committee was unable to regain the initiative for managing the BSTP. The change in direction of the BSTP indicated that the Jamaican government was not necessarily dependent on decisions made by USAID, and that it was still capable of determining the direction of the project.

Nevertheless, the continued support for the BSTP by USAID also suggested that there were no radical differences between the goals of the Jamaican government and those of USAID, namely, to supply skilled labour to the foreign companies involved in export. The other goal of the BSTP was to reduce the country's level of unemployment. The BSTP attempted to achieve this by establishing the HEART Academies in areas of high unemployment. For example, the Garmex Academy was established in one of the poorest areas of Kingston, where unemployment was particularly high.

Following the decision to construct the HEART Academies, a Management Committee was set up to co-ordinate the Basic Skills Training Project (BSTP). The committee comprised of officials solely from the HEART Trust. Under this committee were a number of Project Implementation Units (PIU) which were responsible for the management and implementation of the BSTP at institutional level and for identifying equipment (Tomlin, 1991). For example, a PIU was set up at the Garmex Academy to manage the construction, equipping and development of its courses. Each PIU consisted of representatives from the HEART Trust and from USAID. Only 27 per cent of the total funding was provided by USAID, suggesting that it would have a minimum influence on the components provided under the project. However, according to the officials interviewed at the HEART Trust, the USAID consultants were also responsible for identifying Garmex's equipment, including the sewing machines and workbooks, all of which were obtained from the United States. Similarly, the familiarisation tours were also dependent on First World institutions, and foreign consultants were responsible for designing the Academy's course on garment construction. In fact, Garmex's buildings appeared to be the only part of the Academy that was not totally dependent on materials obtained from the First World. In many respects the Garmex Academy closely resembled a garment training institution in the industrial world, including the way in which it was managed, and in the way in which students were trained to become machine operators.

There had been no major problems with building and equipping of the Garmex Academy. In 1985 the Garmex Academy opened and in its first year, 5,128 full-time students enrolled for the machine operator and mechanic courses. This figure shows that it had almost achieved its full capacity of 6,000 students, suggesting that this component of the BSTP had been successfully implemented. However, if the enrolment figures are analysed in terms of how many students successfully completed the courses, a different picture emerges. A completion rate of only 51 per cent successful students suggests that major problems were experienced during the first year (Ministry of Planning, 1988). There were many factors which could account for this low completion rate, but dependency on foreign components appeared to be one of the major influences. Evidence obtained from interviews with Garmex and USAID personnel revealed that major difficulties were experienced in using the workbooks obtained from the USA and the American style of management. The workbooks had been originally designed in the USA to enable students at American garment academies to study at their own pace. However, no account was taken of the low levels of literacy which existed in certain parts of Jamaica. Yet, as already indicated, Garmex had been established in one of Kingston's poorer areas where the majority of the inhabitants had only been educated to primary school level (Tomlin, 1991). As a result, the trainees at the Academy were inadequately equipped to read, let alone to understand the instructions in the workbooks.

With regard to the American style of management, the familiarisation tours to the USA had enabled the Garmex officials to apply the management techniques which they had observed in American Academies. As a consequence of these familiarisation tours a strict security system was adopted whereby trainees at Garmex were searched every time they left the premises. According to Garmex officials, female trainees in particular, resented being searched. There was, too, opposition to the way in which 'authoritarian' management techniques were used; for example, if female trainees became pregnant they were asked to leave the academy. According to a USAID official this was standard practice at academies in America, but as a member of the staff at Garmex remarked, was alien to Jamaican culture.

The research also found that the Academy experienced difficulties in supplying foreign firms with skilled graduates. Indeed, tracer studies conducted by the BSTP revealed that the majority of Garmex's graduates preferred of working for themselves, supplying to the local market, rather then being employed by one of the large multinational garment construction factories (Tomlin, 1991). According to officials at HEART the graduates disliked working in the foreign-run factories because of the regimented working conditions and low pay. This preference of the typical Garmex graduate had serious implications for the BSTP, which was designed to supply foreign companies in Jamaica with skilled labour, and suggests that there were wide differences between what the Jamaican participants wanted, and what the Jamaican government and the international aid agencies assumed was needed. It also highlighted the need to introduce serious changes to the way in which the Academy operated.

The effects of Jamaican government funded projects on the Garmex Academy

In 1990 the management changed the way in which Academy was managed and also re-designed the courses offered to potential trainees. These reforms were an attempt to overcome the problems which had been experienced through using management techniques and courses 'borrowed' from the USA. According to interviews conducted at the Garmex Academy these changes were funded by the HEART Trust and involved the Academy's own staff. To begin with, the management of the Garmex Academy recognised that an 'authoritarian' style was not conducive to the training needs of Jamaican students. As a result female trainees were no longer searched every time they left the Academy and those who became pregnant were allowed to continue their studies. Furthermore, it was also recognised that the delivery of courses must coincide with the domestic requirements of the women who became single parents and still needed to work. Therefore, the machine operators course was introduced on a staggered basis, allowing women to attend the training sessions either in the morning or in the afternoon.

Secondly, a number of changes occurred to the composition of the Academies courses. Supporting studies in basic English and Numeracy were introduced in the Garment Construction course and in the Mechanics

70

courses. These subjects were intended to upgrade the students' education to CXC level and to provide them with the skills necessary to use the workbooks provided under the BSTP. Managers at the Garmex Academy revealed that, as a result of the introduction of supporting studies, more students had successfully completed the garment construction course. Furthermore, a number of new courses were introduced in order to meet the preference of trainees who wanted to work either for themselves, or in the local garment industry. Garmex staff reported that the Tailoring course had now replaced the Garment Construction course as the most popular option for trainees. The differences between the new courses and those designed under the BSTP can be seen by comparing the content of the two courses. On the Garment Construction course, trainees were taught how to construct only one part of a garment, such as the pocket or a sleeve. However, in the local firms there was no such specialised division of labour to the same degree. The units of production were very small, often involving only two or three people, and individuals had to become familiar with all the different stages involved in constructing a garment. Consequently, the course on tailoring now provided trainees with a much wider range of skills and equipped them for working in the local market. The course also incorporated lessons on entrepreneurship.

Analysis of development at the VTDI

The construction of the VTDI in the 1960s was financed by the UNDP and the Jamaican government; and the development of the institution's courses was dependent on ILO's technical assistance. However, no attempts were made to upgrade the VTDI's courses until the World Bank and USAID projects were implemented in the mid 1980s (USAID, 1990). This suggests that the training and development of the country's instructors had been dependent on a course established over a decade before. Consequently, instructors from the country's former Industrial Training Centres were unable to benefit from recent developments in education and training in Jamaica.

Developments through the World Bank Education III project

The aim of the World Bank project was to improve the quality of training for the country's instructors, and to increase the number of instructors trained at the VTDI. Under this project a local agency (the National Development Agency - NDA) was created to co-ordinate the management of the project. It was anticipated by the World Bank that this would help supply the former Industrial Training Centres with the necessary number of qualified instructors to deliver skills training programmes. There were no noticeable problems with the implementation of the project until the Jamaican government decided to disband the NDA in 1985. Owing to this decision, problems were experienced in synchronising the arrival of different project components. Similar problems to those at CAST were experienced at the VTDI where the foreign consultants arrived in advance of the equipment, and left before it was installed (World Bank, 1990b). Consequently the foreign consultants were unable to train the VTDI instructors either in curricular design or in equipment installation. When the equipment arrived in the mid 1980s the VTDI staff had to install it without the necessary training or support from the overseas consultants. It appears that VTDI staff were not equipped to fulfil this function, as none of the recently established workshops were correctly wired for their equipment. Also, the workshops had to be secured with burglar-proof window guards before equipment could be installed. These difficulties resulted in further costs for the project and evidence suggests that in this case the World Bank may have been justified in using foreign as opposed to local consultants (World Bank, 1990b).

However, a more serious problem occurred in the mid-1980s when the government of Jamaica closed 80 per cent of the country's ITCs. This action meant there was now only a limited demand for the VTDI's courses. All of this evidence suggests that problems experienced in the implementation could have resulted from the disbanding of the NDA and the closure of the ITCs, rather than from the project's financial dependency on the World Bank.

Developments through the USAID's BSTP

The USAID project intended to deal with the lack of pedagogical skills amongst the HEART instructors by developing a new diploma course in Human Resource Development, at the VTDI (see Chapter 3 for details). As described previously, each of the components financed under the project was managed by a Project implementation Unit (PIU). The PIU membership included representatives from the MYCD, USAID and the Institute itself. The project was predominantly dependent on USAID-funded technical assistance, despite the fact that the Jamaican government provided the majority of the resources for the project. This was reflected at the VTDI, where USAID scholarships resulted in four of the institution's instructors studying for B.Eds at Universities in the USA. Similarly, foreign consultants provided seminars on curriculum development and assisted with the construction of the VTDI's diploma in Human Resource Development.

During the first three years of the project's implementation (1983-1987), the USAID consultants developed the Non-Formal-Education Division (NFED) for the Ministry of Youth and Community Development, and assisted with the plans and construction of the HEART Academies (USAID, 1990). However, by 1990, the NFED was not functioning because of the Jamaican government's decision to transfer operational responsibility for the VTDI from the MYCD to the HEART Trust (USAID, 1991). Without the support of the NFED, the VTDI found it difficult to develop the proposed diploma course. It was also impeded by another factor, since 45 per cent of the VTDI staff who went on overseas scholarships left the institution when they resumed work (USAID, 1990). There were also 'problems' with the calibre of ITC instructors who had been chosen to teach at the new Academies. Officials at USAID and HEART commented that the ITC instructors had served their craft apprenticeships over ten years earlier and were therefore not familiar with recent technological developments. Many had also not received any formal training in educational methods Consequently, for the majority of ITC instructors it was not simply a matter of upgrading. Further interviews conducted with VTDI staff revealed that given these 'problems' the USAID consultants were unable to develop the proposed diploma course.

The above evidence suggests that the problems experienced during the implementation of the USAID and World Bank projects had little to do with the VTDI's dependency on foreign aid, consultants or overseas fellowships. The major problem appears to have originated from decisions made by the Jamaican government to disband the National Development Agency and close 80 per cent of the Country's Industrial Training Centres. An additional influence was the decision of the Jamaican government to transfer responsibility of the VTDI from the Ministry of Youth and Community Development to the HEART Trust, and the low educational attainment of the VTDI's instructors. A final consideration was the low level of instructor development in Jamaica.

The effect of a government funded project at the VTDI

In 1990 VTDI attempted to overcome the problems which were experienced during the USAID project through establishing two new courses. The initiative for these courses came from the HEART National Training Agency, and was funded by the Jamaican government. The first course, the Cadet Training Programme enabled the institution to recruit people who had just completed their City and Guilds Craft Certificate and were familiar with recent technological developments, and provided them with training in up-to-date teaching methods. The intention was that this course would improve the quality of basic training for instructors in Jamaica. The second course was on Human Resource Development and at the time of the field work it was at the planning stage. Senior VTDI staff interviewed said that they would collaborate with CAST's Technical Education department to develop the syllabus in 1993. They explained that once the course was established the VTDI would be able to provide further training for those instructors who had completed the Cadet Training Programme. If correctly implemented these courses would clearly help the VTDI to provide high calibre instructors of the type needed by public TVET institutions and private companies.

So far this chapter has dealt with the intricacies involved in implementing projects at TVET institutions. Of the projects analysed in this chapter nearly all experienced some form of difficulty in achieving their stated objectives. A variety of reasons were also identified for these difficulties, ranging from problems associated with their dependence on overseas aid and foreign technical assistance, to the way which they were managed locally. Furthermore, the chapter has also revealed that even if projects are successfully implemented they could still fail to achieve their longer-term objectives (a case in point was the BSTP at the Garmex Academy). These implementation difficulties at public institutions could explain why interest has developed in the private sector as an alternative delivery mechanism. Nevertheless, even within the private sector, the state continues to play an important role in determining the extent to which this type of provision occurs. All of these issues are considered in the final part of this chapter.

Analysis of support for non-governmental forms of training

The movement towards company and non-governmental forms of training could also be viewed as a means of alleviating the financial burden on the state. However, in order for such provision to occur a number of conditions are necessary. To begin with a country must have an economic environment that is conducive for companies and non-governmental organisations to provide training. Secondly, the state must implement programmes that are effective, and efficient, in encouraging this type of provision. All of these issues are analysed by looking at a selection of companies operating in Jamaica, and also by making reference to the activities of Things Jamaica Ltd.

Analysis of in-house company training

Of the companies visited, there was no apparent evidence that they provided structured programmes of TVET, of the type which occurred at institutions such as CAST, without state support or assistance from TVET institutions. Nevertheless, the majority of private companies surveyed did provide training and in most cases it was of a specific nature and normally occurred on-the-job. The majority of companies also had training facilities and access to qualified instructors and trainers. Furthermore, the research found that academic departments at CAST played a major role in assisting private companies with the construction and delivery of their training programmes. Of the eleven companies visited, two had worked with CAST's engineering department to develop their own apprenticeship programmes; another two also had specific training modules designed for them by CAST. This would appear to suggest that the country's economic environment is conducive to supporting collaboration between public and private institutions, of the type required for encouraging in-house company training.

However, the liberalised market environment developed at the beginning of the 1980s underwent numerous changes when PNP came to power in 1989. This administration gave greater recognition to unions at the workplace and introduced a minimum monthly wage of £28 in 1990. In 1992, the PNP administration raised the minimum monthly wage by the equivalent of £12 to £40. These changes appeared to discourage certain companies from conducting in-house training in Jamaica. Indeed, a number of managers at garment construction factories said that the rise in minimum

74

wage costs had raised their company's production costs and acted as a disincentive to other foreign companies thinking of investing in Jamaica. In addition, the pro-labour environment created by the PNP had enabled unions to enforce the demarcation of jobs in the workplace. The effects of this were illustrated in one of the companies visited, where employees were only trained in one specific trade. Nevertheless, the research found that the minimum wage level did not have an impact on the other companies surveyed, or on their decision to provide training.

Nevertheless, a factor which did influence decisions to provide training was the type of help provided by the government. In Jamaica this help consisted of support via the Apprenticeship Board, the school leavers programme and the Tool Makers Institute. Of the companies visited two were registered with the MYCD's Apprenticeship Board, eight employed trainees on the school leavers programme and a further two used training services provided by the Tool Makers Institute. Nevertheless, in order to be effective not only did these programmes have to expand the provision of company training in Jamaica, they also had to be responsive to industry's varied training needs. But at the same time their activities need be carefully monitored, to ensure that certain standards of training are maintained. The effectiveness of the first of these programmes, the apprenticeship scheme, could be questioned on a number of grounds. For one, there are only a limited number of trades which can be mastered under the apprenticeship scheme. Indeed, the Apprenticeship Board appears to have taken no account of the new industries, such as those companies operating in the country's expanding garment construction or service sectors. Even managers of companies who could register with the Apprenticeship Board said that the scheme was a long and costly means of providing training for their employees. This perhaps explains why only 70 apprentices were registered with the Apprenticeship Board in 1983 and a decade later this figure was 68. This brings into question whether the apprenticeship scheme is a very effective means of expanding non-governmental training in Jamaica. Furthermore, the quality of training supported under the apprenticeship scheme is also questionable. A survey conducted by Oliver (1992) found that the majority of apprentices were doing routine, repetitive work, involving little skills development and often, no academic education was provided during their training. The latter of these issues probably relates to the government's decision to close 80 per cent of the country's Industrial Training Centres in the mid 1980s. The senior administrators at the MYCD said that the Apprenticeship programme had also suffered from government under-funding and competition from the school leavers programme.

However, the second of the programmes, the school leavers programme (SLP), appears to have been a more effective means of encouraging company training in Jamaica. Its success probably stems from the programme's ability to respond to the country's growing service sector and apparel industry. In addition, the school leavers programme also provided female school leavers with access to work-based training, an opportunity which had been denied them under the apprenticeship scheme. But at the same time, the school leavers programme has also experienced difficulties in recruiting trainees to meet the growing demands of industry. A manager at a garment factory commented that HEART was unable to supply his company with the number of trainees required. It appears that if school leavers had obtained four or more CXCs they were likely to continue their studies at School rather than attempt to obtain a placement with HEART. The extent of this fall can be seen by the fact that in 1983 a total of 8,109 young people enrolled on the SLP, against a figure of just over 2,000 at the beginning of the 1990s (Planning Institute of Jamaica, 1991). There have also been shortcomings in HEART's monitoring of trainees on the SLP. According to a placement officer at HEART, each officer is given a total of 500 trainees to monitor every year. This large number means that placement officers are able to visit each trainee only once a year. Of the eight companies surveyed (which employed SLP trainees), the present research found that only one had been visited by a placement officer during the last year. Clearly, without adequate mechanisms for monitoring the trainees progress there are no guarantees that trainees will achieve their set competencies. This brings into question the quality of training.

Finally, in regard to the third mechanism of support, the programmes provided by the TMI, the research found that the Institute experienced difficulties in obtaining academically qualified instructors to deliver its training programmes. This restricted the number and type of courses which the institute was capable of delivering. According to one of the managers, there was a shortage of competent instructors in Jamaica. It appears that the most able and qualified instructors worked for companies in the private sector, and that VTDI graduates were regarded by the TMI as not being qualified to deliver their training programmes.

Having discussed the issue of effectiveness, we now turn to the question of whether the programmes discussed above used resources efficiently, both in relation to the actual provision of training and also in relation to the country's development. Interviews conducted with staff at HEART confirmed that the SLP had been designed to subsidise the training activities of multinational companies in Jamaica. In particular, it had been used by the Jamaican government to subsidise the training activities of factories which constructed garments for export. Whilst senior officials at the MYCD commented that the Apprenticeship Programme was dependent on how many trainees were employed by the government-owned utilities. Clearly, the use of government programmes to train employees in large companies could be viewed as an inefficient use of public sector resources, since both multinational companies and government-owned utilities would provide training, regardless of any government programme.

It is also questionable whether using government funds to support the garment industry or state owned utilities is a beneficial way of encouraging long term development in Jamaica. The evidence contained in this chapter showed that components used in the garment industry were imported from the USA. Thus, the industry did little to encourage the use of indigenous resources or to promote production linkages within the local economy. The only benefit to accrue from the garment industry was foreign currency, which could be used to reduce the country's balance of payments deficit.

One could also question why the government should provide additional support to state utilities, given the country's level of development, and when the rest of the world is privatising them.

These government programmes could have played a more positive role in the country's development, had they supported smaller local companies, which lacked the resources to conduct their own training. This is particularly so when one considers that over 50 per cent of the country's employment opportunities are found in small and medium-sized businesses (Hamilton *et al*, 1989). The importance of encouraging training in medium-sized firms was recognised by the government of Singapore in the 1980s when it attempted to improve the country's productivity through providing training subsidies to private sector companies (World Bank, 1991). The target of these subsidies was medium sized firms as the government recognised that large firms were already conducting their own training. In the case of Jamaica, the only programme to support the training needs of small to medium-sized firms was the TMI. This limited government support appears strange given the PNP's commitment to small and medium-sized companies (Planning Institute of Jamaica, 1990). The present research found that the Apprenticeship Board was working with the Jamaican and German Automobile School to restructure the content of its training scheme. Under their proposals, apprentices who wish to train as automechanics will spend their first year studying at the Jamaican and German Automotive School for the City and Guilds London Institute Certificate in Automotive Engineering. During the remaining two years, the apprentices receive practical 'on-the-job training' at a local garage. These two years will be monitored by the Apprenticeship Board. Despite these good intentions without further support, either in the form of subsidies to companies who hire such apprentices or improvements to the way in which instructors in Jamaica are trained, this initiative is likely to experience difficulties in achieving its objective of supporting small to medium-sized firms.

An analysis of support for TVET in the informal sector

The initial manufacturing and marketing activities of *Things Jamaica Ltd* coincided with the PNP's period in office during the 1970s. As indicated in Chapter 3, the PNP's philosophy during this period was based on state ownership and it appears that the activities of *Things Jamaica Ltd* reflected this philosophy. In retrospect the establishment of the craft factory and of the marketing outlets could be criticised since they did little to support small-scale indigenous craft producers or expand the provision of non-formal training. Indeed, it could be argued that this was unfair competition for the indigenous craft producers since the factory at *Things Jamaica Ltd* could benefit from economies of scale and so produce craft items cheaper. This is referred to as 'crowding out' since small producers are being forced out of the market place.

When the JLP came to power in 1981 it was elected on its commitment to private enterprise and the free market. In turn, the JLP's philosophy was reflected at *Things Jamaica Ltd* where the organisation's role had changed to a marketing agent for craft products from the private sector. Private craft producers expected greater support from *Things Jamaica Ltd* under the organisation's new role. However, officials working there commented that the company suffered from underfunding and was unable to provide independent producers support for their training activities. The latter issue had an effect on the quality of the craft products which were collected by *Things Jamaica Ltd.* As a consequence the company was unable to sell its products owing to competition from other producers.

When the PNP returned to power in 1989 the function of *Things Jamaica Ltd* changed yet again. The PNP's philosophy was based on mixture of support from the private sector and the state. Once again, this philosophy was reflected at *Things Jamaica Ltd* where a collaborative venture with the private sector resulted in a number of craft items being produced for export. One official at HEART said that 25 people received 'on-the-job' training as a result of this venture, suggesting that the involvement of the private sector was an effective means of expanding the company's training capacity. Under the PNP administration, *Things Jamaica Ltd* provided support to independent craft producers through the setting up of producer groups. The PNP administration also introduced short-term training courses for leaders from these producer groups. The idea was that these leaders would return to their communities, after they had completed their training at *Things Jamaica Ltd*, and provide further training at the 'grass roots level'. Clearly such a measure was an effective means of supporting and expanding the provision of non-governmental training in rural communities.

Although the company's joint venture with the private sector appeared a successful means of expanding training, it is questionable whether the venture used resources efficiently. According to officials at *Things Jamaica Ltd* the venture proved unsuccessful owing to rising production costs and falling profits. Apparently, the costs of producing the crafts were miscalculated and as a consequence the collaborative venture made a loss. Resources were also inefficiently used when the company provided training to the leaders from the recently established producer groups. Interviews with managers revealed that the company experienced major problems with the quality of the training. Although the instructors were experienced in craft production they had not received any form of 'pedagogical training'. Arguably, the instructors were unable to teach students effectively the skills that were required to manufacture items in the craft bank. And clearly, if students were taught badly they would return to their communities and pass on the bad habits they had learnt, which in turn would affect on the quality of crafts produced in Jamaica. For this reason, *Things Jamaica Ltd* rejected a large proportion of the craft items manufactured by the 14 producer groups.

If the programmes at *Things Jamaica Ltd* had been correctly implemented they could have had a positive impact on the country's development. Not only would these initiatives have helped to expand the provision of training, they would have helped to create employment for people from rural communities, develop linkages within the local economy and increase exports.

In summary, this case study of implementation in Jamaica illustrates how various factors can determine whether a project or programme is successfully implemented. Often the tied nature of overseas aid at public institutions ensured components used in a project were obtained from the First World, and that all decisions in relation to implementation were made by foreign consultants. The effects of this dependency was manifest in a number of TVET institutions and in some cases had a detrimental impact on a project's implementation. Moreover, even if a project was successfully implemented the evidence showed that it could still fail to achieve its longer term goals (due to the use of foreign models). But at the same time the implementation of projects in the public sector was also influenced by a number of more localised factors, such as the macro-economic environment, the behaviour of the state and the way in which it was managed locally.

In the case of the private or non-governmental provision, it was also possible to identify what factors impeded the implementation process. Once again these also related to the broad macro-economic framework and the way in which programmes were managed or mismanaged locally. Furthermore, it could be argued that training in the private sector is also subject to the influence of dependency since certain programmes, such as HEART's SLP, were partly financed by overseas aid.

5 An outline of The Gambian TVET system

Introduction

During colonialism the British were attempting to reduce their liabilities in West Africa and as a result little support was provided for The Gambia's economic development (Hughes, 1991). Consequently, in contrast to Jamaica, The Gambia has an underdeveloped formal sector and the majority of the population until recently were engaged in rural activities. The only TVET institution to be established during colonialism was the National Vocational Training Centre (N'yang, 1984). This was constructed in the late 1960s to provide school leavers with basic craft skills in carpentry and engineering (N'jie, 1983). The other major developments in TVET occurred when the country achieved independence in 1965. The first of which included the setting up of the Directorate for National Vocational Training Programmes (DNVTP) under the 1979 National Vocational Training Act. under this Act the DNVTP was also given responsibility for formulating policies for the country's National Vocational Training Programme and for providing guidelines for their implementation (Jobarteh, Cessay and Sarr, 1992). One of the first initiatives to be implemented by the DNVTP was the Rural Vocational Training Programme (RVTP). The purpose of the RVTP was to equip villagers living in rural communities with the necessary skills to improve their standard of living. The major institution involved in providing training under the RVTP was the Rural Vocational Training Centre (RVTC) at Mansakonko, situated some 120 Kilometres from the country's capital Banjul. Financial support for the RVTP was provided by the EEC.

Another of the other major TVET institution in The Gambia, The Gambia Technical Training Institute, began offering courses in 1983. The funding to construct the GTTI was provided by the World Bank, under the World Bank Education I project. Each of the TVET organisations in The Gambia have also attempted to deal with the country's rising unemployment problem through developing entrepreneurship programmes. For example, at the GTTI an entrepreneurial skill development unit was set-up in 1987 to develop a course on entrepreneurship (N'jie, 1989a). Another of the major providers of TVET in The Gambia, The National Vocational Training Centre, is in the stages of being converted into a Skills Centre. Once operational, this will deliver short, competency-based courses based on identified labour market needs. The RVTP is also being restructured to encourage self-employment amongst rural youths.

80

Besides the institutions discussed above, a number of firms in The Gambia also conduct their own in-house training. Some of these companies, including The Gambia Public Transport Corporation, The Gambia Utilities Corporation and The Gambia Public Telephone Company, have fully equipped training centres. There are also a number of Non Governmental Organisations (NGOs) which provide training for those who work in the country's in-formal sector. Attempts have also been made to encourage greater non-governmental participation in the country's TVET system through the setting-up of a National Council for Technical Education and Vocational Training (to replace the former NVTB). There are plans for the Council to introduce a training levy on all companies operating in The Gambia. All of these developments are discussed in greater depth below.

Provision under the DTEVT

In contrast to Jamaica, there is only one organisational structure for the planning and implmentation of TVET policies in The Gambia (see Figure 5.1). At the top of this structure is the National Council for TVET, and its executive arm, the Directorate of Technical Education and Vocational Traning (this replaced the former DNVTP). The major function of the DTEVT is to co-ordinate and expand post-secondary, public sector TVET in The Gambia including The Gambian Technical Training Institute, the Banjul Skills Centre, and the Rural Vocational Training Centre.

The Gambia Technical Training Institute (GTTI)

The Gambia Technical Training Institute is the only post- secondary technical institution in The Gambia to offer engineering programmes up to the City and Guilds of London Institute Advanced Certificate level. According to the senior managers interviewed, the GTTI is becoming a regional centre for students from the Anglophile countries of West Africa. Enrolment figures for the 1989/90 academic year show that 903 students attended courses at the GTTI; of these 497 were full-time and 406 part-time. During the same academic year 200 students graduated (Jobarteh *et al*, 1992). To be eligible for full-time courses at the GTTI, students must have successfully obtained three or more GCE O-level passes (in the examinations of the West African Examinations Council) at grade C or above or passed an entrance examination which tests students' ability in English and Mathematics (GTTI,1993a).

The Gambia Technical Training Institute has played a major role in supplying the country with skilled manpower at craft and technician levels. Until the mid 1980s, the majority of GTTI leavers were employed in the state sector, either working for parastatal organisations such as The Gambia

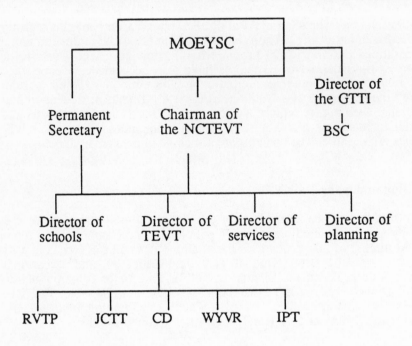

Key

MOEYSC: Ministry of Education, Youth, Sports and Culture
NCTEVT : National Council for Technical Education and Vocational training
RVTP: Rural Vocational Training Programme
JCCT : Job Classification and Trade Testing section
CD : Curriculum Development section
WYVR : Women, Youth and Vocational Rehabilitation section
IPT: In-Plant Training section
BSC: Banjul Skills Centre

(*source*: interviews with senior officials at the DTEVT)

**Figure 5.1 Organisational structure for TVET provision
in The Gambia**

Utilities Corporation, The Gambia Telecommunication Company Limited, or for the government owned utilities such as The Gambia Public Transport Company or The Gambia Product Marketing Board. However, since the government's Economic Reform Programme of the 1980s, employment opportunities in the state sector have declined owing to cut backs in public expenditure (EIU, 1994a). At the same time, employment opportunities in the private sector have increased owing to the growth in foreign investment and the rise in the number of small enterprises operating in the in-formal sector. In response to these changes the GTTI has introduced a number of new courses in the late 1980s. For example, the computer department has developed short-term courses for industry, including one for word-processing, spread sheets and basic computer programming. The Institute has also introduced an entrepreneurial skill development course which is run in conjunction with the Institute's technical courses.

In common with many public institutions around the globe, the GTTI has also had to deal with a declining budget from central government. For example, in the late 1980s central government met nearly 90 per cent of the Institute's re-current operating costs, but by the mid 1990s this figure had fallen to around 72 per cent. As a result of these cuts, the Institute has begun to generate its own funds through charging higher tuition fees and also by setting-up of production centres in certain departments. These Centres have obtained a number of commercial contracts, including one from the Ministry of Education to construct desks for the country's primary schools.

When the GTTI was given its own operating schedule in 1983 it only contained a building and construction department, a clerical studies department and an engineering department. However, over the subsequent fifteen years the number of departments and sections offering courses has expanded. This expansion resulted from a combination of locally funded projects and those supported by overseas aid agencies. The locally funded projects consisted of upgrading the clerical studies department to the department of commerce and arts. This was achieved through the introduction of courses in office practice, accountancy, and economics. The other locally funded projects were the development of an entrepreneurship skill development course in 1986 and the setting-up of a technical teacher education and training section in 1989. Whilst the most influential aid project, the World Bank's Education I project, financed the construction of the Institute's buildings in 1979 (World Bank, 1989a). The Institute's computer department was established as a result of overseas aid, under the ODA Project I in 1985 (Darley and Smith, 1985). The ODA's project II helped upgrade the computer department's IT equipment in 1987 and at the time of the field work was assisting the Institute's staff to establish a Quality Assurance System. Further developments in IT, funded by USAID, have resulted in the establishment of a stenography unit. Nearly all these projects have also provided the GTTI lecturers with overseas scholarships.

The GTTI organisational structure is shown in Figure 5.2. Under the 1983 GTTI Act, a Board of Governors was given responsibility for managing the Institute's activities. In 1992, the Act was amended and a new one (the 1992 GTTI Act) introduced, which gave the Board of Governors greater autonomy in managing the GTTI. Beneath the Board of Governors is the Academic Board which is responsible for academic developments at the GTTI. All Heads of department are on the Board together with an officer from the DTEVT. The GTTI's Director and its two Deputy Directors, together with the department Heads, constitute the Institute's senior management. At the time of the research in 1994, the GTTI offered a variety of training courses ranging from Access Programmes to Advanced Certificate courses and diploma courses. The Basic and Intermediate Craft courses last for two years full-time and successful students obtain the appropriate certificates of the City and Guilds of London Institute. There are also opportunities for students to study for their professional qualifications, such as the Association of Accounting Technician Certificate or the London Stenography Society's diploma.

Many of developments at the GTTI have been guided by the government's Education Sectorial Strategy, the most recent of which covers the years 1988 to 2003 (MOEYSC, 1987). The overall goal of the government's strategy is to increase access to education, and to improve the quality of its provision in a sustainable, and cost effective manner. The government's objectives for TVET have been further defined in a recent paper entitled 'Strategy Formulation for the Development of Vocational Education and Technical Training in The Gambia' (Jobartech *et al*, 1992). The strategy is attempting to ensure that resources are used more efficiently and that alternative measures for funding TVET are considered. At the time of the field work, the GTTI had started to meet some of the objectives outlined in the government's strategy. For example, attempts were being made to improve the cost effectiveness of skills training in The Gambia by annexing the National Vocational Training Centre to the GTTI, thereby ensuring that the duplication of courses in the country are reduced. The overall development of the Institute has also been given more direction through the setting up of a Quality Assurance System (Hough, 1992a). It is anticipated, by GTTI senior managers, that this will assist the Institute to produce a three-year development plan.

Additionally, the Institute has also attempted to make its courses more responsive to the country's manpower needs through modifying existing courses and introducing new ones. This is being achieved, partly through a localisation process, in which the West African Examinations Council (WAEC) will replace the City and Guilds of London Institute, as the body responsible for conducting examinations in technical subjects in The Gambia. The process of localisation has involved a number of workshops jointly funded by the ODA, WAEC, GTTI and the former DNVTP. There have also been major developments in the areas of information technology, including the plans for the computer department to work jointly with other departments to develop new courses. For example, the computer department intends to develop a Computer Aided Design course jointly with the engineering department. The stenography unit has also been equipped with computerised transcript machines by USAID. Other changes include the introduction of the course on entrepreneurial skill development by the recently established entrepreneurial skill development unit. It is hoped that this course will provide GTTI leavers with the skills to become self-employed through establishing their own businesses. Besides these recent course developments the institution has also attempted to upgrade the qualifications and skills of its lecturers through introducing a new Staff Development plan. The developments within each of these areas is discussed in further detail below.

Information technology training at the GTTI

Courses in information technology are delivered in both the computer department and the stenography unit. The computer department is the smallest department at the GTTI and their lecturers teach on the one-year, full-time, diploma in court reporting, delivered by the stenography unit. The GTTI is the only institution in West Africa offering this course.

When the computer department began delivering courses the premises were very basic, but by 1992, the department had two computer Laboratories, one of which contained fifteen IBM compatible computers, and the other, fourteen. The premises for the first computer Laboratory were constructed in 1979, under The World Bank Education I project with the equipment provided by an ODA project. The implementation of the first ODA project commenced in 1985 and its purpose was to provide the GTTI with the equipment necessary to deliver basic courses in information technology. In this respect the project provided twelve BBC micro-computers, twelve Video Display Units and appropriate software (ODA, 1987). The project also funded two consultants to spend two weeks installing equipment and teaching the staff how to deal with maintenance problems.

After the first consultancy had taken place, the ODA consultants recommended that further a two workshops should be delivered in the following year (Darley and Smith, 1985). The first workshop lasted for a week; the object being to familiarise GTTI staff, government Officials and industrialists with the use of computing facilities at the GTTI (British Council, 1986a). The second lasted for three days, and attempted to provide the technical members of the GTTI staff (mainly those in the computer department), with the necessary skills to diagnose and remedy faults when they occurred in the computer system. Under this ODA (I) project there were also plans to provide a consultant, who would be based at the GTTI for three years. According to an unpublished ODA report, the consultant's role would be to assist the computer department to deliver courses and also conduct maintenance work. Other project components financed by ODA included three scholarships, two of which would enable two of the lecturers

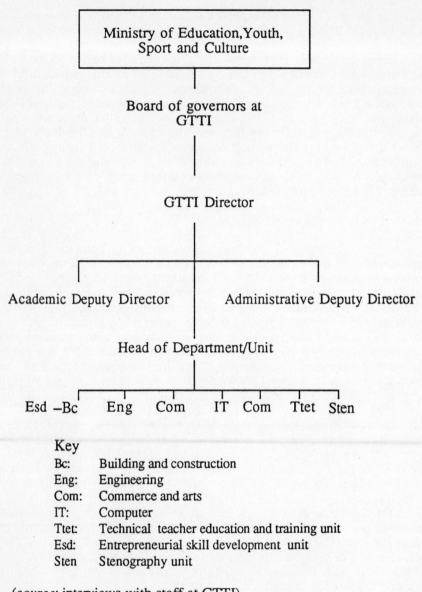

Ministry of Education, Youth,
Sport and Culture

Board of governors at
GTTI

GTTI Director

Academic Deputy Director   Administrative Deputy Director

Head of Department/Unit

Esd —Bc   Eng   Com   IT   Com   Ttet   Sten

Key
Bc: Building and construction
Eng: Engineering
Com: Commerce and arts
IT: Computer
Ttet: Technical teacher education and training unit
Esd: Entrepreneurial skill development unit
Sten   Stenography unit

(*source*: interviews with staff at GTTI)

Figure 5.2 Organisational structure of the GTTI

to study for the RSA Certificate in Information Technology. The third scholarship consisted of an attachment for three months to a technical institution in the UK; the aim of which was to familiarise the member of staff concerned with the processes involved in maintaining and repairing computer systems.

Once the implementation of the ODA(I) project was complete the organisation decided to finance a second project to support the country's National Vocational Training Programme, particularly in the area of information technology (Brown and Lewis, 1992). The project had a life span of three years and its implementation was due to start in 1987. The intention was that this second ODA project would build on the first, and in doing so, enable the computer department to integrate with other GTTI departments, including those in engineering and also to deliver higher level courses in information technology. Thus, under this project, the ODA provided the GTTI with the equipment to furnish a second computer laboratory (Darley and MacDonald, 1991). In order to assist the computer department to deliver higher level courses (and assist with the maintenance of the computers), the GTTI management also recruited a lecturer in information technology from Canada. The lecturer agreed to work on a local contract for two years. The GTTI paid his salary and the President's Office provided residential accommodation. In 1993 the GTTI recruited another expatriate from the USA, through a charity called 'Teachers for Africa', to work as a lecturer in the computer department for two years.

Another important IT development at the GTTI concerned the setting-up of the stenography unit. This Units had been operating for only thirteen months when the field work for the present study was conducted. There was no written documentation of its construction. However, two of the lecturers working there, and one of the GTTIs Deputy Directors, said that USAID was responsible for funding of the equipment, and also of its subsequent installation. Two scholarships from USAID also enabled two lecturers from the computer department to attend a two months intensive training course at the Stenography College in London.

Staff development at the GTTI

Staff development at the GTTI has been guided by two staff development plans, one for the 1983 to 1988 period and the second for the 1989 to 1994. The objective of the first plan was to assist the GTTI to achieve its aim of meeting the country's shortage of middle-level manpower (at technician level) through an appropriate curriculum and a cadre of well-qualified staff. Senior management thought that in order to deliver courses for technicians, GTTI lecturers must hold a subject matter qualification, the minimum being a full technological certificate in their respective subjects and a professional teaching certificate (Source: GTTI, 1983). A survey of lecturers' qualifications conducted in 1984 showed that although the majority of lecturers in the building and construction department lacked a Full Technological Certificate (or equivalent) they did have a professional teaching qualification. It also revealed that the majority of staff in the other departments did not have a pedagogic qualification. As a consequence, the GTTI's first staff development plan proposed to overcome these deficiencies in qualifications by providing in-house training and also by obtaining overseas scholarships.

The in-house training consisted of attending a Certificate Course in Education, delivered by the GTTI, attending a number of short courses, and finally, counterpart training. In relation to the short-courses, interviews conducted with GTTI staff concluded that the majority of courses were delivered by foreign consultants as part of an aid-funded project. For example, in 1985 the ODA delivered a series of one week workshops,on teaching methods. They also delivered workshops lasting a similar period on the subject of information technology in the same year, and additional workshops in the late 1980s on the subject of how to deliver the 730 City and Guilds Further Education and Adult Teachers' Certificate courses. Also during the late 1990s a series of subsequent workshops on micro-computing were also delivered by ODA consultants. Counterpart training also played an important role in the development of the GTTI senior staff. Four foreign consultants, sponsored by CIDA, were responsible for providing counterpart training from 1983 to 1986. One was given the position of Acting Director; the others held positions as Acting Heads of engineering, commerce and arts, and building and construction.

However, the most influential form of staff development appears to be that associated with overseas scholarships. Indeed, to ensure that GTTI staff were equipped with the necessary qualifications to deliver technician level courses the lecturers had to rely on overseas scholarships in order to obtain the qualifications and skills necessary to deliver advanced courses. In addition, the first staff development plan nominated two senior members of the GTTI staff to visit Britain in order to familiarise themselves with the operation of bodies such as the City and Guilds of London Institute, the Royal Society of Arts and the former Industrial Training Boards (Source: GTTI, 1983). During these visits the staff were also to acquaint themselves with examination techniques, with a view to assuming proper responsibility for the CGLI examinations in technical and commercial subjects in The Gambia once these examinations were localised.

The Institute's second plan continued to build on the achievements of the first, with a view to assisting the GTTI to deliver higher level programmes of study and in doing so reduce the need in the long run to send staff on higher level courses at overseas institutions (GTTI, 1989). The second plan also aimed to achieve its objectives by obtaining overseas scholarships and through further in-house training programmes. Indeed, the senior management at the GTTI identified a number of overseas scholarships which would be required to enable the Institute to introduce new courses or enrich existing ones (GTTI, 1989). For example, in the category of new courses, the GTTI had established an electronics laboratory under the World Bank Education II project and there was therefore a need for a Gambian to study overseas for an HND course in electronics (World Bank, 1989). In the Automotive engineering section, there were plans to introduce auto-electronics, so that there was a need for someone to study for an HND in auto-electronics.

The in-house programmes also included plans to further upgrade the management skills of existing staff by developing a Higher Teacher Certificate course. The Certificate would provide senior lecturers with further training once they had completed the 730 C&GLI Further Education and Adult Teachers' Certificate course. Responsibility for developing this course rested with the GTTI's technical teacher education and training section, established in 1993. Another three components of the GTTI's in-house programmes were funded by the British Overseas Development Administration, under the ODA (II) project. The project had a life span of six years and its implementation should have started in 1987. Furthermore, its objectives were to (i) localise the relevant City and Guilds of London Institute examinations in conjunction with the West Africa Examinations Council, (ii) upgrade the management skills of the Institute's senior staff, and finally (iii) to assist the GTTI in providing information technology courses (ODA, 1990). Once again, the ODA financed a series of workshops in each of the above areas. For example, if we take the issue of localisation there were plans in The Gambia to localise the C&GLI examination syllabuses, and for the West African Examination Council in Banjul to take responsibility for validating courses and moderating the examination results (WAEC, 1989). In this respect ODA financed three series of workshops, each lasting three weeks. Topics covered in these workshops were curriculum development, methods of assessment and examinations. The first set of workshops were delivered by an overseas consultant and attended by all Senior Lecturers at the GTTI, by representatives from the DNVTP and by WAEC officers. The ODA had planned that the second series of workshops would take place in February 1993. It was intended that these workshops would focus on the themes of assessment and on the assessment of practical work (Tansley, 1993). However, owing to problems that were experienced in delivering the second series of workshops they were abandoned, and instead a third series of workshops took place in June 1993 and November 1993.

Besides the issue of localisation the ODA (II) project also attempted to upgrade the management skills of the senior staff through providing a series of workshops which focused on the issue of quality assurance. The first occurred in March 1993 and lasted for two weeks. The second lasted for the same period, and was delivered in November 1993. In the first workshop the consultant ran an afternoon session on the basic tools required to establish a Quality Assurance System. This involved familiarising the GTTI staff with operational definitions, including efficiency, effectiveness and the meanings of the terms 'client' and 'customer' (Hough, 1992a). The consultant then ran a workshop on how to conduct external and internal scans of the educational environment.

The first series of workshops enabled the GTTI staff to start the first part of a quality assurance system; namely, to establish a three year strategic plan. At the time of the field work (October 1994), staff were at the stage of writing a three year strategic plan for the Institute. The next series of workshops looked at the roles played by course teams in managing and implementing a Quality Assurance system. The ODA consultant involved in delivering these workshops, said that course teams now have the authority to implement parts of a strategic plan, and the responsibility for ensuring that the quality assurance system is operational (Hough, 1993b).

The entrepreneurship training at the GTTI

Entrepreneurship training at the GTTI was the responsibility of a entrepreneurial skills development unit (ESDU) which was part of the GTTI's building and construction department. This unit was established in 1986 by the Institute's Director in order to develop a course on entrepreneurial skill development and to provide students who successfully completed this course, with the skills to establish their own enterprises (N'jie, 1989a). The course on entrepreneurial skill development lasted for two years, and was specifically designed for craft students from the building and construction and the engineering departments. According to a member of the Institute's senior management the course formed part of a general studies option, delivered to students studying on the Institute's three year basic craft courses. During the first year of the course students studied modules on the subject of setting up a small business. Entry to the second year of the course was determined by the students' motivation towards establishing an enterprise, and by their perceived capability of becoming an entrepreneur. Students attending the second year studied more advanced modules on business development covering issues such as financial planning and legal matters associated with running your own business (Source: N'jie, 1989b)

The modules varied in length, from four to sixteen hours, and each included case studies that made references to the problems of operating an enterprise in The Gambia. At the end of the course, students were provided with a four week placement in a private enterprise. Once students had successfully completed the entrepreneurial skill development course, and graduated from the GTTI, they were entitled to apply for a loan to establish their enterprise from either the Indigenous Business Advisory Service (IBAS) or the entrepreneurial skill development unit. The first of these organisations, IBAS, was set-up by the Ministry of Economic Planning and Industrial Development in 1976 to promote the development of small businesses. One of the primary functions of IBAS is to provide financial loans, ranging from £150 up to £1000 (Sylva, 1991). One of the Institute's Deputy Directors anticipated that the ESDU would manage a revolving loan scheme, and that funding to establish the scheme would be provided by the UNDP.

From this short description of developments at the GTTI it is possible to see that the Institution shares many similarities to the College of Arts Science and Technology in Jamaica, with regard to the way in which it operates. Not only has this enabled the GTTI to respond to the changing needs of students and employers alike, it has also dealt with issues such as efficiency and of the need to gain additional revenue through income generating activities. Unsurprisingly the way in which the GTTI is managed has helped ensure that it is one of the largest, and most successful, post-secondary TVET institutions in English speaking West Africa. The recent proposals to develop a strategic plan should help ensure that GTTI remains so. We now consider another of the major TVET initiatives in The Gambia, namely the RVTP.

The Rural Vocational Training Programme (RVTP)

In the country's second five-year development plan for social and economic development (1979-1984 to 1985-85), The Gambian government emphasised its commitment to rural development through establishing the Rural Vocational Training Programme (MEDIP, 1981). The objective of this Programme was to improve the living standards of rural people by providing villagers with the skills necessary to make home improvements and improve agricultural productivity. In doing so it was also anticipated that this would provide villagers with the ability to earn extra income, outside of the farming season, through sideline activities such as the sale of agricultural products and locally produced handicrafts.

The Rural Vocational Training Programme (RVTP) was started in 1979 and the original institutions involved in its initial implementation are shown in Figure 5.3. Currently, the overall responsibility for co-ordinating the Programme rests with the Directorate of Technical Education and Vocational Training (DTEVT, 1991). The organisations which provided training under the RVTP were the Rural Vocational Training Centre (RVTC) at Mansakonko and numerous In-Village Training Centres (IVTCs) and Mixed Farming Centres situated in the country's provinces. A total of two projects were launched under the RVT Programme and the first of these, the Rural Vocational Training (RVT) Project (I), was funded by the European Economic Community in 1979; whilst the second, the Rural Vocational Project (II), attempted to restructure the RVTP through consolidating the existing number of In-village training centres and by developing a new training course for rural instructors.

The Rural Vocational Training Project (I)

The RVTP (I) was responsible for supporting much of The Gambia's initial skill development in rural areas. The Principal of the RVTC became accountable to the then DNVTP, for: the delivery of courses at the Rural Vocational Training Centre, the Construction of the In-Village Training Centres and the Mixed Farming Centres and delivery of skills training in these Centres (N' yang, 1984). During the first year of the RVTC's operation, volunteer instructors, who were recruited by the organisation Voluntary Services Overseas, provided counterpart training for local Gambians, the assumption being that Gambians would take the places of the volunteers once their training was completed. The counterparts were

91

Gambia High School leavers who had obtained a City and Guilds Craft Certificate in a particular craft area. The RVTP (I) also established a Rural Technical Instructor Training and Service Unit (RTITSU) to provide short skills upgrading courses for successful RVTC graduates once they started work in the rural villages. There was also an Appropriate Technology section at the Centre which promoted the use of technology in conjunction with the Centre's skills training programmes. For example, one of the aims of Appropriate Technology was to provide women in rural areas with the tools and equipment necessary for ground preparation and harvesting, thereby easing their work (Bittaye, 1983).

Under the RVTP (I) students at the RVTC were recruited from villages in the province. Their training periods lasted for a total of twelve months, the first six of which were spent at the RVTC studying home economics, horticulture, metal work and handicrafts. Whilst they were based at the Rural Vocational Training Centre, the trainee instructors received a stipend, (equivalent to seven pounds sterling per month). Following this the students spent six months at one of the village workshops teaching the skills (to villagers) that they had learnt at the RVTC. This latter period was considered to be on-the-job training and was monitored by the RTITSU However, during this second period the payment of this allowance was stopped and instructors were expected to generate their own income through the sale of items such as handicrafts produced in the training process.

The RVTC only delivers instructor training programmes during the non-farming season and the trainees for the RVTC were recruited from what the project defined as 'Key Villages' (N'jie, 1991). In the original EEC project, 60 'Key Villages' were identified and each of these was selected from a circle or cluster of 16 villages (EEC, 1979). The 'Key Villages' were spaced sixteen kilometres apart and the criteria for becoming a Key Village was that the village should have: a good relationship with other local villages; suitable candidates to train as instructors; and also be willing and capable of becoming involved in various forms of income generating activities.

As stipulated previously, graduates from the Rural Vocational Training Centre were to become responsible for delivering courses at the In-Village Training Centres (IVTCs). Under the original project proposal each of the Key villages would contain a multipurpose, in-village training centre and local inhabitants would be responsible for their construction. These centres would contain workshops for carpentry, blacksmiths, building and construction, horticulture, home economics, handicrafts and rural mechanics. The training consisted only of short-term practical activities, as the majority of villagers were illiterate. The content and length of the training activities were determined by the instructors who worked there (Bittaye, 1983). For example, training for carpenters occurred for a period of between nine months and one year and included instruction on how to make household furniture and structures for houses such as doors and window frames.

92

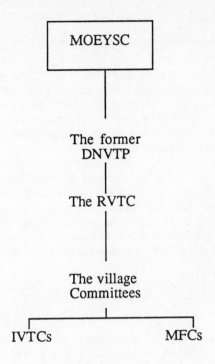

Key

MOEYSC: Ministry of Education, Youth, Sports and Culture.
DNVTP : Directorate for the National Vocational Training Programme.
RVTC : Rural Vocational Training Centre.
IVTCs : In-Village Training Centres (under the original proposal 60 IVTCs
        were to be constructed).
MFCs: Mixed Farming Centres (under the original proposal 22 MFCs were
        to be constructed).

(*source*: interviews with senior officals at the DTEVT)

Figure 5.3   **Organisational structure of the Rural
                  Vocational Training Programme**

The second of the training centres to be established in the Key Villages, the Mixed Farming Centre, consisted of workshops specifically designed to train people to become blacksmiths or to upgrade existing skills, and so enable them to manufacture and repair farmers' tools. The EEC project intended to establish 22 Mixed Farming Centres by the end of the 1980s. However, unlike the 'Key Villages' instructors, those at the Mixed Farming Centres were paid an allowance of the equivalent of seven pounds sterling per month (because they were blacksmiths who had been uprooted from their villages and deprived of their former income).

Under the RVT Project I, a Village Committee was set up in each of the 'Key Villages'. The Committees were each headed by a local chief and comprised individuals representing the views of youths, women and elders. Thus, the committees allowed villagers to participate in the implementation of the Rural Vocational Training Project, with the aim of ensuring that the workshops were constructed. The workshops generated income through the sale of locally produced handicrafts and in the process acted as a vehicle for training rural people. The other functions of the village committee were to select trainees for the RVTC and support income generating activities (DNVTP, 1985).

The Rural Vocational Training Project (II)

The RVT Project (II) started in 1991 when the Principal of the RVTC resigned and a new appointment was made. One of the outcomes of this change was the decision to consolidate the existing number of in-village training centres under the RVTP and to focus resources on a smaller number of Key Villages. It was also decided to develop a new pedagogical programme for the rural instructors who worked at the RVTC. The funding and technical assistance for developing this programme was provided by CIDA. In the mid-1990s the staff at the DTEVT were also attempting to obtain further funding from the German and the Japanese governments for the Rural Vocational Training Programme. The central theme of the proposal was to provide support for unemployed rural youths by establishing a revolving credit scheme. The lack of access to loans under the Rural Vocational Training Project I had been identified by the officials as one of the major reasons why villagers had failed to establish their own enterprises. Having outlined the country's Rural Vocational Training Programme we now consider another organisation in The Gambia which plays a major role in providing skills training, namely the Banjul Skills Centre.

The Banjul Skills Centre (BSC)

The final of the public TVET institutions operating in The Gambia is the Banjul Skills Centre. The BSC was set up in 1989/90 to provide skills training for those who wished to learn the necessary marketable skills in order to establish their own businesses (Jobarteh *et al*, 1992). The origins of the Banjul Skills Centre can be traced back to the establishment of the National Vocational Training Centre in the late 1960s (N'jie, 1983). When the Centre was established towards the end of the 1960s, the initial facilities were basic, consisting of a carpentry and joinery workshop, and a mechanical engineering workshop. There were six full-time instructors, three in carpentry and joinery, the remainder in engineering. The Centre's original training activities were not directly geared to any defined objectives and there was little or no theoretical instruction (N'jie, 1983). Trainees enrolled directly from school at the age of 16 and spent five years at the NVTC. Interviews with former instructors who worked at the Centre revealed that the criteria for assessing good carpenters was an examination of the furniture produced at the end of their five year training period. The Centre's original activities were restricted to the training of carpenters and engineers up to and including craft level. The instructors interviewed also commented that during the 1970s the Centre had an annual enrolment of 35 male students.

In the mid-1970s, the Centre extended its activities to include new courses in Plumbing, Commerce, Telecommunications, Welding and Fabrication and by the late 1970s the annual student intake had increased to 272, an intake which was beyond the Centre's operational capacity (N'jie, 1981). During this period the responsibility for co-ordinating the activities of the NVTC was taken from the Ministry of Education and transferred to the former Directorate for the National Vocational Training Programme (N'jie 1981). This change occurred because of what was perceived as the low priority given to TVET under the Ministry of Education, and because of the need to encourage co-operation between the NVTC and employers.

The annexation of the former NVTC to the GTTI

In 1986 The Gambian government decided to annexe the NVTC to the GTTI and to convert the former into a Skills Training Centre. The mandate for this was given by The Gambian Cabinet in November, 1988. The Cabinet also recommended that a Committee be set up to study and advise on the GTTI's annexation of the NVTC. The committee's recommendations formed the basis for the Centre's annexation to the GTTI, and the World Bank Education II Project was supposed to play a major role in funding and implementing these changes. At the time of the field work (November 1995) the annexation was still in its initial stages and the Banjul Skills Centre was not fully operational. Nevertheless, the Annexation Committee had reported back to the Cabinet on a number of issues relating to the annexation. For example, they stated that the salaries and conditions of employment for the NVTC instructors needed to match those of the GTTI lecturers. However, in achieving the former there was also a need to ensure that NVTC instructors have comparable qualifications.

The committee also decided that new entrants should be at least 17 years old and have successfully completed their schooling at one of the country's secondary technical schools, in an attempt to raise standards. The committee was also given a remit to look at the NVTC's courses in relation to those of the GTTI and to identify where overlaps occurred and also to identify possible new areas of provision for skills training at the BSC. A number of overlaps were identified and it was also suggested that the BSC should diversify its activities to include training in: house decorating, house wiring, out-board motor engineering, typewriting, hairdressing, radio/TV set repairs and office machine repairs. The Committee further recommended that the BSC's training programmes should consist of training modules which would last for a period of between two and six months. For example, in Welding and Fabrication there could be a sudden demand for window and door guards, following the recent construction boom in the country's capital, Banjul. There could also be a demand to repair or make exhaust pipes for motor vehicles. It was thought that if the courses were short and competency-based, people would return to the BSC to continually upgrade their skills, or to learn new ones in response to the needs of the market. It was hoped that this training would enable people to earn an income by constructing items which were readily marketable.

Another recommendation of the committee was that in addition to the provision of technical skills, the Centre should plan to encourage the development of entrepreneurial skills amongst its students, through providing training in basic business skills, (such as book-keeping) and information about how and where to obtain loans. The process of becoming an entrepreneur would be facilitated by creating a 'business incubator' at the BSC. An incubator is basically a workshop equipped with the necessary tools to enable trainees to practice the skills learnt during their training period. According to the senior management of the GTTI, the trainees would thus be able to use the incubators for the six-month period following their training. It was anticipated that this would enable the graduates of the Skill Centre to obtain work contracts, and to earn the income necessary to establish their own workshops. In return for using the Centre's facilities, the graduates would pay a small fee. A further finding of the Committee was the existence of major structural deficiencies in the BSCs workshops. Thus, in order to deliver the new courses at the Centre, promote the development of entrepreneurs and assist with the capital developments, the World Bank Education II project intended to provide technical assistance which would consist of overseas scholarships and consultancy support.

Provision of company and non-governmental training

The final area of provision described in this chapter concerns company and non-governmental provision. In contrast to Jamaica, there are no apprenticeships, or other formalised mechanisms of support to encourage company training in The Gambia. Out of the companies visited during the field work, the only ones to offer any type of structured training within the workplace were those owned, or formerly owned, by The Gambian government. These included The Gambia Public Transport Company, The Gambia Utilities Company and The Gambia Public Telephone Company.

All of these companies played a major role in providing the infrastructure support necessary for the country's development.

The first of these, The Gambia Public Telephone Company (GAMTEL), is responsible for operating the country's telecommunication system. Its training facilities consist of eight classrooms, two small seminar rooms, an electronic workshop containing testing equipment and oscilloscopes, and a fully equipped computer laboratory. The company's apprenticeship programme lasts for two years and enables the trainees to study electronics and telecommunications up to and including technician level. The company also provides continuous skill upgrading courses for its technical and non-technical staff. The upgrading courses have been modularised and can be delivered by the company's instructors when there is an identified need. The finance for establishing the training facilities came from the International Telecommunication Union (in Geneva) in 1992 and advanced training for the company's instructors, up to HND level, was provided through ODA overseas scholarships in the early 1990s.

The second of the major providers of company training in The Gambia, The Gambia Public Transport Company (GPTC), is in charge of the country's public bus company, and the ferry service that operates on the Banjul river. The training centre at the GPTC consists of two classrooms. The training period lasts for twelve months, during which trainees spend time in one of the company's many workshops. The training is based on the concept of 'product orientated training'. During their initial training employees are taught how to repair and maintain various parts of a bus (including the chassis, the engine and the axle) whilst the skill upgrading programmes are designed according to specific needs. For example, in 1994 there was a need to establish a training programme to enable employees to repair the bus fuel pumps which kept breaking down. The former DNVTP assisted the GPTC to obtain funding from the German government to establish and equip the company's new training centre in 1991. The former DNVTP also helped the GPTC to obtain scholarships from the German government and ODA for its employees to study engineering to HND or equivalent level.

At the time of the research, the final company to provide any type of systematic training in The Gambia was The Gambia Utilities Corporation. The GUC manages Gambia's national electricity grid and the country's sewage and water systems. According to officials at the GUC and at the DTEVT, the organisation has one of the best equipped training centres in West Africa. The training centre consists of two electrical workshops equipped with circuits to facilitate training, a third workshop equipped with lathes and other CNC machinery, and a fourth, containing appropriate measuring devices. There is no apprenticeship scheme, although entry-level employees spend six months full-time at the training school where they specialise in either mechanical engineering or electrical engineering. Interviews with GUC senior staff said that this enabled the employees to be trained up to basic craft level. The trainees would then enter the workplace and return for short-term skills up-grading courses, delivered by the institution's own instructors. The funding for the construction and equipping of the training centre came from the German government; whilst technical assistance to set up the training programme was provided by Gesellschaft fur Technische Zusammenarbeit (GTZ). As with the other companies, the former DNVTP assisted the GUC to obtain funds from the German government and from GTZ

In addition to the activities discussed above, The Gambian government is considering the possibility of introducing a training levy into the country. At the time of writing, the finer details had yet to be worked out, although it was anticipated that 50 per cent of the contribution would come from the private sector, since these are the organisations which employ graduates from institutions such as the GTTI and the BSC. Civil servants would contribute 1 per cent of their salary to the fund and workers in the informal sector would contribute an equivalent of thirty pence a month. Under this system, officials at the DTEVT maintained that private sector companies which sent employees to the GTTI or to the BSC would be entitled to a reduction in their levy contributions.

Training in the in-formal sector

The provision of support for those who work in the country's in-formal sector is co-ordinated by an organisation called TANGO (The Association of Non governmental Organisations). This umbrella organisation was set-up in 1979, by 18 NGOs, to co-ordinate the activities of NGOs in The Gambia, to liaise with The government on NGO activities and generally ensure a greater integration of NGOs' efforts in the country's development (TANGO, 1990). When TANGO became operational in 1983 most of its activities were undertaken by volunteers. However, by 1990, TANGO had over 60 members and was able to appoint a full time secretariat (TANGO, 1993). The funding for this expansion came from members' contributions and donations from the Commonwealth Fund for Technical Co-operation and the UNDP. Once TANGO had a secretariat and additional funds, it was able to improve the services offered to its members by documenting members' activities through the circulation of a quarterly newsletter, and by holding quarterly meetings. In addition TANGO started providing funds and technical assistance to groups who wished to establish their own NGOs, or to existing ones who wanted to expand the size of their present operations.

The funding administered by TANGO consisted of grants which varied from the equivalent of £400 upto £1,200. The provision of technical assistance varied according to the NGOs' needs. For example, in 1992, TANGO helped an NGO called 'Partners in Progress' to set up a metal and carpentry workshop to train illiterate Gambians to become self-sufficient, through the construction and subsequent sale of school furniture (TANGO, 1992). TANGO also provided the organisation members with a two week carpentry course on how to construct tables and chairs. This was followed directly by an afternoon workshop on instructional methods. For larger NGOs, such as Action Aid and Save the Children, TANGO acts as a clearing house for overseas scholarships. In 1994 TANGO obtained funding from the Commonwealth Fund for Technical Co-operation to enable five people to study for Forestry Management in Kenya. TANGO also liaises with the government of The Gambia to promote the interests of its members with the result that NGOs were given charitable status. This exempts TANGO and its members from paying customs duty and import tax on materials and equipment used in the implementation of training programmes and also road tax on vehicles. Similarly, expatriate employees working for NGOs in The Gambia are exempt from income tax. The government of The Gambia has also supported NGO activities through providing them with access to government training facilities. An example of this kind of support can be seen by reference to the activities of Action Aid.

Action Aid sponsored training

From the 1970s to the beginning of the 1980s, Action Aid's activities in The Gambia have been confined to the provision of primary education in rural areas. In the mid-1980s the organisation decided to extend its activities to include the provision of basic skills training through a project called the Continuing Village Education Programme (CVEP). Under this Programme, Action Aid planned to operate nine Village Training Centres; six of which were to be constructed using the organisation's own resources, and the other three were to be provided by the former DNVTP. It appears that many of the government's Rural Training Centres were not being used and as a consequence it was decided that Action Aid could use the Training Centre at Jali on a pilot basis and that other government centres could be brought into use over the next two to three years. The type of training provided at the Action Aid Vocational Training Centres depended on the artisans' needs and in the majority of cases involved practical nature involving 'hands-on-experience'. According to sources interviewed, the training period varied from two to six months with supervision by local instructors. But in contrast to the former government's Rural Vocational Training Programme, Action Aid's CVEP provided its instructors with salaries and its trainees with a stipend and a grant at the end of their training (to purchase the tools, and materials necessary to establish their own enterprise).

This outline of developments within The Gambian TVET system illustrates the rapid progress that has been made since the country achieved independence in the late 1960s. This has resulted in a variety of organisations providing different types of TVET. At one end of the scale are organisations such as TANGO, and the government's Basic Skills Centres, who provide basic skills training for those who earn a living in the country's informal sector. At the other end of the spectrum are institutions such as the GTTI, and certain state owned companies, which deliver some of the most technologically advanced training courses in West Africa. This chapter has also shown how these developments have occurred and whether they resulted from locally supported initiatives or projects financed by a donor agencies. However, it has not looked at the processes involved in implementing such projects. Neither has it considered their impact. All of these issues are analysed in the following chapter.

6 An analysis of the implementation process in The Gambia

Introduction

There are two parts to this chapter and the first of these focuses on the process involved in implementing projects at public TVET institutions in The Gambia, including how they were initiated, managed and implemented. Not only does this allow us to discuss the possible impact of these projects, it also enables the chapter to analyse one of the central themes of the present study - namely, how the dependence on overseas aid and foreign technical assistance has affected the implementation process. This is achieved through focusing on projects implemented at the GTTI, and those that were implemented at institutions operating under the DTEVT, or as it was formerly known the DNVTP. The second part of the chapter reflects upon how effectively, and efficiently the government has supported company and non-governmental provision of training in The Gambia.

Analysis of developments at the GTTI

As previously mentioned, the GTTI is one of the largest post-secondary TVET institutions in West Africa. In analysing the implementation process at this institution we start by focusing on those initiatives which supported developments in information technology. This is followed by an analysis of the GTTI's programmes for the continuing and professional development of its staff. Finally the analysis turns to the institute's attempts at developing entrepreneurship training programmes for their students.

Developments in information technology

Information technology projects at the GTTI supported initiatives at the computer department and also at the stenography unit. Both the computer department and the stenography unit were dependent on aid projects for their development. As can be recalled from Chapter 5 the development of the computer department was heavily influenced by two projects, both of which were financed by ODA, under the ODA (I) and (II) projects. Whilst the construction of the stenography unit was supported by funding from the United States Agency for International Development (USAID).

The first ODA project was initiated because of the demand for training in information technology in The Gambia, and owing to the lack of facilities to respond to this demand. Thus, ODA decided that information technology would be a beneficial area to develop at the GTTI. However, this financial dependency on British aid enabled the ODA to determine the type of equipment provided under the project. According to the GTTI managers interviewed, in selecting this equipment ODA had been influenced by the type of computers being used at the time in British technical institutions, namely BBC micro-computers. None of the academic members of staff at GTTI were involved in constructing the project proposal. Furthermore, they felt that the provision of IBM computers would have been more appropriate since these are the type of machines most commonly used by businesses in The Gambia.

Despite ODA's control over the management and implementation process, problems were experienced when the foreign consultants came to install the computer equipment in the mid-1980s. The first of these was only minor and related to faults with the BBC computers (Darley and Smith, 1985). But the second problem was more serious and concerned the physical conditions of the computer laboratory. According to an unpublished consultancy report, the computer Laboratory had not been adequately prepared to house the computer equipment when the project started in 1985 (Darley, 1985). The computer laboratory, a former classroom, had not been made dust-proof and the ODA consultants were concerned about the damage this could cause to the computers. This concern was justified a year later, when four of the computer terminals ceased functioning as a result of dust entering the electrical circuits.

As a result, the machines were sent back to the UK for repairs. At first it appeared that the damage had resulted from negligence on the part of GTTI, rather than on the part of the ODA. Although, closer examination revealed that in managing the implementation of the project, the ODA had assumed that before the equipment arrived, the computer laboratory would be dust proof and secondly that the GTTI would finance the necessary capital developments, including the installation of new doors and windows. However, in reality the GTTI was unable to meet the cost of such developments because it had committed its finances to other ventures, and according to one of the Institute's senior managers they were unable to raise the necessary funds until the following year. In retrospect, the ODA could have prevented this damage. For example, they should have delayed the installation of the computers, or alternatively they could have assisted with the capital developments. This support would have amounted to only a small proportion of the project's total budget.

Another problem occurred with the project in 1987 and concerned the GTTI lecturers who had completed their overseas training. Under the original project proposal the overseas training was supposed to have provided the GTTI with a cadre of qualified staff who would be capable of maintaining the department's equipment and in doing so reduce its dependence on overseas expertise. However, unpublished documents indicate that this was not the case. Indeed, in 1988 the department's computer networking system stopped working and the GTTI management contacted the ODA consultants in the UK for advice. The ODA consultants responded with fax communications suggesting ways in which the GTTI staff could repair the fault. However, none of these suggestions proved successful. The impact was devastating since those students studying word processing were unable to take the practical part of their RSA examination. During the same year, the computer department also encountered staffing problems when two of the lecturers decided to leave the GTTI for the private sector. This resulted in the Institute having to rely on part-time staff to deliver the computer courses. Thus, by the end of the 1980s the computer department was experiencing staffing problems and difficulties in maintaining its equipment.

The GTTI had clearly benefited from its financial dependency on the ODA in that it had obtained a fully equipped computer laboratory. But at the same time the department lacked the qualified staff necessary to maintain and repair the computers. Arguably, in order to become more sustainable, the computer department needed either to upgrade the qualifications of its existing staff though further overseas scholarships, or to recruit additional, better qualified, and more experienced lecturers. The former strategy has already been tried by the ODA with limited success. By providing overseas scholarships for the lecturers, the ODA was equipping them with skills which were well in advance of those held by technicians working in the country's private sector. This resulted in the GTTI staff being head-hunted by the private sector. The ODA recognising this dilemma, attempted to recruit a long term expatriate consultant to work at the GTTI for three years. While such a measure would have benefited the department, it would have done little to reduce its dependence on overseas assistance. As it happened, ODA was unable to recruit a suitable candidate and so no one was appointed.

The management and implementation of the ODA project II

ODA decided to implement a second project in an attempt to resolve some of the problems associated with the first project and also in order to expand the capacity of the existing computer department by providing equipment for a second laboratory (Brown, 1991). A member of the Institute's senior management said that the decision occurred because of the fact that students had to wait for two years before they could obtain a place on one of the computer department's courses.

However, in contrast to the first ODA project, the Institute's senior management now had a considerable input into determining the equipment provided. For instance, their preference for IBM compatible computers rather than BBC machines was accepted by the ODA. The ODA also provided a scholarship for one of the lecturers to study for an HND in computing at a University in the UK. The ODA project II was managed by an ODA consultant in collaboration with the Director of the GTTI, and an official from the former DNVTP (ODA, 1987). The ODA had planned to implement the project in 1988 with the assistance of a long-term consultant. However, as explained earlier, they were unable to recruit a suitable person for the post. This delayed the implementation of the project for three years. Further complications arose when the Head of the computer department suddenly died in 1992. As a result of this unfortunate incident, the Institute was left with another major staffing problem and attempts were made to fill this vacuum through recruiting an expatriate lecturer from Canada. Senior managers at the GTTI and the ODA consultants hoped that this lecturer would ease the staffing problem, and enable the department to deliver courses, assist with the maintenance and repair of the department's equipment and also respond to the demand for higher level courses in information technology.

Unfortunately, the Canadian lecturer commenced work at the GTTI in 1993 and remained there for only two weeks. Therefore, the department was unable to achieve any of the above aims. Besides the problem of dependency on foreign lecturers, the GTTI had also experienced difficulties in retaining local lecturers, with good IT qualifications, owing to their marketability. Senior managers at the GTTI were aware of this problem and hoped that the recently recruited lecturer from America, through the organisation 'Teachers in Africa', will help the department to overcome its staffing problems. There was also anticipation that the situation would improve when the lecturers from the computer department have completed their overseas scholarships and returned to the GTTI. Perhaps when The Gambia becomes more economically advanced the GTTI will not face the problem of staff turn over.

Information technology at the stenography unit

The initiative for the development of a stenography unit at the GTTI came from USAID, who approached The Gambian government to ask if they were interested in computerising the country's system of court reporting. Two of the GTTI senior managers said that USAID represented the interests of an American organisation called the Stenography Corporation. This Corporation is the only company in the world to manufacture and market computerised stenography equipment. As a consequence, USAID enabled the Stenography Corporation to obtain a ready made market for its products in West Africa. The effect of USAID's project was that GTTI was dependent on the Stenography Corporation for the computerised stenography machines, the software, the installation of the equipment and the delivery of the course in Court Reporting.

The consultants successfully installed the equipment in 1992, but the unit soon experienced problems with the computer software provided by USAID and also with the course in Court Reporting, which was moderated and validated by the Stenography Corporation in America. According to lecturers at the unit, the software package 'Premier Power' stopped working soon after it had been installed. As a consequence students were unable to transcribe their work for over a month. The problem was then solved by advice from the Stenography Corporation and through re-installing the software package. Whilst with regard to the second issue the lecturers also said that it was difficult to deliver the course in the time allocated by the Stenography Corporation because of language differences. Indeed, because English is the students' second language it took them longer to learn the phonetics used to operate the computerised stenography machines. However, there were plans made to solve this problem by extending the duration of the course.

This example of problems experienced with information technology illustrate that it is not only dependence on foreign components which can influence the implementation process, but also the conditions of the local infrastructure and labour market. Indeed, the marketability of lecturing staff with IT qualifications appears to have created major problems for the GTTI's computer department, both in terms of project implementation and in the actual delivery of its courses. This issue of staffing is further explored in the section below.

An analysis of GTTI's dependency on the First World for staff development

When the field work for the present research was being conducted the GTTI had implemented two staff development programmes. The first of these covered the 1983 to 1988 period, and the second, 1989 to 1994. In analysing these programmes we assess the extent to which each of them is dependent on First World institutions, and overseas aid, and whether other factors, such as the managing of the Institution, have had an effect on the provision of staff development at the GTTI.

GTTI's first five year staff development plan (1983 to 1988)

Interviews with department heads and information obtained from policy documents revealed that under the Institute's first programme of staff development there were a total of 19 initiatives, out of which 15 were dependent on scholarships to overseas institutions. The majority of the overseas training was financed by ODA, the German government and CIDA, respectively. This high level of dependency reflects the fact that the GTTI was in its early stages of development and lacked the necessary qualified staff to deliver technician-level courses and also that The Gambia lacks the organisations necessary to conduct such training. However, the significance of the dependency on ODA scholarships also relates to The Gambia's historical relationship with its former colonial power, the United Kingdom.

The interview data gathered from ODA consultants and senior GTTI officials revealed that the ODA was keen to invest in The Gambia owing to the fact that it is a relatively small country, and consequently the outcomes of aid projects could be more clearly identified than in other Third World countries in Africa. It is clear that the provision of ODA scholarships has assisted the Institute to build a cadre of qualified staff who are capable of delivering technician level courses. However, senior lecturers at the engineering and computer departments revealed that about half of the staff who had completed their overseas studies and returned to The Gambia had left the Institute. A solution to this problem could lie in providing scholarships for short courses (in overseas institutions) which do not lead to academic awards. This occurred with some of the former CIDA scholarships, and more recently with ODA's three month scholarships which provided training through work placements. Another possible solution could be in the improvement of remuneration's and conditions of service for GTTI lecturers.

Besides the overseas scholarships discussed above, the present study identified four major in-house initiatives (counterpart training, workshops and the development of the 730 CGLI Further Education and Adult Teachers Certificate). All of these were dependent on overseas aid or foreign personnel to varying degrees. But the present research found no adverse problems with the first initiative for staff development, namely, counterpart training. According to the GTTI staff involved, they were able to take on the responsibilities of department Heads at the end of the counterpart training. They thought that this form of training could be regarded as an efficient means of training local staff to manage the GTTI and that it was also a more effective way of retaining trained staff than overseas scholarships. For the second group of initiatives, the workshops on entrepreneurship and teaching methods, the research again, found no significant problems.

However, in relation to the third of the initiatives, the development of the 730 CGLI Further Education and Adult Teachers Certificate, the implementation process was significantly more complicated and influenced by a variety of factors. Despite being initiated and funded by the GTTI and the West African Examination Council, this course continued to be dependent on the City and Guilds Institute of London for its validation. Furthermore, it was also dependent on overseas consultants for the moderation of the students' examination marks. This made the course particularly expensive to administer and resulted in high fees for the GTTI staff who were taking these examinations as part of their staff development (TETOCb, 1985). For example, during the early 1990s the average GNP per capita in The Gambia was £187 per annum and the estimated cost for taking the examination was £53. Under these conditions it is not difficult to see why the decision was taken, by the GTTI senior management, to localise the examination. Nevertheless, quite apart from the issue of costs, and the common criticisms of syllabuses imported from overseas, there was another justification for localising the examination. A number of senior officials at WAEC commented that GTTI lecturers and teachers who had successfully obtained their C&GLI(FE) 730 Teachers Certificate were not recognised by the country's Ministry of Education as having qualified teacher status. As a consequence, GTTI lecturers were not placed on the same salary scale as other qualified teachers. According to reliable sources, the Ministry of Education was unable to raise the salaries owing to the provisions of the 1982 Education Act, under which, The Gambia College was the only post-secondary institution in the country with a mandate to train school teachers.

The College offered a two-year, full-time teacher training course, at the end of which successful students were awarded a Teachers Certificate.

Thus, in an attempt to gain recognition from the Ministry of Education for the 730 C&GLI Further Education and Adult Teachers' Certificate, the GTTI set-up a Technical Teachers Development Committee to manage the implementation of the localisation process. The Committee was made up of representatives from the Ministry of Education, The Gambia College, the GTTI, the DTEVT and the WAEC.

It was anticipated that the localisation process would take three years, but no available records were found to indicate the extent to which the localisation process was dependent on overseas aid or on foreign consultants. Nevertheless, the interview data revealed that the funds for the localisation process came from the ODA and were used to finance the appointment of a Chief Assessor from the City and Guilds of London Institute. During the first two years of the localisation programme (1985-87) the course was validated jointly by WAEC's office in The Gambia and the City and Guilds Institute in London. The local assessor was a lecturer from The Gambia College and he was responsible for vetting the examination marks which the GTTI students obtained, and for making recommendations to the Technical Teachers Development Committee. The Chief Assessor from CGLI came to The Gambia once a year to ensure that the assessment was taking place according to the CGLI guidelines. After the third year of the localisation process, WAEC was given the authority to validate the 730 C&GLI Further Education and Adult Teachers' Certificate course, and to award the Certificate.

No adverse effects could be found from the use of foreign consultants and overseas aid to fund the localisation process. However, problems were experienced in validating the course after the localisation process had been completed. According to members of the GTTI's senior management there was a dispute between the GTTI, the WAEC and The Gambia College over who should pay the Chief Assessor's fees. Prior to the completion of the localisation process the Chief Assessor was an overseas consultant, and was paid by the City and Guilds Institute in London. Once this process had been completed, the local assessor replaced the Chief Assessor, and became responsible for the validation of the course and for the moderation of the examinations. However, the newly appointed local Chief Assessor, was not awarded an allowance for this added responsibility. Consequently at the time of writing, the new Chief Assessor had not assessed any of the students' work. Hence the students were still waiting to receive their examination results.

GTTI's second five year staff development plan (1989 to 1994)

Information obtained from further interviews showed that under the second five year staff development plan the GTTI continued to be dependent on overseas institutions for the upgrading and training of its staff. By continuing to depend on overseas institutions for staff development, the Institute faced the ever present problem of lecturers leaving the GTTI once they had completed their studies overseas and returned home. For example, a further lecturer who successfully completed studies overseas, and had obtained a certificate in information technology, remained at the GTTI for only one year. In an attempt to tackle this issue, the senior management of the GTTI now have a deliberate policy of attempting to obtain concurrently two similar scholarships rather than just one. This is done in anticipation that at least one of the two lecturers will remain at the GTTI, following overseas training. For example, in the field of computing the Institute was allocated a two-year ODA scholarship to enable one of its lecturers to study for an HND in computing; at the same time in conjunction with the University of Huddersfield, GTTI financed a three-year scholarship for another lecturer, also in computing. Similarly, in the field of engineering the ODA provided funding to enable one of the lecturers to study for an HND in auto-mechanics at an institution in the UK; and the German government sponsored another lecturer to study for a diploma in auto-mechanics in Germany.

By pursuing a policy of obtaining scholarships from donor agencies, the senior management are making the GTTI more dependent on First World institutions for Staff Development. The effect of this strategy has been to create what amounts to a *dependency culture.* This was evident in the building and construction department where lecturers viewed overseas training as far superior to local, in-house training. This attitude created a resistance to local forms of in-service training. For example, two assistant lecturers at the building and construction department were offered the opportunity of studying for the Technician Certificate in Construction at the GTTI. However, according to the GTTI staff interviewed, none of the lecturers attended the course.

The provision of in-house training under the second staff development plan also consisted of counter-part training, training for localisation, the setting-up of a Quality Assurance System and the development of a Higher Technical Teachers Certificate. By its very nature the first of these, counterpart training, was evidence of dependency on expatriates. In the case of Motor Vehicle maintenance and Electronics, the expatriates providing counterpart training were funded by VSO. In computing, the expatriate was recruited by the Institute's Director from Canada and employed on a contract drawn locally (in The Gambia). According to the senior management of the GTTI, there has also been a deliberate strategy to recruit expatriates into lecturing posts at the GTTI for subject areas where there is a shortage of staff or a lack of local expertise. By so doing the Institute is attempting to ensure that it will have qualified lecturers who will not be recruited by the private sector.

The training, in relation to the localisation of the Institute's examinations, came from senior GTTI management who approached the City and Guilds of London Institute in the late 1980s when it had just completed the localisation of their examinations in Ghana and Nigeria. Initially, the C&GLI was reluctant to localise its examinations in The Gambia because of the small number of students who took the course and the correspondingly high unit cost. However, when ODA agreed to fund the localisation process, the CGLI agreed to provide the necessary assistance. Under this arrangement ODA was responsible for the preparation of the teaching/learning materials necessary to run the workshops and also for the actual delivery of the workshops. The GTTI and WAEC were jointly responsible for ensuring that the UK consultants were provided with copies of the syllabuses for the subjects to be localised; and for providing consultants with transport and the premises necessary to deliver the workshops (ODA, 1987).

The localisation process was to have been completed by June 1993 when WAEC would assume responsibility for the validation of the examinations in The Gambia. However, at the time of the field work for the research, the localisation process had not taken place, and the City and Guilds Institute in London, was still responsible for moderation and for awarding the certificates. The slow progress in localisation can be explained by a number of related issues. To begin with, although the first of ODA's workshops were subsequently delivered, and subsequent committees were established to adjust the C&CLI syllabuses to local needs and prepare the corresponding examination syllabuses, the research found that there were deficiencies in the questions and also in the marking schemes. Furthermore, a consultancy report revealed that the majority of the papers had not been modified according to the guidelines stipulated by ODA and over half of the examination syllabuses had not been prepared (Tansley, 1993). According to the GTTI lecturers interviewed, there were a number of reasons for the poor preparation of examination papers, the main one being that they had only been given five months to prepare the examination papers and to agree on their standards. Apparently, these 'problems' were not related to the consultancies on which localisation depended, but to the management of the localisation process by the GTTI. As a result the second ODA workshop focused upon issues which were covered in the first workshop, including the aims and objectives of assessment. Problems were also experienced during the delivery of the second training workshop when one of the Institute's senior managers withdrew all but two of the Institute's staff from the workshop. According to an unpublished ODA report, the staff were also involved with the World Bank Education II project which was being implemented at the same time. Seemingly, the World Bank project took precedence over the ODA one. Furthermore, difficulties in transportation resulted in the consultants arriving at the workshops one to two hours late each day. This situation was made worse by the failure of the West African Examination Council to appoint someone with a technical background to the Joint Validation Panel.

Arguably then, the 'problems' experienced during the localisation process have so far related mainly to the local management of the project in The Gambia, and not to its dependency on ODA funding, or on overseas consultants. An unpublished ODA report commented that these 'problems' resulted mainly from the lack of support provided by WAEC during the localisation process. This was confirmed by a number of GTTI staff. It appears that during the initial stages of the localisation process, GTTI liaised with ODA to plan a timetable for its implementation and excluded WAEC during negotiations. It was only later that WAEC became involved and it seems that some of its senior officials resented not being involved earlier. As a consequence, WAEC was making it difficult for the localisation process to be completed successfully and on time.

Another major in-house development in the GTTI's second staff development programme concerns attempts to upgrade the skills of the Institute's management through the implementation of a Quality Assurance System and also by developing a Higher Technical Teachers Certificate. The initiative for establishing a Quality Assurance System came from the anticipated upgrading of the GTTI to a Polytechnic. The senior management at the GTTI thought that this upgrading would require them to develop validated courses, such as those offered by the former British BTEC, as opposed to the existing WAEC/CGLI externally examined courses. Thus, in order to deliver such courses GTTI had to develop and implement a Quality Assurance System for their courses. Consequently, GTTI sponsored one of its departmental Heads to look into the development and establishment of Quality Assurance Systems in UK institutions which offered BTEC validated courses.

In order to set-up a Quality Assurance System, the GTTI became dependent on an ODA consultant who delivered a series of three workshops. The teaching/learning materials used in the workshops were obtained from the UK and consisted of a strategic plan, obtained from a Further Education College, and some questionnaires which had been used to collect the information required to construct this plan. The materials were used during the workshops to show what could be done at the GTTI. The first training workshop was successfully implemented and resulted in a series of internal and external scans, which are now being used (by one of the Institute's Deputy Director, himself an expatriate funded by CFTC) to develop a three-year strategic plan. The development of the Quality Assurance System was dependent on overseas help. In contrast to the first workshop, the second experienced difficulties in achieving the objective of establishing effective formal Course Committees for GTTI courses. Yet, without these Committees the Institute would have difficulty in operating a Quality Assurance System. According to the foreign consultant who delivered the second workshop, cultural differences between The Gambia and the UK made it difficult to introduce effective Course Committees at the GTTI. The consultant said that institutions in The Gambia have a more rigid hierarchical system than in the UK; consequently, all departmental heads at the GTTI waited for the Director's permission to introduce changes instead of using their own initiative to do so. This cultural factor illustrates the difficulties of borrowing concepts from the First World, such as the democratisation of course management, and applying them in the context of a Third World country. However, the consultant succeeded in persuading the senior management of the benefits of a Quality Assurance system and the importance of Course Committees in helping to implement such a system. This resulted in the senior management requiring each department to set up a Course Committee, and in doing so, taking more initiatives in implementing changes within the department.

109

The initiative for the final of the in-house programmes, the Higher Technical Teachers Certificate was a local one, financed by The Gambian government. The technical teachers education and training section at the GTTI was responsible for developing the Course, and for managing its implementation. The curriculum was the only part of the initiative dependent on resources in the First World. When the technical teacher education and training section was given the mandate to develop the programme, the section's Head looked at the courses being delivered at Huddersfield University and at Southgate College respectively, and considered their appropriateness for The Gambia. After consultation with the GTTI senior management it was decided to base the programme on the University of Huddersfield's twenty-one month course leading to the award of B.Ed in vocational education. The section decided to use the content of this course because it had been designed specifically for students from developing countries. It was also decided to call the programme 'The Higher Technical Teachers Certificate' and to introduce another core element into the course, namely, an option on project management and implementation. This option was introduced because of the increasing number of aid projects that were being implemented in The Gambia, and specifically at the GTTI. The option would deal with issues such as how to write a project proposal, project costing, and project evaluation. It was planned to start delivering the course on a part-time basis in September 1994, the first students would be GTTI lecturers.

At the time of the research in October 1994, the Head of the section was at the stage of adjusting the content of the proposed Higher Technical Teachers Certificate. The intention was that when the adjustments were completed the course would then need to be approved by the Technical Teachers Development Committee. There was also the issue of who was going to be responsible for validating the course. At first, senior GTTI management thought that Huddersfield University could validate the course since the GTTI had close links with the University and the GTTI was basing the proposed course on the University's B.Ed course. However, the senior management of the GTTI thought it would cost less for the programme to be validated by the University of Cape Coast in Ghana. By using another institution in Africa, the GTTI would not have to meet the travel and other costs of staff coming from Huddersfield to validate the course each year. The setting up of the Higher Technical Teachers' Certificate course shows that the GTTI is able to reduce dependency on First World institutions through co-operating with other institutions in West Africa.

From this evidence it is clear that the GTTI is dependent on First World institutions and overseas aid for its programme of staff development. Although, there are clear advantages to this dependency, in terms of the continuing and professional development of its staff, there are also disadvantages. Indeed, the predominant use of overseas scholarships appears to have had a detrimental effect on the institute's attempt at capacity building. Nevertheless, the development of the Higher Technical Teachers Certificate also highlights what can be done when institutions in neighbouring Third World countries work together.

A number of senior staff at the GTTI said that the entrepreneurial skill development course was initiated because craft students, from the building and construction department and the engineering department, were experiencing difficulties in obtaining employment after they had graduated. In developing this course the lecturers from the entrepreneurial skill development unit collaborated with officials from the Indigenous Business Advisory Service, and from the former DNVTP. The course was not dependent, in any way, on overseas aid or foreign consultants for its development. The first entrepreneurial skill developmentcourse was delivered in 1987 to 55 of the Institutes students, as planned. Of these, 25 students were chosen by the Unit's lecturers to take the course's second year (N'jie, 1989a). The Unit's staff said students recognised that starting a small business was a possibility once they graduated. Another consideration is that the development of the course, independently of foreign consultants and overseas aid, could explain why it had a positive impact on students at the GTTI. Indeed, reference to one of the course case studies illustrates how the case study relates to the socio-economic and cultural circumstances in The Gambia (and contrasts with the case studies used by the entrepreneurial extension centre in Jamaica). Within each of the case studies attempts were made to show how cultural aspects of Gambian society could impact on a person's business. For example, in one case study it was shown how the practice of polygamy resulted in a young man facing bankruptcy as his small enterprise was unable to simultaneously support two households. However, another case illustrated how the extended family helped a young person to obtain initial funding to start their own business.

Only minor problems could be identified with the delivery of the course. This related to the GTTI student's work placements in small enterprises. In an interview, one of the ESDU lecturers said that a large number of business owners believed that the students were government spies who had been placed in their enterprises to collect information for tax purposes. As a result such businessmen were reluctant to reveal some of their commercial activities to GTTI students. However, despite these minor difficulties only three GTTI graduates had established an enterprise by the end of the 1980s. It appears that the UNDP, upon whom the GTTI was financially dependent, decided not to support the Institute's revolving loan scheme. As a consequence, the only source of finance available to GTTI graduates (outside of the commercial banking system) was the Indigenous Business Advisory Service (IBAS). However, IBAS required that applicants should provide 20 per cent of the amount being borrowed, but in the majority of applications such borrowing was still beyond the capability of most students. In response, the GTTI decided that the course in Entrepreneurial Skills Development should be concerned with developing entrepreneurial values. It was hoped that this would encourage students to look for work in the small business sector when they graduated. GTTI also planned to extend the course to include students from the GTTI commerce and arts department and computer department.

This final example of entrepreneurship training at the GTTI illustrates once again that initiatives in the Third World are not necessarily dependent on overseas aid for their implementation. Nevertheless, it also shows how dependence on donor funding can result in an initiative failing to achieve its long term aim (which in this case was the development of entrepreneurs). We now analyse provision under the DTEVT and comment on whether the implementation experiences are similar or different to those of The GTTI.

Analysis of developments under the DTEVT

We saw in Chapter 5 how the Directorate for Technical Education and Vocational Training (DTEVT), or as it was formerly known the DNVTP, was responsible for the Rural Vocational Training Programme (RVTP) and until recently the country's National Vocational Training Centre (NVTC). In analysing the RVTP this chapter focuses on the two projects which contributed towards its development, namely the RVTP (I) and the RVTP (II). And in the case of the NVTC we analyse how the Centre was established and the processes involved in its recent conversion to a skills centre.

An analysis of the Rural Vocational Training Programme

The origins of the Rural Vocational Training programme can be traced back to the Rural Vocational Training Project (I) which was initiated in 1979 by a UNDP consultant. Evidence from the interview data showed that the dependency of the former DNVTP staff on the 'alleged expertise' of the UNDP consultant meant that no Gambians were involved in writing the project proposal. The effect of this dependency was apparent in the strategy which was used to implement the project. This strategy was based on the concept of 'tesito' or self-reliance. According to interviews conducted at the DTEVT, it was concerned with meeting the basic needs of people living in rural areas through the mobilisation of the traditional system of mutual aid (MEDIP, 1981). Thus, under 'tesito' it was envisaged that local people would play a central role in supporting the Rural Vocational Training Project through constructing In-Village workshops and Mixed Farming Centres and supporting their operations and recurrent costs (Bittaye, 1983). The assumption underpinning this strategy was that collective support would be provided by villagers and that the Village Committees would be responsible for mobilising this local labour power.

The management and implementation of the RVTP (I)

Despite the influential role played by a foreign consultant in formulating the original proposal a number of Gambian bodies were involved in managing the project's implementation including former DNVTP officials, the

112

Principal of the Rural Vocational Training Centre, the Village Committees and the EEC (as the funding agency). The DNVTP was responsible for managing the project's recurrent costs including the wages for the instructors employed at the RVTC and also the stipends for the students studying there. The DNVTP also worked in conjunction with the Public Works department to ensure that project vehicles were kept on the road, by providing fuel and carrying out repairs when necessary. The Village Committees were concerned with managing the part of the project which was implemented at village level, namely, the construction of the workshops and their recurrent costs.

Thus, although Gambian nationals did not develop the proposal they had considerable involvement in managing the project's implementation. However, the EEC was also able to influence the implementation process; for under the project's guidelines, an EEC (1985) office in The Gambia was responsible for managing the project's capital funds, and for determining the components provided under the project. For instance, when the former DNVTP required either building materials or equipment for the project's workshops, the DNVTP applied to the EEC stating what components were needed, as well as their intended use. If the EEC approved the application European firms were invited to tender for the supply of materials. Such control of funds demonstrates the EEC's intention to determine the conditions under which the project would be implemented and to ensure that materials were used for their stated purpose. It is difficult to determine the exact dependence of the project on the EEC owing to the finance provided by The Gambian government, the support in kind provided by the villagers in the form of unpaid labour and also because of the lack of accounting records for the project. Using these resources and forms of support the original project proposal anticipated that a total of 60 In Village Training Centres (IVTCs) and 22 Mixed Farming Centres (MFCs) would be established. However, by 1988 only 4 IVTCs and 2 MFCs were operational (RVTC, 1989a). A number of reasons can be suggested as to why only a fraction of the anticipated IVTCs or MFCs were built. This ranged from the effects of dependence on overseas aid and foreign technical assistance, to the way in which the project was managed locally.

The effects of dependency

The dependency on overseas volunteers had a major impact on the project during the early implementation stages. It took the EEC's Projects Office two years to recruit volunteer instructors for the RVTC (N'jie, 1989a). Consequently, there was no 'Counterpart Training' at the RVTC for two years and skills training (at the RVTC) was delayed for a further year. This delay would have been one of the factors which prevented the project achieving its stated objective of establishing 60 Village Training Centres and 22 Mixed Farming Centres by 1988. The dependency of the project on the UNDP consultant's formulation of the strategy for implementing the project was an additional factor. The strategy assumed that African societies were communal and that the Village Committees would provide collective

113

support for the project. However, interviewees observed that many of these assumptions were unwarranted, particularly those relating to the role of the Village Committees. This observation was confirmed in a survey of the RVTP which was conducted by the Directorate of the NVTP in 1985. The report showed that in 10 of the 20 Key Villages surveyed there were no Village Committees to oversee the construction of the workshops. The report concluded that 'the villagers' lack of support was one of the major reasons why only a small proportion of the training workshops were ever constructed' (DNVTP, 1985 p3.). But even if the villagers had had an effective Committee and a supportive workforce, they were still faced with the problem of having to use unfamiliar building materials (such as building bricks and scaffolding). This unfamiliarity stemmed from the project's dependency on the EEC for procuring building materials from the First World rather than from other countries in West Africa. The effects of such unfamiliarity were to cause further delays to the construction of the workshops.

The implementation strategy had also neglected the specific cultural circumstances under which blacksmiths' skills and other skills are acquired in The Gambia. Under the original strategy, the RVTP project intended to train blacksmiths and to upgrade the skills of existing ones through establishing Mixed Farming Centres. However, according to a number of RVTC staff one could only become a blacksmith in The Gambia if one's father was himself a blacksmith, and not through attending institutionalised courses at the Mixed Farming Centres. This patriarchal system of acquiring and transmitting skills was probably not unlike the Caste system in India. A number of senior officials at the DTEVT also said that some of the Village Committees were reluctant to allow women to become trainees at the IVTCs. Given these cultural mores and lack of financial incentives, it is not surprising that the local villagers did not support fully the construction of either the MFCs or the IVTCs.

The full effect of financial dependency on the implementation process was evident in 1987, when the EEC decided to cease funding the Rural Vocational Training Project (I). The decision came as a result of a surprise visit of an EEC delegation to the Rural Vocational Training Centre and to nine of the country's Key Villages in June 1986 (EEC, 1988). The purpose of the visit was to conduct an audit of the RVTP and to see how resources from the EEC's capital fund were being used. The major findings of the audit were that of the nine Key Villages visited, only four had constructed IVTCs. It was further found that because the building materials and equipment provided by the EEC were lying around the Key Villages unused, it was impossible to make an inventory. However, a more worrying factor was that the EEC official found that some of the project building materials had been used by the instructors to build their own houses (EEC, 1988). Consequently, the official wished to discuss what decision could be taken by the government in order to improve this very critical situation and avoid the complete failure of the project (EEC,1987). However, the former DNVTP argued that they were unaware that the EEC's Technical Adviser had visited the project, and that if he wished to conduct an inventory of equipment, these were stored in three containers anchored at the side of the RVTC in Mansakonko (DNVTP, 1987). There was also a question as to whether the EEC Technical Adviser understood the rationale underpinning the Rural Vocational Training Project (namely, that in-village training was given only during the non-farming season), since he conducted his survey during the farming season.

There was also some unpublished correspondence between the former DNVTP and the EEC which suggested that the EEC was uncertain about how project resources were actually being used during the implementation process and indeed whether they were being used for their intended purpose. The upshot of the EEC's visit and of the subsequent correspondence with the former DNVTP, was that the EEC decided to close the project's account owing to what was seen as the slow progress with the implementation of the project (EEC, 1988). Without such access to EEC funds the former DNVTP was no longer able to obtain the building materials necessary to construct the remaining In-Village Training Centres.

The local management of the project

But although financial dependency and dependency on overseas personnel had a detrimental effect on the implementation of the RVTP, this was probably made worse by local management of the project. Yet, the former DNVTP decided to continue implementing the Rural Vocational Training Project (I), (albeit in a modified form). It was decided to establish 22 In-Village Training Centres and 11 Mixed Farming Centres. However, in spite of these revised targets, by 1989 the Directorate had not constructed any more IVTCs and only a fraction of the established IVTCs were still in operation. The reason for the project's continued failure appears to relate to local management issues, particularly in relation to those of transportation and personnel.

With regard to transportation the interview data showed that the Project's vehicles suffered from a lack of available spare parts and an inadequate supply of fuel. Under the Rural Vocational Training Project (I), the EEC had provided one truck to transport building materials from the port (at Banjul) to each of the Key Villages in the provinces, some of which were over 200 miles away. In 1987, the truck went out of action owing to air locks in the braking system (DNVTP, 1987). The vehicle went to the Public Works department for repairs, and was still there at the time of writing! As for the supply of fuel, under the RVT Project (I), the organisation responsible for allocating petroleum was the Public Works department and 'problems' began in 1986. For, under the country's Economic Reform Programme, only a limited amount of fuel could be supplied by government for use in the provinces and emphasis had to be given to ambulances and medical officers (Ministry of Works, 1985). Furthermore, there was a large discrepancy between the amount of petrol supplied by the Public Works department and that actually received by the RVTC for its own vehicle, thus casting doubt on the use of such a scarce resource as fuel in practice (Ministry of Works, 1985).

For the second of the issues, personnel, the present study found that in 1987, the RVTC instructors petitioned the former DNVTP because of what they regarded as an excessive work load (RVTC, 1987b). In point of fact they were responsible for: the initial pre-service training of IVTC instructors; monitoring the construction of the village workshops in the provinces; and for providing in-service short courses for IVTC instructors. The second and third of these responsibilities were particularly demanding since the RVTC instructors, at Mansakonko, had no means of transport to the Key Villages. As a consequence, the RVTC instructors had to walk long distances to the Key Villages in order to provide short-courses and this often involved overnight treks. Furthermore, the RVTC instructors felt that they were being badly treated, compared to the staff who worked at other government Training Centres. The feeling of the entire RVTC staff was that all training centres under the former DNVTP should have equal opportunities for staff development for their staff and that all instructors who worked at government training centres, and held similar qualifications, should receive comparable rates of pay (RVTC, 1986). The point was that the instructors of the RVTC received no form of staff development under the RVTP. This contrasted with the National Vocational Training Centre instructors who benefited from training programmes, ranging from six months to two years.

There were also differences between the rates of pay for the RVTC instructors and those for the NVTC instructors. The differences had occurred as a result of the government's retrenchment programme, which attempted to reduce overmanning in the public sector and to increase the productivity of the remaining employees by placing them on a higher pay scale. As a consequence, all lecturers and instructors who worked in government institutions were placed on a higher grade and were given an increase in salary. Those who worked at the RVTC did not have a similar rise in salary despite a petition. The only concession made to them was to provide Staff Development for four senior RVTC instructors. This consisted of attending the 730 CGLI Further Education and Adult Teachers Certificate Programme at the GTTI. There were also 'problems' with the way in which the RVTC instructors were paid. The salaries for government employees, including instructors, were administered by the Ministry of Economic Planning and Industrial Development, in Banjul. Thus, in order to receive their salaries, the RVTC instructors had to travel from Mansakonko to Banjul each month, a distance of about 120 miles.

In summary then, with lower rates of pay, long working hours, limited opportunities for further training and difficulties in collecting their pay, the RVTC instructors were at a severe disadvantage compared to those working at the National Vocational Training Centre in Banjul. This is particularly true if the conditions under which the RVTC instructors had to live and work at Mansakonko were also taken into account. These were the frequent cuts in the supply of electricity and running water, and the lack of other infrastructure developments generally associated with living in an urban area. The extent of their dissatisfaction became apparent in the late 1980s when a large number of staff resigned and the RVTC had difficulty in recruiting instructors. This shortage of instructors combined with the lack of motivation amongst the instructors in post, made it difficult for the RVTC to train instructors for the Key Villages in those subject areas or to monitor the training activities at each of the Key Villages and provide support where necessary. Unsurprisingly, these factors further impeded the implementation process and prevented the project from providing the necessary skills training at the village level.

The RVTC students also petitioned the Directorate of NVTP in 1987, complaining about the lack of sufficient financial support both during their training period at Mansakonko and when they returned to their own Key villages. The students felt that the stipend they received during their initial training at Mansakonko was too low, considering that most had families to support (RVTC, 1987a). The problem was compounded during the second part of their training owing to the fact that they received no allowance when they returned to their villages. As a consequence, the RVTC graduates found it difficult to purchase tools, and so were unable to become involved either in training villagers or in production related activities. The lack of support for the RVTC under the RVTP compared unfavourably with the relatively greater support given to the NVTC, suggesting that there might have been some form of urban bias in the allocation of resources.

The Rural Vocational Training Project (II)

Owing to the difficulties discussed above, and of the continual problem of rural to urban drift, whereby people from the provinces came to Banjul in search of jobs, it was decided to modify the way in which the Rural Vocational Training Programme operated. This resulted in the Rural Vocational Training Project (II) which attempted to address the overambitious nature of the former RVTP (I) and at the same time provide additional support for RVTC instructors and RVTP graduates. Thus, in order to achieve the first of these aims the RVTP (II) decided to support only a fraction of the original 60 Key Villages. However, in the absence of EEC funding, the necessary resources had to be obtained through closing down the RVTC and by diverting the corresponding resources to the In-Village Training Centres. Thus, from 1992 onwards, the training programme at the RVTC ceased and the instructors were deployed to the Key Villages to provide extension services to trainees. In relation to the lack of support for the former RVTC instructors, the RVTP (II) planned to equip the RVTC instructors with a four wheel drive vehicle and a number of motor bikes to facilitate the monitoring of the in-village training programmes. It was envisaged that this would enable the RVTC instructors to act as extension workers and at the same time provide pedagogical support for the IVTC's staff. An additional consideration was the introduction of staff development for the RVTC instructors. This latter objective was to be achieved through the setting-up of a Rural Instructors Training Programme leading to a Certificate awarded by the GTTI (the funding for which came from CIDA). Finally, in order to provide additional support to the programme's graduates the RVTP (II) proposed to provide them with the tools necessary to practice their trade. At the same time the RVTP graduates were also going to be given access to a revolving loans system. It was hoped that these facilities would improve the employment prospects for self-employment in rural areas (DTEVT, 1992a).

Because the RVT project (II) had a number of components, different organisations managed its implementation, including:, the DTEVT the GTTI Board of Directors, CIDA, and the Canadian Community Colleges. The DTEVT was totally responsible for funding and managing the first phase of the restructuring, the consolidation phase. However, the DTEVT worked in conjunction with the GTTI staff and the Canadian consultants (from the Community Colleges) to manage the next phase, namely, the development of the Adult Rural Instructor Certificate programme for the RVTC staff.

The development of the instructors' programme was totally dependent on CIDA for its funding. This financial dependency resulted in the project using Canadian consultants to deliver the instructor programme. At the time of the research, the project was still in the early stages of its execution. Nevertheless, CIDA attempted to ensure that the project was not implemented in isolation from the country's national development programme, and that there was considerable Gambian involvement in the implementation process. Thus, CIDA recognised the need for a well integrated project and decided that this could be achieved through a Rural Adult Instructors Certificate course which incorporates issues relevant to The Gambia, such as the training of villagers to become entrepreneurs. The project proposal also outlined the need for a complete revision of the adaptation of the Instructor Certificate course offered in Canada, and for involving both the DTEVT and the GTTI staff in this process. The proposal hoped that this new approach would enable the Canadian inspired Rural Adult Instructor Certificate course offered in The Gambia to be culturally sensitive to the native population of The Gambia (CIDA, 1992).

At the time of writing, the RVTC had stopped running courses and the consolidation phase was under way and the Adult Rural Instructor Certificate course was due to start in October 1994. Nevertheless a factor which will have a major influence on the restructuring process is the availability of vehicles to transport the materials necessary to construct more In-Village Training Centres and also to enable the former RVTC instructors to visit the In-Village Training Centres.

The key informants interviewed claimed that without transport the DTEVT would find it difficult to complete even the first phase of the RVT project (II) (the consolidation phase). The lack of vehicles would result in a lack of support for the In-Village Training Centres by the DTEVT, and as a consequence villagers would not become involved in the construction and/or running of the workshops. To break this vicious circle, the DTEVT must have reliable transport and access to a regular supply of fuel. However, there were no plans to cater for transport, aside from application for funding from other donor agencies besides the EEC. The nature of this dependency needs to be questioned. Why is the Rural Vocational Training Programme continually dependent on overseas aid for transport? The EEC project had provided funding for a number of vehicles. Yet, the way in which the use of these vehicles was managed, and the inability to repair them, were two of the main reasons why the RVT project (I) came to a halt. Clearly, without proper maintenance of the vehicles, the RVT project (II) would experience similar problems to those experienced by the EEC funded RVT project (I). The continued dependence on overseas-aid for funded transport may be regarded as evidence of 'self-perpetuating dependency'.

The experience of the RVTP illustrates the added complexity surrounding the implementation process in a rural area. Indeed, although dependence on foreign consultants and overseas aid influenced the way in which implementation occurred, the situation was compounded by how the process was managed locally. In particular, owing to limited incentives locally the RVTP(I) had difficulty in obtaining commitment from its instructors, trainees and villagers, all of whom were essential for successful implementation. The experience of the RVTP(I) also highlights how instructors at rural centres are treated less favourably than those who work at urban centres, such as the National Vocational Training Centre. Given these differences between rural and urban centres you might expect the implementation experiences to be less problematic at the NVTC. This issue is dealt with in the following part of the chapter.

An analysis of the dependency of the Banjul Skills Centre on overseas aid

This part of the chapter analyses the role played by international aid organisations in establishing the National Vocational Training Centre and in its subsequent conversion to a Skills Centre. The implications of these developments for the future of skills training in The Gambia are also considered.

The establishment of the National Vocational Training Centre (NVTC) in Banjul

The present research found no record of the early development of the National Vocational Training Centre. However, the interview data revealed the extent to which these early developments were dependent on overseas aid. The Gambian government was responsible for constructing the Centre's original buildings and for equipping it with the machinery necessary for conducting training. However, the lack of suitably qualified local staff during the early 1970s meant that the Centre's initial courses and their subsequent delivery were dependent on overseas technical assistance. This consisted of four UNESCO consultants who were based at the NVTC for a period of four years to act as instructors. Further training for the NVTC students was also dependent on overseas aid in the form of four fellowships, one being financed by ODA and the others by the German government. The ODA scholarship enabled one of the NVTC graduates to study Motor Mechanics in England for two years and to obtain the City and Guilds Technician Certificate in that subject. As a result of the fellowships provided by the German government, three NVTC graduates were each able to study in Germany for three years; two obtained a diploma in engineering

119

and the other a diploma in Welding and Fabrication. The idea behind these fellowships was that on completing their studies the former NVTC graduates would return to The Gambia and become instructors at the NVTC.

The effects of the Centre's initial dependency on overseas aid are difficult to determine. It could be argued that the foreign consultants and fellowships contributed towards the Centre's sustainability by providing it with a nucleus of qualified staff who were capable of delivering courses (and so reduce dependency on foreign technical assistance). However, the interview data showed that the Centre experienced difficulties in delivering its courses as The Gambian instructors were transferred to other posts once they had completed their overseas fellowships. It appears that they took up senior posts in the recently established Directorate of the National Vocational Training Programme. Thus, the difficulties experienced in delivering the courses stemmed not from the Centre's dependency on overseas technical assistance but from the management of human resources in a developing country, and from the need for continuous training to meet the requirements of organisational growth.

The NVTC experienced other problems, during the 1980s, none of which were related to the Centre's dependency on overseas aid or personnel, but stemmed from the way in which the Centre's staff and equipment were managed. Indeed, from the interview data the author was given to understand that the majority of the junior instructors were more committed to undertaking private jobs than to discharging their responsibilities in official capacity as trainers. As a consequence these instructors neglected their teaching duties and used the Centre's equipment and materials for private gain rather than for the training purposes for which they were intended. Furthermore, with regard to the Centre's equipment the senior staff had a policy of providing its graduates with tools once they had completed their period of training. However, this practice served only to deplete the NVTC's stock of equipment, thereby impeding the training of subsequent cohorts of students (DNVTP, 1990c).

This part of the analysis has shown that although the NVTC was dependent on overseas technical assistance during its initial development this resulted in no major difficulties. Instead there were more problems relating to the way in which the Centre was managed locally. Indeed, officials who worked in the country's technical education and vocational training sector commented that only a very small proportion of the students were competent enough to enter for the appropriate City and Guilds examinations at the end of their training. As a consequence, local industry in The Gambia was unwilling to employ the NVTC's graduates (World Bank, 1990b); and it seems that towards the end of the 1980s, school leavers became aware of the Centre's low reputation, with the annual intake falling to around 40 students.

The conversion of the NVTC to the Banjul Skills Centre

The initiative for converting the NVTC to the Banjul Skills Centre was a local one, and originated from The Gambian government. No overseas

120

agency was involved. As can be recalled from the previous chapter, The Gambian government was concerned with establishing a Skills Centre to promote self employment and also to improve the poor reputation of the former NVTC. An interview conducted with senior officials at the DTEVT showed that the Banjul Skills Centre was a pilot project which, if proved successful, would form the model for the establishment of a further thirty Skills Centres in the country's provinces.

One of the first components of the conversion consisted of upgrading the pedagogical and technical skills of the NVTC instructors in order for them to be on the same pay scale as staff at the GTTI. This was achieved through the staff attending appropriate courses at the GTTI. According to the staff concerned no problems were experienced with this process.

The other components of the NVTCs conversion to a Skills Centre involved capital developments and the introduction of new programmes of study. In the original proposal it was anticipated that the funding for both of these components would be provided by the World Bank in the form of a loan under the World Bank Education II project. One of the first effects of dependence on World Bank funding was that the Bank was able to determine how many man-months of consultancy support and overseas fellowships were to be provided under the project. However, there was a disagreement between the World Bank and GTTI's senior management over the number of man-months of consultancy provided. In particular, the GTTI management requested a reduction in consultancy support for teaching methods from seven to four man-months, and in Production Management from seven to four man-months. The rationale for this reduction was that the ODA had already conducted a number of audio-visual workshops for technical teachers; this reduced the need for a World Bank consultant to run a similar workshop. It was further argued that a reduction in the number of consultancy man-months would free resources and enable additional fellowship man-months for Gambian instructors. The DTEVT proposed that the first of these additional fellowships would include a further four man months' fellowship for The Gambian instructor who was studying Production Management at Birmingham University. This additional training and experience would reduce the BSC's dependency on the assistance of a World Bank consultant for Production Management.

The DTEVT also requested a fellowship extension of two man-months' for the instructor who was studying outboard motors, since the original attachment occurred during the winter, making it impossible for the lecturer to have a practical, on-site attachment (DTEVT, 1992c). Despite the Directorate's requests and justifications, the World Bank refused to divert resources from consultancy support to fellowships and commented that the budget for technical skills training was already overextended and that no further resources were available for this area (World Bank, 1992a). Thus, ensuring that World Bank consultants played a prominent role in the project's implementation.

The World Bank Education II project had a life span of six years and was expected to be completed by January 1997. However, by 1994 the conversion of the NVTC to a Skills Training Centre was behind schedule and none of the proposed workshops had been built nor the existing ones upgraded. The reasons for this delay, in part, relate to the project's dependence on the World Bank. Senior officials at the DTEVT and at the GTTI disagreed with the World Bank's implementation plans for the BSC capital developments, arguing that DTEVT and GTTI resources would be sufficient to construct new workshops and upgrade existing ones, at one-sixth of the costs estimated by the World Bank. However, after negotiations with The Gambian government, the World Bank agreed that the GTTI could take responsibility for the BSC's capital developments using their own resources rather than using a loan under the Education II project. This example illustrates how the local organisations were not always dependent on decisions made by the World Bank consultants and that they were capable of determining for themselves how local resources were to be invested in a project. However, partly as a result of this disagreement between the DTEVT and the World Bank, the construction and upgrading of workshops at the BSC were delayed by three years.

Nevertheless, another reason for the delay in converting the NVTC to a Skills Centre related to what could be called the machinery of government. For example, once the DTEVT and the GTTI had become responsible for NVTC's capital developments, they had to find local architects to provide detailed plans for the building work at the BSC. Once designed, these plans were sent to the government's Project Implementation Unit where local firms were invited to tender for the proposed capital developments. At the time of writing the Project Implementation Unit was waiting for tenders from local companies. When these have been obtained, they will be passed on to the Cabinet for approval. In brief, The Gambia bureaucracy also played its part in delaying the construction work at the BSC.

Having documented the process leading the conversion of the NVTC to a Skills Centre, we now need to briefly comment on the possible implications of these changes. Interviews of officials in the technical education and vocational training sector prompted the question of whether the BSC would equip people with the skills necessary to set up their own businesses, owing to the quality of the student intake. GTTI staff and NVTC staff also questioned whether in future entrants to the Banjul Skills Centre would have the technical ability and aptitude to acquire the skills taught there. Indeed, the government's annexation document had recommended that all entrants to the BSC must have successfully completed their secondary technical education, the assumption being that these students would have acquired certain technical skills prior to starting their training at the BSC. However, the World Bank has influenced, indirectly, the quality of future entrants to the BSC; for, under its Education II project, they decided that no further secondary technical schools should be constructed in The Gambia and that existing ones should be converted into Middle Schools.

The decision was in line with World Bank policy world-wide. According to senior managers at the GTTI the World Bank was opposed to secondary technical schools because it thought that The Gambian government was incapable of supporting their recurrent running costs.

The Gambian government disagreed with the World Bank's decision since it was contrary to the country's 1988-2002 Education Plan to expand secondary technical education. In consequence, The Gambian government approached the EEC and the Islamic Development Bank for financial support in the construction of more secondary technical schools. The EEC and the Islamic Development Bank agreed to support these proposals. However, according to unofficial sources in The Gambia, the World Bank would have withdrawn its funds from the Education II project and ceased funding future projects if The Gambian government had accepted financial support from these other agencies. The effect of this financial dependency on the World Bank, is that in future BSC students will not have acquired any technical skills at school before starting their Skills Training at the BSC. The GTTI staff interviewed thought that this was particularly worrying since students studying at the BSC will have only a short period in which to acquire their technical skills(in most cases between two and six months). When interviewed, GTTI managers involved with the development of the BSC, questioned whether in future BSC graduates will have the experience to set up their own workshops, or the ability to establish successful businesses given the short period of their training, and given that they will have no work experience having just left school or being unemployed. If these doubts prove to be true the BSC will have difficulty in facilitating employment prospects among school leavers and the unemployed.

Up until now the present chapter has illustrated the complex process involved in implementing projects at public institutions in The Gambia. As in the case of Jamaica a variety of factors were shown to impede the implementation process, ranging from their dependence on overseas aid and foreign technical assistance, to the way in which the implementation process was managed locally. However, in contrast to Jamaica the implementation experience in The Gambia appears to have been made much worse by the undeveloped nature of the country's physical and political infrastructure. In the final part of this chapter we analyse whether support for company and non-governmental forms of training was influenced by similar factors.

Analysis of support for non-governmental forms of training

The final part of this chapter looks at support for company and non-governmental forms of training. This is achieved by looking at whether The Gambian government has created a favourable policy climate for encouraging company training and the extent to which it has used resources effectively and efficiently to support this type of provision. Finally, a similar approach is used to analyse the activities of TANGO, an organisation which supports training for those who work in the country's informal sector.

With regard to the policy environment The Gambia, like Jamaica, has also recently implemented an Economic Reform Programme. Furthermore, the country has limited unionisation and no minimum wage legislation. However, unlike Jamaica, the size of the formal sector in The Gambia is relatively small and consequently there are limited opportunities for in-house company training by the private sector. Of the 8 companies visited nearly all provided some form of in-house training. However, the only companies which had equipped training centres, and which delivered any type of structured training, were those owned by the state (as opposed to those privately owned). Under the country's Economic Reform Programme (ERP) the government removed all import tax on equipment used in the training process. Such a measure might have reduced the costs of establishing training centres, especially for companies such as GUC and GAMTEL which use technologically advanced equipment in the process of training. However, there was no evidence to suggest that such a saving encouraged further in-house company training. Nevertheless, the country's Economic Reform Programme (ERP) appears to have facilitated the expansion of in-house company training in another way. During the implementation of the ERP, the GUC, GAMTEL and GPTC all constructed and equipped new training centres. One might have expected that, under the ERP (with its enforced reduction in government expenditure), the amount of public resources available for training in government-owned companies would have declined. Although the former is probably true the resources for establishing these training centres came from overseas funding. This evidence suggests that, these agencies may have a preference for establishing training centres within companies rather than in public TVET institutions.

Turning to the next issue, whether the government has used resources effectively to support company training, the only form of support related to state-owned companies which offered in-house company training and the possible introduction of a training levy. With regard to the first of these issues, there was some evidence that steps were being taken to ensure that parastatal companies were effective in expanding the provision of training. This particularly relates to the GUC and GAMTEL where managers said in interviews that they had plans to operate their training centres as business centres. Indeed, in 1993, the training centre at GAMTEL started to increase the number of its trainees, through developing specific training modules and delivering them to employees from the Police, the Army and the country's Airport Authority.

Besides expanding the provision of training, the issue of effectiveness also needs to take into account quality. At the time of the field work, there was no concrete evidence that the DTEVT monitored the training activities of either parastatal or private companies. Nevertheless, according to senior officials at the DTEVT, there were proposals for all companies operating training programmes to register with the DTEVT, and for the DTEVT to monitor their training activities; and for companies that reach a specified standard, to be officially recognised as approved training centres. However, it is questionable whether the other government measure, the training levy, will help to expand the provision of company training in The Gambia. According to unpublished government documents and officials at the DTEVT, the levy is likely to be used as a means of recovering the costs of running public institution such as the GTTI, and not as a means of encouraging in-house company training. This contrasts with the example of levying in Jamaica, where the levy was used as a measure to encourage private companies to provide in-house training. If implemented as planned, the levy would probably discourage companies from providing training, because they would be entitled to a rebate only if they sent their employees to the GTTI for training, and not if they conducted their own training.

There was also a general feeling amongst the representatives from the companies who were interviewed, that the government already imposes enough taxes and that a levy would place an additional financial burden on them, making it unprofitable for them to continue to operate in The Gambia. The proposal for a levy also suggested that some of the taxation burden could be placed on public sector employees. If implemented, this could be regarded as inequitable, since these employees have already experienced a decline in their standard of living following the country's currency devaluations in the mid 1980s.

Finally in relation to the last of the issues, efficiency, the government's support for in-house company training could be regarded as inefficient since it did not draw on non-governmental sources of finance. Nevertheless, the recent decision of GUC and GAMTEL to operate their training centres on business lines will provide a means of obtaining revenue from the private sector. Another consideration is the need to look at the external benefits which arise from supporting training at the GUC, GPTC and GAMTEL. In most Third World countries there has been a trend towards the privatisation of state-owned industries, in the name of efficiency and its promotion through the operation of market forces. This would suggest that supporting in-house, company training is an inefficient use of resources. However, this assumption needs to be considered within the context of the country's development. The Gambia is in the early stages of its development, and without an adequate infrastructure (such as that provided by GUC, GAMTEL and GPTC) and a trained workforce to operate it, the country's development will, clearly, be constrained. Another external benefit can be identified from supporting the product-orientated training at the GPTC. According to GPTC staff, such training enables the company to recondition two buses every six months. Clearly, support for this type of training will reduce the company's need to import new buses and, in turn, contribute towards reducing the country's budget deficit.

We now turn to the type of support available for those who work in the country's informal sector.

An analysis of support for TVET in the informal sector

As can be recalled from Chapter 5 one of the main forms of support for those working in the country's informal sector came from the organisation TANGO. In analysing the activities of TANGO, we consider how effectively the organisation has helped expand the provision of non-governmental training in The Gambia, and also how effectively it has liaised with the government on NGO activities to ensure a greater integration of NGO efforts in the country's development. For the first of these issues TANGO appears to have been successful in expanding the provision of non-governmental training in the informal sector, especially if one considers that TANGO's membership had grown from 18 to 60 members in a period of just over 8 years. However, it is questionable whether TANGO was very effective at achieving its main objective of 'liaising with the government on NGO activities'. This can be seen by reference to the activities of Action Aid. As explained in Chapter 5, TANGO assisted Action Aid by making use of some of the government's rural vocational training centres in its Continuing Village Education Programmes. One might have expected that by using these facilities Action Aid would have contributed towards the costs of running these government centres and at the same time have been an effective way of helping the government to expand the provision of skills training in rural areas.

However, there was a lack of co-ordination between Action Aid's Continuing Village Education Programme and the former DNVTP's Rural Vocational Training Project (I). The point is that there were considerable differences between the two programmes. For example, we have seen that the former DNVTP's RVT Project (I) was based on the concept of 'self reliance' and trainees had to be financially independent, whereas under the Action Aid's Continuing Village Education Programme trainees received a stipend and a grant to establish their own businesses once they had completed their period of training. Also, the instructors working at Action Aid's Training centres were paid a salary, unlike their colleagues who worked at the former DNVTP's In-Village Training Centres for no financial reward. Consequently, villagers were more likely to be attracted to Action Aid's programme than to the DNVTP's In-Village Training Centres. Interviews with former DNVTP officials about the In-Village Training Centres said that the activities of Action Aid helped to undermine the government's Rural Vocational Training Programme, and were one of the reasons why there was a lack of support for the RVTP at village level.

Interviews with representatives from the Catholic Relief Services and Christian Aid revealed that, despite being members of TANGO, they had no formalised links with the former DNVTP, or with the DTEVT. A recent report commented that the majority of TVET programmes in rural areas were organised and sponsored by NGOs without prior notification to the DTEVT (Jobarteh et al, 1992). This evidence suggests that TANGO is failing to play one of its vital roles, that of a co-ordinating body. As a consequence, NGOs such as Action Aid are concerned with developing their own Vocational Training programmes, separately from those at government owned Vocational Training Centres and Skills Centres. This brings into question whether TANGO is an effective way of expanding non governmental training in The Gambia. But at the same time it is important to realise that in a predominantly Muslim country, such as The Gambia, the state may have a legitimacy problem if it openly advocates support for Christian or Catholic backed organisations.

In terms of resourcing TVET, TANGO can in theory be regarded as an efficient means of expanding the non-governmental provision of training (since it uses non-governmental sources of finance) assuming that NGOs are efficiently run. However, at the time of the field work, its survival was questionable, owing to a financial crisis in which TANGO was unable to meet its recurrent costs. Action Aid was attempting to assist TANGO through providing a large donation and TANGO staff hoped that further resources would be obtained from international donors such as the UNDP. However, even if such funding was obtained, it is questionable how long these donors would continue to support TANGO's recurrent running costs. This raises the issue of whether TANGO is a sustainable means of supporting TVET in the country's informal sector. The sustainability of one of its member's programmes could also be questioned. For example, in the case of Action Aid, if the resources were withdrawn from the Continuing Village Education Programme the instructors would be left without salaries and the students without stipends, and there would probably be a lack of support for the programme by local villagers.

So what can be said about market-led TVET and the provision of TVET by companies and non-governmental organisations? The evidence presented in the last part of this chapter points to the importance of the state and international donor organisations in supporting this type of provision. However, the involvement of donor agencies raises a number of important questions. For example, are private companies and non-governmental organisations subject to the same influences of dependency as public TVET institutions? Moreover, does the role of external donors in supporting the non-governmental provision of TVET ensure that local labour market needs are being met? These and other similar issues are discussed in the concluding chapter.

7 Conclusion

Introduction

The present study has analysed the process of implementing Technical and Vocational Education and Training (TVET) policies in Jamaica and in The Gambia. This was achieved through looking at strategies for implementing projects at public TVET institutions, and also those programmes which supported or encouraged company or non-governmental forms of TVET. This concluding chapter begins by re-considering the implementation process within public TVET institutions, commenting on the operational levels at which dependency on overseas aid has occurred. By adopting such an approach we can examine the influence of dependency on the implementation process, as well as the longer term impact of overseas aid-funded projects on TVET institutions. Furthermore, it also enables us to discuss the different implementation experiences of public institutions in the two countries and whether such processes were influenced by factors other than their dependency on foreign consultants and overseas educational material. This part of the chapter concludes by commenting on the limitations of the dependency concept and how it could be improved.

The second part of the chapter presents the study's findings in relation to company and non-govermental provision. This allows us to discuss the market approach and to comment on its limitations, particularly in relation to the important role played by state and aid agencies in supporting the implementation of TVET programmes in the private sector.

Finally, the third part of this chapter re-examines the assumptions underpinning the two approaches used in the present study. In particular, questions are raised about the appropriateness of the 'market approach' and the assumption that private provision is not subject to the influences which generate dependency. This enables the chapter to argue that the concept of dependency is applicable whether applied to public or private provision. Furthermore, what is at issue is not public or private TVET, nor the market verses the state, but the effectiveness of TVET provision in terms of promoting independent decision-making processes. That is to say decision-making processes which ensure that the implementation of TVET projects or programmes meet the particular labour market conditions in which training is provided. Nevertheless, what is even more important is how dependency is overridden to ensure that decisions meet 'real market' conditions.

Implementation within the public sector

A total of 19 projects (10 in The Gambia and 9 in Jamaica) were analysed using the dependency concept, all of which were implemented between the

1970s and the mid-1990s. Of the 10 projects studied in The Gambia, 9 were dependent on overseas aid. Whereas, of the 9 projects analysed in Jamaica only 6 were dependent on overseas aid, with the remaining three being funded locally. The higher dependence of The Gambia on overseas funding probably reflects the underdeveloped nature of the country's economy, and the comparatively fewer opportunities for locally funded activities. From these projects it was possible to identify the operational levels at which dependency occurred. For the first of these, the central government level, the analysis found that four projects in Jamaica and four projects in The Gambia were dependent on overseas aid. All of these projects financed developments in basic skills training and in both countries they were used as a vehicle for socio-economic development. For example, in Jamaica the USAID Basic Skills Training Project supported the PNP's economic policy of attracting foreign investment to the country, whilst in The Gambia the EEC's Rural Vocational Training Project (I) was concerned with promoting 'self-reliance and sustainable development' in rural areas.

The second operational level on which dependency occurred was at the institution. Indeed, the present study indicated that both countries were dependent on international aid organisations for the funding of projects in their post-secondary, technical training institutions. Six projects in Jamaica and five projects in The Gambia were implemented at this level. The interesting contrast between projects implemented at central government level and those implemented at the institutional level was that both the Jamaican and The Gambian government contributed financially towards the costs of implementing projects at central government level, whereas the projects implemented at the institutional level were, in the majority of cases, totally dependent on overseas aid.

The final operational level where dependency occurred relates to the way in which various components of the different projects depended on overseas countries. These two countries were dependent on donor agencies for various project components, including educational materials, technical equipment, overseas scholarships and foreign consultants.

Having described the operational levels on which dependency occurred we now turn to the more important issue of the influence and effects of dependency on the different implementation stages. Although it might be possible to distinguish between the different stages of implementing a TVET project, in practice it is a complex process and these distinctions often become blurred (Dyer, 1994). In this respect it was sometimes difficult to know whether the life of a project begins with the approval of the project proposal, or with the provision of funding for the project's implementation, or with the actual launching of a project. In this study all of these stages were classified as the project's initiation stage. The next stage, for purpose of classification, was designated as the management and implementation stage. A final consideration in this classification typology was the project's overall impact upon the TVET institution where implemented. However, it should be noted that although these categories provide a useful framework for purposes of analysis, they are nevertheless artificial since, it is only through a comprehensive analysis of the *whole* project that the overall effects of dependency can be seen.

Dependency at the initiation stage

There was evidence in the present study that the dependence of institutions and governments in the Third World on overseas aid, enabled international aid organisations to determine if a particular project was going to be implemented and how. In Jamaica, for example, the World Bank refused to fund an entrepreneurial development project at the entrepreneurial extension centre because the institution wanted non-governmental organisations to manage the project's funds. Also the World Bank Education III project in Jamaica was postponed for four years because the World Bank failed to process the necessary loan to implement the project. Similar problems were found in the initiation of projects in The Gambia. The RVTP(I) project, for example, experienced delays because the aid agency had difficulty in recruiting qualified instructors. Again it was found that the failure of the UNDP to provide funds for entrepreneurs at the GTTI, prevented the project from achieving its stated objective.

The involvement of local personnel in initiating aid projects varied in each of the countries studied. Of the seven projects funded by international aid organisations in Jamaica, only two were initiated solely by an international aid organisation. In the case of The Gambia four of the ten aid-funded projects were initiated by international aid organisations. In both countries the exclusion of local personnel from the implementation process had a direct impact upon a project's implementation. For example, the project Education and Entrepreneurship at the EXC, in Jamaica, failed to achieve its stated objectives because local personnel were not involved; and the exclusion of Gambian personnel from formulating project proposals for the RVTP (I) resulted in the project being based on cultural assumptions that were alien to the context in which the project was being implemented.

It was also clear from the analysis that local TVET officials in The Gambia were more likely to be excluded from the initial stages in the development of a project than their counterparts in Jamaica. The greater involvement of Jamaican personnel may be explained by the fact that the country has a longer history of implementing aid projects and perhaps more experience. Nevertheless, the involvement of Jamaican personnel in aid projects, raises the question of whether overseas aid has become institutionalised in the country, or whether TVET institutions have improved their managerial capacity, and what are the corresponding implications for reducing dependency or encouraging it?

However, at the same time it should be pointed out that international aid organisations will only fund projects if certain conditions are met by the recipients in the Third World. Indeed, Third World countries receiving aid are facing an increasing and elaborate array of red, green and blue conditionality (Westlake, 1992). The emphasis on equitable development has seen aid organisations emphasise projects which enhance the role of women (red conditionality). The green conditionality places emphasis on

130

projects which support environment-friendly developments, and blue conditionality is concerned with moving countries towards democracy and political pluralism. Examples of the red and green conditionality were apparent to varying degrees in both Jamaica, and in The Gambia. All of this suggests that it is the international aid organisations that are instrumental in determining which project proposals are likely to receive funding, and the way in which Third World governments need to respond accordingly. There may be some political reasons for guiding Third World countries in certain directions. For example, with the end of the cold war, international aid organisations can no longer continue to support authoritarian regimes just because they are anti-Communist (Harber, 1994). Instead aid agencies are more prone to support democratic societies and exert pressure for democracy, which together with the creation of accountable and representative political systems, can only help governments in the Third World to implement successfully aid-funded TVET projects.

Not withstanding the level of control over the initiation of projects by the aid agencies, the question still remains of the control of the relationship between the aid agency and the recipient in terms of the establishment or otherwise of dependency factors. Crucial to an understanding of this relationship are not only the motives of the donor at the initiating stages, but also, the level of dependency established during the management and implementation stages.

Dependency at the management and implementation stages

Local TVET personnel were involved in managing the majority of projects that were implemented in Jamaica and in The Gambia. However, the local TVET personnel only played a limited role in identifying the project components. Indeed, the present study found that there was only one project in The Gambia, and two projects in Jamaica where the project components were identified by the local TVET personnel. What this seems to indicate is that no matter how well the initiation process is designed, dependency can be generated at the subsequent stages of the implementation process.

Often the dependency of projects on the First World for technical equipment and machinery is probably justified given the level of industrial development in both Jamaica and The Gambia (King, 1991). But it is questionable whether aid-funded projects should be completely dependent on educational materials from the First World or on foreign consultancies. It was clear from the case study data that TVET institutions in Jamaica did have the necessary capability for producing educational materials for use in aid projects. Also, there were probably qualified Gambians who could have played a more active role in implementing the aid-funded projects.

The decision by aid agencies to use foreign consultants had a direct impact on the projects investigated. Indeed the uncritical promotion of foreign educational models by aid agencies can lead to problems in managing the implementation of aid projects. For example, in Jamaica the dependence of the CIDA phase I project on the supposed expertise of foreign consultants resulted in the project not being implemented in its intended form. The

131

World Bank Education III project also experienced implementation difficulties because the foreign consultants failed to provide the expected technical support. In The Gambia, the dependence of projects on overseas aid and foreign components also resulted in implementation problems. In the case of the Rural Vocational Training Project (I), the EEC withdrew funding half way through its implementation, resulting in the project being implemented in a modified form. The difficulties associated with the RVTP (I) were also related to another factor, namely, the design of the project. According to Craig (1990), if the design of an education project is overambitious, or is based on unrealistic expectations, then the project will have difficulty in achieving its stated objectives. In this respect, the objective of the RVTP(I) to provide skills training to 135,849 villagers by the end of the 1980s was in all probability overambitious.

All of this evidence indicates the degree to which recipients are dependent on decisions made by donors at the management and implementation stages. Whatever the donor's justification for controlling the implementation process during these stages, such as the need to achieve certain goals within specific time periods, the overall effects of dependency need to be examined over a longer time period. In this respect, the problems associated with dependency might be outweighed by the overall benefits to accrue to an institution, from implementing an aid-funded TVET project. But the important issue is how to move from dependency to independent market-related decision-making processes.

The overall effects of a project on the institution where it was implemented

The majority of the aid-funded projects studied appeared to have a positive impact on the TVET institutions where they were implemented. For example, the projects upgraded equipment at these institutions, developed new and higher level courses, localised existing courses and upgraded the skills of existing staff. However, some of the projects failed to achieve their longer term objectives, and in the case of Jamaica had what could be regarded as a distorted effect on the institutions where they were implemented. Hence, the dependence of CIDA's Education and Entrepreneurship project, and of the Basic Skills Training Project, on overseas components resulted in the development of First World enclaves at the institutions where they were implemented. Attempts by international organisations (whether deliberate or unintentional) to replicate conditions in the First World, resulted in these projects failing to achieve their stated objectives. Indeed the CIDA project failed to develop any of the hoped for entrepreneurs and the BSTP had difficulties in supplying the garment construction factories with the quantity of skilled labour that they required.

The implementation of aid-funded projects and their isolation from the country's educational infrastructure have been identified by King (1991) as one of the major limitations of overseas aid. Furthermore, King argues that owing to the austerity of the socio-economic conditions in which projects are implemented, funding agencies, such as the World Bank, have to continue funding projects even after their original completion dates had passed. Examples of projects, in Jamaica, which required additional time for their implementation were the CIDA projects and the World Bank (III) project; and in The Gambia, the ODA I and the ODA II projects, the World Bank (II) project and the Rural Vocational Training Project(I).

However, the failure of aid-funded projects in The Gambia to achieve their stated objectives is more likely to be related to the country's economic and political infrastructure, than to the overseas components and foreign assistance on which the projects depended. For example, although the two ODA funded projects financed the equipping of two computer laboratories at the GTTI, the Institute lacked the necessary staff to maintain or repair this equipment; the effect of this was apparent when the installed networking system ceased functioning and the Institute's students were unable to take the practical part of their RSA examinations. Given these conditions the project did not have the beneficial impact that was originally intended.

The analysis of the data in the two countries also indicated the negative effects of training TVET staff at institutions overseas. Indeed, the prominent dependence of TVET personnel in Jamaica, and in The Gambia, on project-based scholarships prevented institutions in either of these countries establishing a full programme of staff development based on identified local needs. Furthermore, the dependency of the GTTI on overseas institutions for staff development has resulted in some of the lecturers regarding local forms of staff development as somewhat inferior.

This raises questions about the efficacy of aid-funded TVET projects on the dependent TVET institutions. But what about the effects of locally funded projects on TVET institutions? An interesting observation was that the TVET projects funded by the Jamaican government itself appeared to be concerned with modifying the negative effects of the aid-funded projects in the country after the latter had been implemented. However, these locally-funded projects in Jamaica were less likely to experience problems during their implementation than the aid-funded projects, and were more likely to have a beneficial impact on the institution where they were implemented. Examples of beneficial projects included the one which provided entrepreneurship training to students from the Garmex Academy who wanted to work in the local economy.

Turning next to The Gambia, the four projects that were initiated locally, were nevertheless dependent on overseas aid and specifically on foreign project 'components' for their implementation. Furthermore, the locally funded projects in The Gambia also experienced difficulties in achieving their longer term objectives owing to what has been termed the *underdeveloped* nature of the country's economic and political infrastructure.

Thus, the evidence suggests that it is far too simplistic to evaluate the development of a project at any particular point of delivery. In the end, the project needs to be considered in terms of its overall achievements in the long run. But this raises the question of how long is the long run? However one looks at it, one is still left with the problem of understanding the implementation process; a process which itself may be totally undermined by a country's inadequate economic and political infrastructure. As a consequence, if these conditions are not accounted for in a project's design then dependency may be automatically built in.

The influence of the economic and political infrastructure

So far in this chapter the theme of dependency has been the focus, and this has been evaluated using a framework of implementation stages (initiation, management and implementation, and the overall effects). But this framework has shown that in order for effective implementation to occur, the project design needs to take into account the different political and economic conditions. Indeed, it cannot be taken for granted that the donor country's economic and political environment exists in the recipient country. For example, North Western European countries have political infrastructures which support their development; this is achieved through the provision of a rule of law, and the maintenance of political stability; also by the promotion of a national sense of identity, all of which are essential to economic and commercial activity. They also have developed road networks, a regular and stable supply of electricity and water, good telecommunication systems and the existence of financial markets.

In contrast to the countries in North Western Europe, The Gambia's economic infrastructure is relatively underdeveloped, a fact which explains why that infrastructure affected projects that were implemented in the country. For example, because of the underdeveloped road system in The Gambia (there is one major trunk road and this is only seven miles long!) the RVTP(I) experienced difficulties in moving building materials, often a distance of over 100 miles, from Banjul to villages in the provinces, where the In-Village Training Centres were being built. The problems with the RVTP(I) were compounded by the absence of a developed monetary economy in the rural provinces, with the consequence that the RVTC instructors had to travel 120 miles each month to collect their wages.

Other effects of the poor infrastructure in The Gambia (such as the impact of irregular supplies of electricity) were evident at the GTTI where the ODA had established two computer laboratories. According to senior GTTI managers, owing to the frequent cuts in electricity supply, and the sudden surges in voltage, the Institute had to purchase two standby generators, and several voltage stabilisers. But although this equipment may have solved one problem, it created another since The Gambia lacks the necessary qualified personnel to repair the machinery; and another consideration is that the new equipment has raised the cost of providing courses in information technology owing to the Institute's higher overhead costs.

In contrast, the analysis of the Jamaica data revealed that there were no projects which experienced implementation difficulties because of the country's economic infrastructure. Indeed, unlike The Gambia, Jamaica has a relatively advanced infrastructure, and consequently the implementation of TVET projects in Jamaica were in any case less likely to experience difficulties.

The political infrastructure also had a major influence on TVET projects which were implemented in The Gambia and in Jamaica, although the political nature of the state and its influence were quite different in the two countries. For example, the state in The Gambia can be seen as a false structure imposed on the country by its former colonial power (Sandbrook, 1989; Clapham, 1990; Ayittey, 1992). On achieving independence, the composition of the state changed and the former colonialists were replaced by a local indigenous elite. Nevertheless, despite the changes in its composition, the function of the state remained the same, namely to extract resources from the domestic economy (Sandbrook,1989). Subsequently, some of the extracted resources were then used by indigenous politicians and civil servants to achieve private goals or as a form of political patronage, rather than to support the country's development (Sandbrook, 1989).

The issue of 'patronage' needs to be considered within the context of the fragile nature of the state in Sub-Saharan Africa. For example, the majority of states are fragile owing to the lack of shared values between those who operate the state (that is, the civil servants) and the rest of society who live in the rural areas and/or work in the informal sector. Without the shared values of citizenship the state faces the continual problem of having to achieve and maintain legitimacy (Clapham, 1990). This problem of legitimacy has been described by Harber (1994) as a lack of articulation between the state and the nation; whereby the state is an apparatus which rules over a particular geographical area, and a nation consists of a group of people who share common attitudes and values, and a common religion.

The issue of legitimacy becomes more severe in African countries which lack a democratic political system. Even The Gambia, which held elections after independence and until the early 1990s, cannot be regarded as having a developed democracy since there are no true 'multi-party' elections in the country. Indeed, Sandbrook (1986) has described the political complexion of The Gambia as a 'pseudo-democracy'. Furthermore, overseas aid is viewed as playing a prominent role in perpetuating this system since such aid provides lucrative opportunities for those working in the post-colonial state to engage in patronage and corruption (Clapham, 1990). Although the above may seem to be an extreme description of the state in Africa, it nevertheless suggests why resources may have been mis-managed locally in The Gambia under the RVTP(I), and why difficulties were experienced with the RVTP(I)'s equipment.

The state had also impinged on the implementation of TVET projects in Jamaica, although the implementation process was more likely to have been affected by external influences (such as the use of foreign consultants or equipment) than by the political system of the country. Jamaica has a genuine two party political system (with competitive elections), which in many ways resembles the classic Westminster system (Huber, 1993). In such a developed political system there are more likely to be checks and balances for accountability, and consequently civil servants are less likely to use their office for private gain. Also, the state is given more legitimacy due to the competitive elections, and so it is argued, the public service officials are less likely to engage in patronage (Clapham, 1992). Under these conditions the ruling administration was more likely to be concerned with development goals, than solely with the issue of legitimacy. Nevertheless, the state in Jamaica could still have an unexpected impact on the implementation process, as was shown in the Basic Skills Training Project. When this project was initially implemented one of its major objectives was to upgrade the country's Industrial Training Centres and the MYCD's apprenticeship scheme. However, three years later the mandate of the project had changed and it became concerned with supporting the construction of the HEART Academies, and also in establishing a school leavers programme. This sudden change in the project's mandate relates to the fact that a general election was held at the start of the project's implementation, and that the newly elected party was attempting to make its mark on society by changing the aims and objectives. This behaviour of the Jamaican state is evident in other areas of the country's public policy. For example, the Manley airport in the country's capital Kingston was named after a former prime-minister, Michael Manley.

All of the evidence presented so far suggests that TVET projects need to be considered in terms of their articulation within the local cultural, economic and political environment. It is therefore curious that not just the construction of project proposals, but also their monitoring and evaluation quite often take place in a cultural, economic and political vacuum. When this happens the creation of dependency is much more likely, indeed whether consciously or unconsciously, the donor is generating built in dependency.

The appropriateness of the dependency concept

In sociological literature, dependency theory is often criticised for being too deterministic and for focusing on external conditioning factors at the expense of internal ones. Given these reasons, Noah and Eckstein (1992) argue, from a survey of its use in educational literature, that dependency theory can only make a limited contribution to the study of comparative education. This view is further endorsed by Craig (1990) who dismissed the approach in a World Bank publication. Nevertheless, the present study has highlighted the usefulness of the dependency concept in analysing how both internal and external factors influenced the implementation of TVET projects in Jamaica and in The Gambia. Furthermore, in using this concept the present study has revealed that it also has numerous facets, ranging from imposed dependency to dependency reversal. By looking briefly at each of these facets we are able to further refine the concept of dependency.

At one end of the spectrum is *imposed dependency* which occurs where overseas aid agencies impose projects on TVET institutions in the Third World. In this type of dependency, local TVET personnel are not involved either in initiating the project or in managing its implementation. The project serves the need of the donor, and is completely dependent on the use of educational materials from the First World, and/or foreign consultants,

136

for its implementation. Examples of imposed dependency were apparent with the CIDA Education Phase I project.

A second facet of dependency, identified in the present study, was *perpetual dependency*. This occurs when a project is not sustainable on its own and requires additional, and continual overseas aid over a long period of implementation. This type of dependency may result from the way in which a project's resources were managed locally during implementation, as was apparent with the RVTP(I) in The Gambia. Alternatively, perpetual dependency may result from the decision of an overseas aid agency to continue funding projects at a specific institution under the policy of Institutional Building in Third World countries. The risk with perpetual dependency, however, is that the implementation of such a policy can lead to the development of a 'dependency culture' in which the Third World institution fails to develop its own capacity to implement projects.

Closely related to perpetual dependency is *ideological dependency*. The concept of ideological dependency is drawn from Sklair's (1992) theory of the global system and is used to describe the process whereby products manufactured in the First World are regarded as superior to those manufactured in the Third World. In the case of TVET, ideological dependency occurs where the qualifications awarded by examining or validating bodies in the First World, or the training provided by TVET institutions in the First World, are regarded as superior to those provided by institutions in the Third World. Some academics prefer to use the term *cultural dependence*, rather than ideological dependence, in order to explain the influence that overseas training and foreign consultants have on the attitudes and aspirations of people in the Third World (see, for example Leach, 1994).

A fourth facet identified in the study was *self-imposed dependency*. This occurs when a TVET institution in the Third World is responsible for putting itself unnecessarily into a position of dependency on overseas aid (or on foreign consultants) through a deliberate policy decision (by its institutional managers) to use the institutional resources of the First World, or to draw on additional sources of overseas aid. An example of 'self-imposed dependency' was apparent in The Gambia in its provision of staff development for the GTTI's lecturers.

Another facet, *reciprocal dependency*, occurs when donors and recipients benefit mutually from the implementation of projects. The concept of reciprocal dependency also brings into question the issue of mutual collusion and the relationship between an aid agency, an institution in the First World, and an institution or ministry in the Third World. For example, a Higher Education institution in the First World may be partially dependent in financial terms on the recruitment of students from the Third World for certain courses, and the aid agency will provide the necessary funding for these overseas students.

Finally, at the other end of the spectrum is *dependency reversal*. As the term applies this situation refers to cases of TVET institutions that were once dependent on overseas aid and have now reversed that situation, or are in the process of doing so (Frobel *et al*, 1980). For example, a technical

137

training institution in the Third World might wish to reduce its dependence on overseas awarding bodies such as the City and Guilds Institute of London by localising the examinations. A TVET institution in the Third World could also reduce its dependence on overseas scholarships from the aid agencies through developing advanced courses as a form of in-house staff development. Yet another procedure through which institutions in the Third World can reduce their dependence on the First World is by collaborating with other institutions in neighbouring Third World countries. This allows Third World countries to pool their resources and talents, thereby reducing their dependence on overseas aid and foreign consultants from the First World.

Thus, the examination of the TVET projects using various classifications of dependency illustrates the continued value of this concept in analysing TVET provision. Having vindicated and improved the sophistication of dependency we now turn to the use of the market approach.

The application of the market approach

This part of the chapter turns to the assumptions underpinning the market approach in the light of findings from the case studies of Jamaica and The Gambia. This will be achieved through focusing upon the provision of TVET by companies and non-governmental organisations. In looking at non-governmental TVET, the chapter comments on the limitations of the market as a means of encouraging private sector provision, and to the importance of support from either the state or international aid agencies for providing TVET. Then, the chapter looks at the effectiveness, and efficiency, of state support for in-house company training or training in the informal sector; and how various factors such as aid agencies and the state facilitate or impede the non-governmental provision of TVET. In doing so the chapter is able to comment on the complex nature of funding non-governmental provision and the important role played by aid agencies and the state in this process. This also enables us to highlight that it is not only public TVET institutions which are subject to the influence of dependency, but also companies and NGOs.

The provision of TVET by the private sector

The market approach would seem to assume that provided a country has a liberalised economy, including the abolition of minimum wages, then the private sector could play a major role in providing TVET (World Bank, 1991c). These conditions were apparent in varying degrees in Jamaica and The Gambia where both countries have undergone reform programmes to liberalise their economies. Despite this liberalisation, of the private companies visited in Jamaica, and in The Gambia, none provided a formalised programme of TVET which was completely independent of state

138

support or overseas aid. In fact, the evidence points to the contrary because the only companies which provided formalised TVET were those which had received considerable state support or financial assistance from overseas aid. For example, in The Gambia, the companies with the best equipped training centres and classrooms were at the government owned utilities; and the funding for their construction and technical equipment was provided by international aid organisations. Also the majority of private companies in Jamaica which provided on-the-job training received support or help from the government.

So, what about the role of the free market as a strategy for providing TVET for those working in the informal sector of the economy? The World Bank (1991) assumes that the free market is the most effective way of providing skills training to craftsmen working in the informal sector of the economy. This would involve leaving the provision of skills to the traditional master apprentice relationship; and if this occurred training would be based on the skills associated with a particular occupation. Consequently, the apprentice would lack the opportunity for general skills development, let alone theoretical study. Furthermore, if there was no market demand for the product associated with an apprentice's skill, then his/her skills would be redundant. In contrast, if the state acted as a provider of training for those who work in the informal sector, and as a marketing agent, as occurred in the case of '*Things Jamaica Ltd*', then craftsmen would be provided with access to continuous skills training that had an identified market demand. Further, if the provision of TVET for those in the informal sector was left totally to the market, some groups would be excluded from acquiring certain skills. Therefore, to give one example, in the case of the RVTP(I), in The Gambia, it was shown that the acquisition of certain skills were related to a Caste type system.

The present study's findings contrast with the apparent free market approach of the World Bank (1991c), which seems to equate free markets with the provision of TVET by the private sector. Indeed, there appears to be confusion over the use of the term 'free market' and the assumption that this is synonymous with the private provision of TVET. For, more often that not, in-house company training is initiated through government funding or overseas aid, as occurred in the case of the GUC and the GPTC in The Gambia. Furthermore, private organisations do exist even in an economy organised by centralised planning. For example, private organisations operate quite effectively in totalitarian states, such as in parts of China (Sklair, 1991). The World Bank's approach appears questionable given the increasing emphasis on the provision of state funded TVET in Europe (Funnel and Muller, 1991). Also, evidence from recent studies shows that the success of the Korean economy's initial take-off was made possible, not only by the abundance of cheap labour and an unregulated labour market, but by the availability of skilled manpower generated by government initiated vocational training programmes (Asian Development Bank, 1991).

The findings from the case study data suggest that it is not so much a matter of the role of the market in the provision of TVET, as a matter of the responsiveness of institutions, whether they are private or public, to labour market development needs (FEU, 1987). In this respect we now re-assess the effectiveness, and efficiency, of organisations TVET programmes for supporting private organisational delivery.

The effectiveness and efficiency of TVET programmes

In Jamaica a variety of methods were used to support the provision of in-house company training and TVET in the informal sector. As can be recalled from Chapter 3, the government supported in-house company training using a school leavers programme and an apprenticeship scheme. Additional support was provided by departments at CAST and by the TMI, and included the design and delivery of modules for companies. Neither the government's school leavers programme nor its apprenticeship scheme was a very effective means of supporting in-house company training. There are a variety of reasons for this and the data analysis suggested one of the major reasons was that these schemes were not responsive to market conditions. For example, the SLP failed to provide adequate incentives to attract school leavers, despite the fact that companies were willing to employ trainees under the SLP. Similar circumstances occurred under the government's apprenticeship scheme; here companies did not want to employ apprentices under the government's scheme because the period of apprenticeship was too long and the scheme lacked the appropriate incentives for companies to do so. The most effective means of supporting in-house training in Jamaica came from the Tool Makers Institute (TMI) and from academic departments at CAST. Their effectiveness probably relates to their autonomy (in decision-making) from the state, and to their corresponding ability to earn revenue from providing tailor-made TVET modules for private companies.

The organisation responsible for supporting training in the informal sector was *Things Jamaica Ltd.* The organisation was not privately owned, nevertheless it did operate as a limited company. The analysis suggested that Things Jamaica was effective at expanding the provision of training for those working in the informal sector. However, the efficiency of the organisation was deemed questionable as instructors were not trained teachers; as a consequence the rural communities were not provided with adequate skills training. Presumably, the company could become more efficient by allowing its instructors to attend a formal course of teacher training at CAST.

In relation to the issue of efficiency, the TMI and CAST in Jamaica proved to be the most efficient at supporting in-house company training because they did not directly use public resources to support this type of provision, but instead used private sector resources. In contrast, the SLP and the apprenticeship scheme could be deemed inefficient since they utilised public resources to support the training activities of large organisations, such as multinational companies and government-owned companies, who would have funded their own training anyway, regardless of government incentives or support. Also, in considering efficiency there is a need to look at the wider effects that such programmes have on a country's development. The analysis also questioned whether the use of government resources to

140

support the school leavers programme or the apprenticeship scheme would have a beneficial impact on the country's development. For example, the analysis questioned the long-term development benefits to be gained from using the school leavers programme as a means of encouraging foreign companies to invest in Jamaica.

Whilst in the case of The Gambia, only two measures were used for supporting in-house company training; a proposed levy, and financial support for state-owned companies. The data analysis showed that the proposed levy might discourage companies from providing training since it would place an additional financial burden. However, the Utility companies, particularly the GUC and GAMTEL, appeared to be a more effective way of expanding in-house company training. As with the TMI and CAST in Jamaica, their effectiveness stemmed from their ability to operate as profit-making centres by providing training for other companies. As regards the issue of efficiency, the analysis suggested that the TVET provision of these companies was clearly efficient, particularly in the light of their contribution to the country's development.

The support for training within the country's informal sector was provided by the DTEVT. As we saw in Chapter 6, this enabled one of TANGO's members - Action Aid - to use the DTEVT's In-village Training Centres. However, this proved counterproductive and was partly responsible for undermining the DTEVT's Rural Vocational Training Programme. Furthermore, it seemed to have created some antagonism between NGOs operating in The Gambia and the government organisation responsible for co-ordinating TVET (DTEVT). This presumably explains why the research could find no formal links between Action Aid, Christian Aid, the Catholic Relief Services and the DTEVT. Furthermore, the analysis also questioned the sustainability, and hence efficiency, of TANGO because the organisation was having difficulties in meeting its recurrent costs. But at the same time it also revealed that the organisation's recurrent costs would be met by a grant from the UNDP. This example points to the importance of the provision of external aid, and indeed dependency, within the informal sector in The Gambia.

So, what can be said about state intervention to support in-house, company training, and training in the informal sector? As in the case of implementing projects at TVET institutions, the effectiveness of programmes to support in-house training, or training in the informal sector, depended on a number of influences. Some of the most important of which related to the way in which a particular programme was initiated and managed. For example, in regard to the issue of initiation, the HEART Trust failed to incorporate adequate incentives into the school leavers programme to attract school leavers. The issue of poor management, was particularly apparent in the quality of skills training that was delivered by instructors at *Things Jamaica Ltd.* But without doubt, amongst the most influential factors, in the present study, were the political motives of the state and of international aid-agencies.

Political motives of the state were particularly apparent with the implementation of the apprenticeship scheme. The analysis in Chapter 4 showed that the apprenticeship scheme was facing competition from the SLP and it appears that the PNP administration was using the SLP, via the HEART Trust, as a means of undermining the MYCD's apprenticeship scheme. The reason for this was to enable the PNP administration to gain greater control over the co-ordination of the country's TVET system.

All of this suggests that the politics of TVET were closely tied up with the complex nature of the state in that country, for as Migdal (1988) has shown, the state consists of a set of agencies and organisations each having its own interests. The relationship between these agencies can prove difficult as was the relationship between the Ministry of Youth and Community Development (responsible for operating the apprenticeship scheme), and the recently established HEART Trust, which set-up the school leavers programme. The relationship, between the SLP and the apprenticeship scheme, was further complicated by the fact that the SLP was established under USAID's Basic Skills Training Project. It is difficult to comment on whether USAID had a direct influence on the PNP's administration decision to use the SLP as a means of gaining greater control over the country's TVET system; but what is known, is that under the BSTP's original mandate, USAID had anticipated that the project would be concerned with improving the co-ordination of the country's TVET system.

However, the influence of aid agencies was more apparent in The Gambia where they initiated and financed the construction of a number of training centres. This evidence suggests that the move towards in-house company provision, particularly in The Gambia, has been guided by aid agencies such as USAID, the World Bank and GTZ. The extent of support of such agencies for non-governmental provision of TVET can be seen by reference to the allocation of ODA funds in the Third World. For example, in 1980, ODA disbursed £11 million for NGO activities in the Third World (which included training); this increased to £25 million in 1990, and in 1994/95 it was targeted to reach £64 million (Booth, 1994). All of which highlights the move towards public expenditure on non-governmental delivery systems for TVET.

Private versus public sector views

The increased emphasis on non-governmental training brings into question why the state either in Jamaica or in The Gambia should want to directly support this type of provision, especially as post-secondary, academic and technical institutions are the means by which states in Third World countries are able to maintain their legitimacy (Hughes, 1994). However, the movement towards non-governmental forms of delivery has been justified by international aid agencies, such as the World Bank and ODA, on the grounds of efficiency and sustainability (World Bank, 1991c; Gray *et al*, 1993). In particular, the World Bank has argued that governments in the Third World are unable to support the recurrent operating costs of providing TVET, particularly in secondary education institutions, and that instead, they should cease providing technical education at the secondary level and divert resources to the provision of primary education. At the same time, if they wish to expand training they should, according to the World Bank, encourage the provision of training by non-governmental organisations.

This approach became apparent in The Gambia, when the majority of senior TVET officials in the country disagreed with the World Bank's decision to cease funding the construction of further secondary technical schools. In particular these officials argued that The Gambia did have the funding and capacity to support the recurrent costs of operating these schools. Furthermore, they argued that this move would have a detrimental effect on the quality of graduates who entered The Gambia Technical Training Institute or the Banjul Skills Centre.

Arguably, this external pressure for non-governmental forms of training is an imposition, and the discouragement of TVET by public institutions, is an example of what dependency theorists called 'neo-colonialism' (Frank, 1981). That is to say, external conditioning influences, such as international aid agencies, are determining the type of TVET provision which occurs in The Gambia. Although apparently initiated by 'free market philosophies', the 'free market approach' rests on the assumption that those working in the private sector are more likely to use resources for their intended use, than those working in the public sector (Todaro, 1989). But in each TVET project or programme, it would be naive to assume that this is the case. The analysis of the school leavers programme in Jamaica suggested that private companies were using funds from this training programme to subsidise their overall operating costs. In point of fact, the misuse and abuse of funds by the private sector is analysed by Martin (1995) who argues that privatisation has all too often led to rich pickings for the unprincipled few.

All of this would seem to indicate that dependency is a relevant concept whether we are talking about public or private provision. However, whilst this may be the case, on balance, the data collected in Jamaica, and in The Gambia, tells a much more confusing and complicated story about the effectiveness of the many different types of public and private resourcing and delivery of TVET. But at the same time, dependency would appear to be a concept which can be applied in the analysis of the support given to TVET systems whether in the public sector or in the private sector. Furthermore, the implied assumption that a 'free market' approach to TVET is synonymous with providing TVET in the private sector is not necessarily so. And finally, it is questionable whether a public versus private dichotomy actually exists in the provision of TVET, because neither type of provision can be seen in isolation from the other. On this point, the evidence from the present study shows that the private delivery of TVET rarely exists without public initiation. As a consequence, there are grounds for assuming that the private provision of TVET is also subject to the undermining consequences of dependency.

From these discussions it is clear that the concept of dependency is applicable to both public and private delivery systems. Furthermore, the present study has shown that it is possible to define a typology encompassing the following types of dependency: imposed, self-imposed, ideological, perpetual, reciprocal, and reversal. It is also important to note

143

that a project may be subject to the influence of one or more types of dependency. However, further conceptualisation of dependency could be developed by considering at what point in time, particular types of dependency began to operate. In this respect the relationship between dependency and time (representing the different stages of implementation) can be represented by the two boxes in Figure 7.1.

These two boxes could provide us with a framework for understanding the relationship between types of dependency and the stages in which they are generated. At one extreme there would be no links between the two boxes, as generally occurred with locally financed projects. At the other extreme there may be many links between the two boxes, indicating when dependency was generated and the type of dependency that was generated. Thus, by examining the stages at which the effects of dependency are observable, that is in the initiation, management or implementation stages, the theoretical sophistication of the concept is being further developed, as it allows us to put together empirical data about past mistakes in implementing projects, which can be used as a reference point to pre-empt ineffective decision-making about project implementation in the future. So, data which indicated that a particular project went wrong at a particular stage can be used to ensure that the same mistakes are not made in future projects. This would necessitate the building up of a data base reflecting the past experiences of projects which have been implemented in the Third World. Although such an exercise would prove expensive, it would probably be less so than the costs associated with projects which continually fail to achieve their objectives, or require additional technical or financial support.

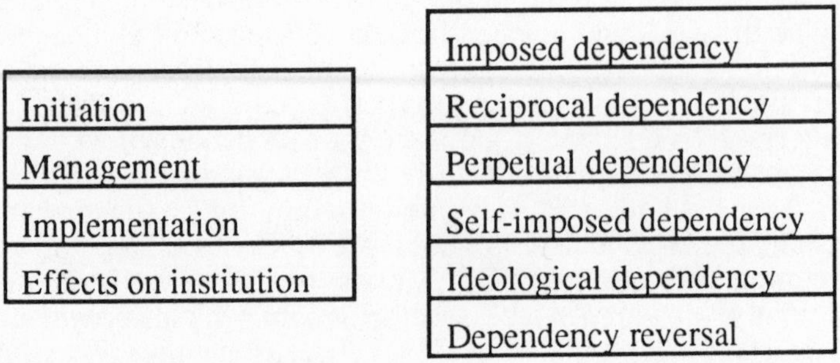

Initiation		Imposed dependency
		Reciprocal dependency
Management		Perpetual dependency
Implementation		Self-imposed dependency
Effects on institution		Ideological dependency
		Dependency reversal

Figure 7.1 The links between the generation of dependency and the life cycle of a TVET project

In conclusion, it can be argued that the concepts of dependency and the market approach provided useful frameworks for collecting and analysing the case study data. However, when the two approaches were considered in the light of key concepts, such as public and private delivery systems for

TVET, a number of questions were raised about their theoretical assumptions. In part this questioning occurred because of the fact that both approaches were too simplistic for dealing with the complexities surrounding TVET provision in the Third World. Indeed, the orthodox political left and the radical right have produced world views which, when transferred to particular events, have proved to be more like ideological differences, than theoretical aids. Nevertheless, the concept of dependency has proved useful and valid for depicting tendencies for projects to move away from an independent, market-led process when making decisions about TVET. Thus, the study has proved to be rewarding in that by following the Weberian voluntaristic tradition, not only have the deterministic tendencies of both theoretical approaches been challenged, but a method has been found for assisting researchers in their analysis of the implementation of TVET policies in the Third World.

Bibliography

Abercrombie, N., Hill, S. and Tumer, B. (1984), *Dictionary of Sociology*, Penguin: London.

Action Aid (1987) Action Aid's strategy for development in The Gambia, Action Aid: Mansakonko.

Adams, A.V. and Schwartz, A. (1988), *Vocational Education and Economic Environments*, The World Bank: Washington DC.

Altbach, P. and Kelly, G. (1984), in Noah, J.N. and Eckstein, M. (1992).

Altbach, P.(1988), 'Introductory remarks on a critical symposium on the World Bank report on education in Sub-Sahara Africa', *ComparativeEducation Review*, Vol.33, pp.93-133.

Altbach, P. (1991), 'Focus on comparative perspectives trends', *Comparative Educational Review*, Vol.35, No.3, pp.491-509

The Apprenticeship Board (1973), *The Apprenticeship Act*, Ministry of Youth and Community Development: Kingston.

Arnove, R. (1980), 'Comparative education and world system analysis', *Educational Review*, No.24, pp.54-67.

Ashton, D. and Green, F. (1996), *Education, Training and the Global Economy*, Edward Elgar: Cheltenham.

Asian Development Bank (1991), Human Resource Policy and Economic Development, Asian Development Bank: Manila.

Association of Canadian Community Colleges (1989), *Evaluation of the Education and Entrepreneurship Project*, The College of Arts, Science, Technology: Kingston.

Ayittey, G. (1992), *Africa Betrayed*, St.Martin's Press: New York, Ch.1-5.

Babbie, E. (1990), *Social Research Methods*, Wadsworth: California.

Baker, C. A. Holohan and Marenga, E. K. (1984), A Joint British Government and Tanzanian Government Evaluation of Training Programme Collaborations, The Overseas Development Administration: London.

Bauer, P. (1991), *The Development Fontier*, Harvard University Press: Cambridge, Ch.9.

Bittaye, A. (1983), *The Place of Technology in Rural Education in TheGambia*, Diploma in Further Education: University of Huddersfield, Ch.10.

Blaug, M. (1967), *Economics of Education*, Penguin: London.

Blaug, M. (1985), 'Where are we now in Education ?' *Economics of Education*, Vol.4, No.8.

Blomsstrom, M. and Hettne, B. (1988), *Development Theory in Transition: Dependency debates and beyond*, Zed books: London.

Bobillier, W. and Cole, J. (1993), *Technical education and vocational training in The Gambia and its financing*, The Ministry of Education, Youth, Sports and Culture: Banjul.

Booth, D. (ed.) (1994), Rethinking Social Development Theory, Research and Practice, Longman group: London, Ch.10-12.

Bottomore, T. (1983), A Dictionary of Marxist Thought, Blackwell: London.

Boyne, I .(1992), 'The apparel sector - still a major player', The Daily Gleener, 30th January, Kingston.

Bray, M. (1990a), 'Provision of higher education in small states: demands, constraints and strategies', *Higher Education Quarterly*, Vol.44, No.3. pp.265-279.

Bray, M. (1990b), 'Economics of Education' in Thomas, M. (ed.) (1990).

British Council (1985a), [*Unpublished briefing report from the British Council to the DNVTP on technical education operations in The Gambia*], British Council: London.

British Council (1985b), [Unpublished report from the British Council to the DNVTP on the proposed programme of activity for technica education in The Gambia- April 12th], British Council: London.

British Council (1985c), [Unpublished letter from the British Council to the GTTI on the condition of the institute's computing laboratory -16th Dec.], British Council: London.

British Council (1985d), [Unpublished consultancy report on technicaleducation in The Gambia] ,The British: Council London.

British Council (1985e), [Unpublished consultancy report on the second workshop for BBC micro-computers at the GTTI], British Council: London.

British Council (1986a), [Unpublished briefing report from the British Council to the DNVTP on objectives for micro-computing work-shop and staff development programmes- 20th Feb.], British Council: London.

British Council (1986b), [Unpublished letter on the subject of BBC micro-computers, from the British Council to the DNVTP-25th Feb.] British Council: London.

Brown, K. (1991), Monitoring visit - under assignment of the Overseas Development Administration, Centre for International Technical Education: Huddersfield.

Brown, K. and Jones, G. (1992), Monitoring visit - under assignment of the ODA, Huddersfield, Centre for International Technical Education: Huddersfield.

Brown, K. and Lewis, C. (1992), Monitoring visit - under assignment of the ODA, Centre for International Technical Education: Huddersfield.

Brown, K. (1992), Monitoring visit - under assignment of the ODA, Centrefor International Technical Education: Huddersfield

Browns College (1986), Education and training for productivity project submission to CIDA, The Associations of Canadian Community Colleges: Ontario.

Bryman, A. (1988), Quantity and Quality in Social Research, Unwin Hyman:London.

Bryman, A. (1989), Research Methods and Organisation Studies, Routledge: London.

Cardoso, F. and Faletto, E. (1979), Dependency and Development in Latin America, University of California Press: California.

The Community Secretariat (1988), Survey of Technical and Vocational Education and Training, CARICOM Secretariat: Kingston, Appendix 1.

The Community Secretariat (1990), Regional Strategy for Technical and Vocational Education and Training, CARICOM Secretariat: Kingston.

Carron, G. (1984), 'Educational planning: past approaches and newprospects', in Hetland, A. and Ishumi, A .G. M. (1984).

CAST (1970), CAST The Beginning, CAST: Kingston, Ch.1.

CAST (1981), CAST The beginning, CAST: Kingston, Ch.3.

CAST (1985), CAST Year Book, CAST: Kingston, Ch.1.

CAST (1986a), Against All Odds, CAST: Kingston, Ch.2.

CAST (1986b), 'A brief overview of the structure, organisation, function and operation of the College', The Jamaican Gazette Supplement, CAST: Kingston.

CAST (1988), New horizons proposals for restructuring CAST, CAST: Kingston.

CAST (1989a), College of Arts Science and Technology Prospectus 1989-90, CAST: Kingston.

CAST (1989b), CAST year book 1989-1990, excellence against all odds, CAST: Kingston.

CAST (1991), College of Arts Science and Technology Prospectus - the way forward, CAST: Kingston.

Catholic Relief Services (1990), Summary of activities in The Gambia, CRS: Banjul.

Chalmers, A. (1994), What is this thing called Science ?, Open University Press: Milton Keynes.

Christian, K. (1990), [Unpublished report on staff qualification at the College of Arts Science and Technology], CAST: Kingston.

CIDA (1992), Rural Vocational and Adult instructor programme draft -proposal, GTTI: Kanifing.

CGLI (1992), [Unpublished memorandum on the localisation of Vocational Examination subjects in The Gambia 1992-94], City and Guilds Institute of London: London.

Clapham, C. (1990), Third World Politics - An introduction, Routledge: London, Ch.1 -5.

Cohen, L. and Manion, L. (1981), Research Methods in Education, Croom Helm: London, Ch.6.

Cohen, L. and Manion, L. (1994), Research Methods in Education, 4th Edition, Routledge: London and New York.

Cole, P. (1990), Implications of the non-formal apprentice system for the development and utilisation of manpower in The Gambia, ScholarshipPaper: University of Huddersfield.

Commonwealth Secretariat (1983), Innovation in Technical and Vocational Education and Training in Island Developing and other Specially Disadvantaged States, Commonwealth Caribbean Regional Meeting Nassau, The Commonwealth Secretariat: London.

Commonwealth Secretariat (1988), *Education, Training and Work, SomeResponses to Youth Unemployment*, The Commonwealth Secretariat: London.

Craig, J. (1990), *Comparative African Experiences in Implementing Educational Policies*, World Bank: Washington D.C, pp.1-59.

Darley, R. and Smith, R. (1985), [Unpublished report on the installation of microcomputers at the GTTI by British Council 13th Sept.], Centre for International Technical Education: Huddersfield.

Darley, R. (1985), [Unpublished progress report on the computing facilities at the CTTI - 4th Dec.], Centre for International Technical Education: Huddersfield.

Darley, R. (1986), [Unpublished progress report on the state of the computer equipment at the GTTI - 10th March], Centre for International Technical Education: Huddersfield.

Darley, R. (1991), Progress report on the ODA II project in The Gambia, Centre for International Technical Education: Huddersfield.

Darley, R. and Macdonald (1991), Micro-computer consultancy under assignment of the ODA, Centre for International Technical Education: Huddersfield.

Directorate for the National Vocational Training Programme (1983), Report on the state of the Rural Vocational Training Programme, The Ministry of Education, Youth, Sports and Culture: Banjul.

DNVTP (1985), The Rural Vocational Training Programme Unpublished report, MOEYSC: Banjul.

DNVTP (1986), [Unpublished letter from the DNVTP to the permanent secretaries office], Ministry of Education,Youth, Sports and Culture: Banjul.

DNVTP (1987a), [Unpublished letter to the Permanent Secretary from the DNVTP], MOEYSC: Banjul.

DNVTP (1987b), [Unpublished letter from the Directorate to the Permanent Secretaries Office] MOEYSC: Banjul.

DNVTP (1987c), [Unpublished letter from the Directorate to the EEC], MOEYSC: Banjul.

DNVTP (1990a), [Unpublished letter from the Auditors office to the Director of the National Vocational Training Centre], MOEYSC: Banjul.

DNVTP (1990b), [Unpublished memorandum from the Director of the National Vocational Training Programme to the World Bank], MOEYSC: Banjul.

DNVTP (1990c), [Unpublished memorandum on the subject of private jobs, from the DNVTP to the NVTC 14th Nov], MOEYSC: Banjul.

DNVTP (1991a), Annual Report of Training Activities in The Gambia forthe years 1988-90, MOEYSC: Banjul.

DNVTP (1991b), Unpublished minutes of a meeting held at the RVTC on Nov 21st, MOEYSC: Mansakonko.

DTEVT (1992a), Financial proposal for vocational training and extension services to promote self employment for the rural youth, MOEYSC: Banjul.

DTEVT (1992b), [Unpublished Minutes from the opening ceremonies of the workshop for the localisation of external examiners], MOEYSC: Banjul.

DTEVT (1992c), [Unpublished letter on consultancies and fellowships under the World Bank II project, from the DTEVT to the World Bank-15th May], MOEYSC: Banjul.

Durkhiem, E. (1984), The Divsion of Labor in Society, Macmillan: London.

Dyer, C. (1994), 'Education and the state: policy implementation in India's federal polity', International Journal of Educational Development, Vol.14, No.3. pp.241-253.

Economist (1994), 'Foreign aid the kindness of strangers', The Economist, May 7th, London. pp.21-26.

EEC (1979), Project proposal for the Rural Vocational Training Project the EEC: Banjul.

EEC (1985), EEC requirements for evaluating vocational training projects in selected countries, the EEC: Banjul.

EEC (1986), [Unpublished letter from the EEC's project office to the DNVTP], the EEC: Banjul.

EEC (1987), [Unpublished letter from the EEC's project office to the DNVTP], the EEC: Banjul.

EEC (1988), [Unpublished letter from the EEC's project office to the DNVTP], the EEC: Banjul.

The Economist Intelligence Unit (1994a), The Gambia Country Profile: Annual survey of Political and Economic Background, Business International: London.

The Economist Intelligence Unit (1994b), The Gambia Country Report, Business International: London.

The Economist Intelligence Unit (1994c), Jamaica Country Profile: Annual survey of Political and Economic Background, Business International: London.

The Economist Intelligence Unit (1994d), Jamaica Country Report, Business International: London.

Eisemon, T.,Elkana, O. and Hart, L. (1988), 'Schooling for self employment in Kenya: the acquisition of craft skills in and outside schools', International Journal of Educational Development,Vol 8. No. 4.

ERNWACA (1991), State of the Art Review - Primary, Junior, Secondary and Non-formal Education, The Ministry of Education,Youth, Sports and Culture: Banjul.

Europa Publications (1994), The Europa World Year Book, Europa Publications: London, pp1600-1605.

Faraja, A .H. (1988), 'Higher education and economic development in south Asian countries', Higher Education Review, Vol.21, No.1. pp.9-26.

Fluitman, F. (1994), 'Some global trends in training policy', TheInternational Journal of Vocational Education and Training,Vol.2 No.1. pp.5-8.

Forrest, R. (1991), 'Lending agencies ripping the nation', The Daily Gleaner: Kingston.

Frank, A .G. (1967), *Capitalism and Underdevelopment in Latin America,*

Monthly Review Press: New York.

Frank, A. G. (1981), *Crisis: In the Third World*, Heineman: London

Frederiksen, B. (1990), *Increasing foreign aid for primary education; the challenge for donors, PHREE back-ground paper series*, World Bank: Washington DC.

Frobel, F. Heinrich, J. and Kreye, O. (1980), *The New International Division of Labour: Structural Unemployment in industrialised countries and industrialisation in developing countries*, Cambridge University Press: Cambridge.

Futher Education Unit (1987a), *Marketing Adult/Continuing Education*, FEU: London.

Further Education Unit (1987b), *Planning Staff Development: Monitoring and evaluation of Staff Development*, FEU: London pp. 1-5.

Funnell, P. and Muller, D. (1991) (ed.), *Vocational Education and the challenge of Europe*, Kogan Page Limited: London.

The Gambia Government (1979), *The Gambia National Vocational Training Act 1979*, Government Gazette: Banjul

The Gambian Government (1992), *The amendments to the National Vocational Training Act 1979*, Government Gazette: Banjul.

Giddens, A. (1984), *The Constitution of Society*, Polity Press: Cambridge.

Glasgow, S. (Nov.1989), 'The extension centre linking CAST to the business community', *The CAST Review*, No.13, Kingston.

Glasgow, S. (1992),'What is the GON-GOJ Micro Enterprise Project?' *The Micro- Enterprise Project News*, Volume I , issue I p.2, Kingston.

The Government of the Netherlands (1990), *Proposal for the Micro-Enterprise Project by the Government of the Netherlands and the Government of Jamaica*, The Government of the Netherlands: Amsterdam, Ch 1.

Godwin, D. (1990), 'Technical education in Sub-Saharan African countries; a review of developments and strategies', *The Vocational Aspect of Education*,Vol.XLII, No.113. pp.91-99.

Goodwin, J. (1997), 'The Republic of Ireland and The Singaporean model of skill formation and economic development', *Centre for Labour Market Studies Working Paper No.14*, University of Leicester.

Gray, L. *et al* (1993), *Cost-effective Technical and Vocational Education in Developing Countries*, Coombe Lodge Report: Bristol.

Grubb, W. N. (1985), 'The convergence of educational systems and the role of vocationalism', *Comparative Education Review*, No.29, Vol.4. pp.526-548.

GTTI (1983), *Proposals for staff development*, The GTTI: Kanifing.

GTTI(1984), [*Unpublished GTTI records the qualifications held by GTTI lecturers during the period 1983/84*], The GTTI: Kanifing.

GTTI (1989), *Staff Development Policy and Scheme of Service for the GTTI*, The GTTI: Kanifing.

GTTI (1992a), [*Unpublished minutes of a special meeting on localisation held Monday 18th May at the GTTI*], The GTTI: Knifing.

GTII (1992b), [*Unpublished letter from the Director of the GTTI to the Banjul Annex instructors*], The GTTI: Kanifing.

GTTI (1992c),[*Unpublished figures of ODAs contribution to micro-computing developments at the GTTI*],The GTTI: Kanifing.

GTTI (1993a), *GTTI Prospectus 1993-95*, The GTTI: Kanifing.

GTTI (1993b), *GTTI's Income and expenditure account for the period ending 30th June 1992*, The GTTI: Kanifing.

GTTI (1993c), *GTTI's Trial Balance as at 30th June 1992*, The GTTI: Kanifing.

GTTI (1994), *Programme Development and staff training schedule1990 to 1995*, The GTTI: Kanifing.

Halls, W. D. (1974), 'Towards a European education system?', *Comparative Education*, No.10,Vol.4.

Hall, W. D. (1990), (ed.) *Comparative Education - Contemporary Issues and Trends*, Jessica Kingsley: London.

Halliwell, J. (1986), *Directory of Further Education and Training in Jamaica*, University of the West Indies: Kingston Jamaica.

Ham, C. and Hill, M. (1993), *The Policy Process in the Modern Capitalist State*, Harvester: London.

Hamilton, G. and Glasgow, S. (1990), *Support for enterprise pathways to success a case study of the Entrepreneurial Extension Centre*, CAST: Kingston Ch 2.

Hamilton, T. and Associates (1989), [*Unpublished consultancy report on the structure of the Jamaican economy*], Hamilton,T. and Associates: Kingston.

Hanna, N. (1991), 'Informatics and the developing World', *Finance and Development*,World Bank, December Edition. pp.45-47.

Harber, C. (1994), 'Ethnicity and Education for Democracy in Sub- Saharan Africa', *International Journal of Educational Development*, Vol.14, No.3, pp 255-264

HEART-Trust (1989), *Annual Report for the HEART-Trust*, HEART-Trust: Kingston.

HEART (1990), *The aims and objectives of the HEART - Trust (unoffical paper)*, The HEART-Trust: Kingston.

HEART-Trust (1992), *School Leavers Training Opportunities Programme* (employers information sheet), HEART-Trust: Kingston.

Hendrikson and Associate consultants (1991), *Review of small scale industries in The Gambia*, Hendrikson Associates: Banjul.

Hetland, A. and Ishumi, A. G. M. (1984), 'Educational Planning in developing countries' in Almquist and Wiksell (1984), (ed).

Hickey, D. (1992), 'CAST's Entrepreneurial Extension Centre: Mandated to Provide Training and Technology Development', *Micro-Enterprise Project News*, CAST, Vol. I, No.1, p.3.

Hinchlifee, K. (1989), *Is vocational training effective ? Considerations of some training routes in Botswanna*, University of Sussex: East Anglia.

Hill, M. (1993), *Understanding Social Policy*. Blackwell: London.

Hogwood, B. and Gunn (1984), *Policy Analysis for the Real World*, Oxford University Press: Oxford.

Holmes, B. (1965), *Problems in Education - A Comparative Approach*, Routledge and Kegan Paul Ltd: London.

Hough, A. (1992a), *Technical Education Management Consultancy; managing quality assurance, under assignment of the ODA*, Centre for International Technical Education: Huddersfield.

Hough, A. (1992b), *Workshop tasks and worksheets sheets on the management of technical education institutions, under assignment of the ODA*, Centre for International Technical Education: Huddersfield.

Huber, E. (1993), The future of democracy in the Caribbean in Pastor, R. and Worrel, R. (1993), (eds) *Democracy in the Caribbean, Political, Economic and Social Perspectives*, London: John Hopkins University.

Hughes, A. (1991) (ed.), 'The Gambia: Studies in society and Politics', *Centre for West Africa Studies*, The University of Birmingham.

Hughes, R .(1994), 'Legitimation, higher education, and the post-colonial state: a comparative study of India and Kenya', *Comparative Education*, Vol. 30, No.3, pp.193- 203.

Hultin, A. (1987), *Vocational education in developing countries*, Education Division Documents no.34, Stockholm, SIDA.

Huseon, T. and Postlethwaite, T. N. (1985) (ed.), *The International Encylopodia of Education*, Pergamen Press: Oxford, Vol.19.

IBAS (1986), *Comprehensive report on IBAS's activiites from 1976 to 1986*, Ministry of Economic Planning and Industrial Development: Farifeeni.

IBAS (1990), *Comprehensive report on IBAS activities*, MEPID: Farifeeni.

IBAS (1991), *Comprehensive report on IBAS activities*, MEPID: Farifeeni.

IBAS (1992), *Comprehensive report on IBAS activities*, MEPID: Farifeeni.

Inkeles, A. and Smith, D. (1974), *Becoming Modern, Individual Change in Six Developing Countries*, Heinemann Part III: London.

Irizarry, R, L. (1983), 'Technological dependence and the failure of educational institutions to support development', *International Journal of Educational Development*, No.3. pp.163-174.

Ishumi, G. M. (1988), 'Vocational training an educational and development strategy:conceptual and practical issues', *The International Journal of Educational Development*, Vol.8, No.3. pp.162-173.

Jampro (1992), *Industrial Training and Engineering Services Division programme schedule for July - September*, JAMPRO: Kingston.

Jennings, D, Z .(1985), 'Education and Productive Work Linkages in the Formal and Non-formal Education Systems of the Commonwealth Caribbean' in Commonwealth Secretariat (1988).

Jobartech, E., N'jie, O., Ceesay , M. and Sarr, B. (1992), *Draft report on strategy formulation for development of vocational education and technical training in The Gambia*, Ministry of Education: Banjul.

Kerneke L. J. (1994), 'Implementing Development Projects: A Paradigm for Decision Making', *International Journal of Vocational Educationand Training*, Vol.2, No.1. pp.9- 20.

Killick, T. (1984), *The IMF and Stabilisation in Developing Countries Experiences*, Heineman: London.

King, K. (1986), 'Education and youth unemployment in Commonwealthcountries', *Labour, Capital and Society*, Vol.19, No.2.

153

King, K. (1988), 'The new politics of job training and work training in, Africa',*International Journal of Educational Development*, Vol.8, No. 3, pp.153-161.

King, K. (1991), *Aid and Education in the Developing World*, Longman: Hong Kong, pp.257-263.

King, K. and Sing, S, J. (1991), *Quality and aid - background paper*, Commonwealth Secretariat: London.

King, K. (1992), 'The external agenda of aid in internal reform', *International Journal of Educational Development*, Vol.12, No.4, pp257-.263.

Kiros, R. (1990), *Implementing Educational Policies in Ethiopia*, World Bank:Washington DC.

Larrain, J (1989), Theories of Development. Cambridge: Polity Press Part 3.

Lauglo, J. and Lillis, K. (1988) (ed.), *Vocationalising Education an International Perspective*, Pergamon Press: Oxford.

Leach, F. (1994), 'Expatriates as agents of cross-cultural transmission', *Compare*, Vol.24, pp.217-227.

Lewin, M. and Stuart, S. (1991) (ed.), *Education Innovation in Developing*

Lewins, F. (1992), *Social Science Methodology*, Macmillan.

Lewin, K. (1986), 'Educational finance in recession', *Prospects*, Vol. XVI, No.2. pp.215-227.

Lewin, K. (1993), 'Investing in technical and vocational education:a review of evidence', *Vocational Aspect of Education*, Vol. 45, No.3, 1993, pp.217-227.

Lindsay, B. (1989), 'Redefining the educational and cultural milieu of Tanzanian teachers: a case study in development or dependency?' *Comparative Education*, Vol.25, No.1, pp.87-95.

Lipsky, M. (1980), *Street-Level Bureaucracy - Dilemmas of the Individual in Public Services*, Russel Sage Foundation.

Magalula, C. (1990), *Implementing Educational Policies in Swaziland*, World Bank: Washington DC.

Majchrzak, J. (1984), *Methods for policy research*, Sage: London.

Maliyamkono, T. (1980) (ed.), *Policy Developments in Overseas Training*, *Eastern African Universities research project*, Heineman: London Ch.1

Maliyamkono, T., Ishumi, A. and Wells, S. (1982), *Higher Education and Development in Easten Africa*, Heinemann: London, Ch1-3.

Manley, M. (1982), *Jamaica's Struggle in the Periphery*, Media Ltd/Writers: Kingston.

Marshall, A. (1994), 'Economic consequences of labour protection regimes in Latin America', *International Labour Review*, Vol.133, No.1, 55-73

Marsden, K. (1990), *African Entrepreuers: Poineers of Development*, The World Bank: Washington.

Martin, B. (1995), *In the public interest? Privatisation and Public Sector Reform*, Zed books: London.

McDonald, B. and Sanger, J. in Powney, J. and Watts, M. (1987) (ed.).

Merriam, S. (1989), Case Study Research in Education - A qualitative Approach, Jossey-Bass: London.

Middleton, J .(1988), 'Changing patterns in World Bank investments in vocational education and training: implications for secondary vocational schools', *International Journal of Educational Development*, Vol.8, No.3. pp.213-225.

Middleton, J. and Demsky, (1989), *Vocational Education and Training: A review of World Bank Investment*, World Bank: Washington DC, pp.64-78.

Migdal, J. S. (1988), *Strong Societies and Weak States: State-Society Relations and State Capability in the Third World*, Princeton University Press: Princeton NJ.

Ministry of Development, Planning and Production (1990), *Science and Technology a National Policy*, Ministry of Development, Planning and Production: Kingston.

Ministry of Economic Development and Industrial Planning (1981), *Five year plan for economic and social development 1981/82-1985/86*, MEDIP: Banjul.

Ministry of Education,Youth, Sports and Culture (1987a), *Outline of Education Policy for The Gambia 1988 to 2003*, First Edition, MOEYSC: Banjul.

Ministry of Education, Youth, Sports and Culture (1987b), *Outline of Education Policy for The Gambia 1988 to 2003*, MOEYSC: Banjul.

Ministry of Works (1985), [*Unpublished letter from the store branch at the Ministry of Works and Communications to the RVTC- 7th October*], Ministry of Works: Banjul.

Ministry of Youth and Community Development (1984*), Report on the state of the institutions operating under the MYCD*, MYCD: Kingston.

Ministry of Youth and Community Development (1990), *Information on Apprenticeship Training in Jamaica*, MYCD: Kingston.

Misiska, F. (1994),'Some practical limitations of curriculum vocationalisation as a remedy to school leavers unemployment: focus on Malawi', *International Review of Education*,Vol. 40, No. 2.

Mosha, H. J. (1990), 'Twenty years after education for self-reliance: A critical review', *International Journal of Educational Development*, Vol.10, No.1, pp.59-62.

Mosley, P. (1991), *Aid and Power and Policy-based lending, vol 2 case studies*, Routledge: London.

Mouzelis, N.(1994), *The state in late development: historical and comparative perspectives*, in Booth, D. (1994) (ed).

National Vocational Training Board (1989), *National Vocationa Training Centre / Gambia Technical Training Institute Annexation Report*, The Ministry of Education,Youth, Sports and Culture: Banjul.

Nettleford, R. (1989) (ed.), *Jamaica in independence - Essays on the Early Years*, Heinemann Caribbean: Kingston.

N'jie, M. (1983), *Vocational and Technical Education in The Gambia The Road- ahead*, MEd dissertation: University of Sheffield.

N'jie, M. (1987), [*Unpublished report on Mr N'jies visit to CGLI-April 21st*], GTTI: Kanifing.

N'jie, M. (1989a), *Entrepreneurial Skill Development Programmes in Common wealth Countries: case study The Gambia*, GTTI: Kanifing.

N'jie, M. (1989b), *Curriculum Guidelines for Entrepreneurial Skills Development*, Commonwealth Secretariat, Ministry of Education: Malaysia.

N'jie, O. (1981), *The needs of technical education and training in The education training system in The Gambia, Scholarship Paper*: The University of Huddersfield.

N'jie, O (1992), *An investigation into how to narrow the gap between manpower needs, technical/vocational training and employment, Scholarship Paper*: The University of Huddersfield.

Noah, J. N. and Eckstein, M. (1992), 'Dependency Theory in Comparative Education: Twelve lessons from the literature' in Schriewer, J (1992) (ed.).

N'yang, O. (1984), *A historical overview of technical education and vocational training in The Gambia*, MEd dissertation: Bolton Institute.

Oliver, G. (1992), *Submission to The National Training Agency on the rationalisation of instructor grades - Part I*, Oliver and Associates: Kingston.

Okwuanaso, S .I. (1985), 'Vocational education in developing countries: What is it worth?' *Vocational Aspects of Education*, Vol.XXXVII, No.96,pp.9-11.

ODA (1987), *ODA draft Revised Project memorandum for The Gambia*, Centre for International Technical Education: Huddersfield.

ODA (1990a), *Final version; ODA project memorandum the National Vocational Training Programme*, Centre for International Technical Education: Huddersfield.

ODA (1990b), *Into the 1990's - An education policy for British Aid*, London: ODA.

ODA (1993a), *Reducing the cost of technical and vocational education*, Research Paper, The Staff College: Bristol, pp.9-21.

ODA (1993b), *Aid to Education in 1993 and beyond*, Education division ODA: London.

Oxenham, J. (1984), *Education Versus Qualifications*, Alien and Unwin: technical and vocational education and training in developing countries: editorial introduction', *Vocational Aspects of Education*, Vol.45, No.3, pp.195-200.

Parks, D. (1986), *The responsive Colllege: A progress report*, Further Education Staff College Coombe Lodge: Bristol.

Parsons, T. (1951), 'Modernisation Theory' in Webster, A. (1984) *Introduction to sociology of development*, Macmillan: London.

Powell, M. (1997), Economic Restructuring and Human Resource Development: A discussion of events in Mexico, *Centre for Labour Market Studies University of Leicester*, Working Paper No.19.

Powney, J. and Watts, M. (1987), *Interviewing in Educational Research*, Routledge and Kegan Paul: London.

Planning Institute of Jamaica (1990), *The Government's five year Social and Economic Development Plan*, Planning Institute of Jamaica: Kingson.

Pressmen, J. and Wildavsky, A. (1973), *How great expectations in Washington are dashed in Oakland*, University of California Press: California.

Project Implementation Unit (1990), *Scholarships to be provided under the World Bank Project*, The Ministry of Education, Youth, Sport and Culture: Banjul.

Project Implementation Unit (1991), *Terms of reference for the design of new resources and training facilities at the GTTI and BSC*, MOEYSC: Banjul.

Project Implementation Unit (1991), *Terms of reference for consultancy on the establishment of a teacher resource centre*, MOEYSC: Banjul.

Project Implementation Unit (1992), [*Unpublished letter from a World Bank representative at the Project Implementation Unit to the Director of the GTTI*], MOEYSC: Banjul.

Psacharopoulos, G. (1990), 'Priorities in the financing of education', *Journal of International Educational Development*, Vol.10, No.2/3, pp.157-162.

Psacharopoulos, G. (1991a), 'Education and work; The perennial mismatch and ways to solve it', *The Vocational Aspect of Education*, No.114, pp.127-132.

Psacharopoulos, G. (1991b), 'Vocational education theory, VOCED101: including hints for vocational planners', *International Journal of Educational Development*, Vol. ll, No.3. pp. 193-199.

Psacharopoulos, G. (1991c), 'Higher education in developing countries: the scenario of the future', *Higher Education*, 21. pp. 3-9.

Reimers, F. (1991), 'The impact of economic stabilisation and adjustment on education in Latin America', *Comparative Education*, Vol.35, No.2. pp.319-353.

Reimers, F .(1994), 'Education and structural adjustment in Latin America and Sub-saharan Africa', *International Journal of Educational Development*,Vol.14, No.2. pp.119-128.

Review Committee Report (*Government of The Gambia submitted to the World Bank Funding Mission*) (Sept.1988), Ministry of Education: Banjul, Appendix IV.

Ritchie, J. (1985), 'The contribution of Qualitative Methods to Social Policy in ESRC Survey Methods', *Newsletter*, Winter 1985/86.

Robson, C. (1993), *Real World Research, a Resource for Social Scientistsand Practioner Researchers*, Blackwell: Oxford.

Rostow, E. (1960), *The Stages of Economic Growth*, Cambridge University Press: Cambridge.

RVTC (1986), [*Unpublished letter from the RVTC to the Permanent Secretary at the Vice Presidents Office*], RVTC: Mansakonko.

RVTC (1987a), [*Unpublished letter from students at the RVTC to the DNVTP 13th April*], RVTC: Mansakonko.

RVTC (1987b), [*Unpublished letter from instructors at Mansakonko to the DNVTP - 8th February*], RVTC: Mansakonko.

RVTC (1989a), [*Unpublished letter from the RVTC to the DNVTP, Mansakonko- 20th July*], RVTC: Mansakonko.

RVTC (1989b), [*Unpublished letter from the Head of the RVTC to the DNVTP 27th March*], RVTC: Manasakonko.

RVTC (1989c), [*Unpublished report on the state of the In-Village Training Centres*], RVTC: Manasakonko.

Samoff, J .(1990), 'The politics of privatization in Tanzania', *International Journal of Educational Development*, Vol.10, No.1, pp. 1-15.

Sandbrook, R. (1986), *The Politics of Africa's Economic Stagnation*, Cambridge University Press: Cambridge.

Sangster, A. (1989), 'Decision makers Sangster looks at 89-90' in *The CAST Year Book*, CAST: Kingston, p.5.

Schriwer, J. (1989), 'The two fold character of comparative education: cross-cultural comparision and externalisation to world situations', *Prospects* Vol.XIX, No.3. pp.389- 406.

Schriwer, J. and Holmes, B. (1992) (ed.), *Theory and methods incomparative education*, Peter Lang: Frankfurt, pp.165-192

Seaga, E. (1988), *A craft development policy for Jamaica. Kingston*, Ministry of Youth and Community Development: Kingston.

Selvaratnam ,V. (1988), 'Limits to vocationally-orientated education in the Third World', *International Journal of Education Development*, Vol.8, pp.129-140.

Sender, J. and Smith, S. (1984), *The Development of Capitalism in Africa,* Oxford University Press: Oxford.

Shafer, S. M. (1986), 'Persistent issues in bilingual education', *Compare*, No.16, pp. 189-197.

Sifuna, D. N. (1992), 'Pre-vocational subjects in primary schools in the 8-4-4 education system in Kenya', *International Journal of Educational Development*, Vol. 12, No.4, pp133-145.

Sklair, L. (1973), *Organised Knowledge*, Paladin: St.Albans.

Sklair, L. (1992), *Sociology of the Global System*, Wheatsheaf: Newyork.

Smith,A. (1973), *The Concept of Social Change*, Routledge and Kegan Paul: London, Ch 4.

Sonko, E. B. (1984), [*Unpublished progress Report on the Rural Vocational Training Programme - Third Quarter*], DNVTP: Banjul.

Sonko, E. B. (1985), *Proposals for the reorganisation of the Rural Vocational Training Centre at Mansakonko, Scholarship Paper*: The University of Huddersfield.

Sonko, E. B (1989), [*Unpublished report on the handing over Jali Training Centre*], DNVTP: Banjul.

Sonko, E. B.(1991), [*Unpublished notes on the handing over of the RVTC, from the Principal of the RVTC, to the DTEVT*], DNVTP: Mansakonko.

Sosseh, B. M. (1991), *Is there the need for developing further the vocational and Career Guidance and Counselling Service in The Gambia, Seminar Paper*: The University of Huddersfield.

Sosseh, B., N'jie, O and Nyang, O. (1992), *Categorisation of vocational education and training establishments in The Gambia*, DTEVT: Banjul.

Steele, D. (1991*), What work requires of schools; A SCANS report for America 2000*, US Department of Labour: Washington.

Stone,C. (1989), 'Policy and Politics in Independent Jamaica' in Nettleford, R. (1989) (ed.).

Sylva (1991), *Indigenous Business Advisory Service's Proposal on Small Industries Promotion*, Ministry of Economic Planning and Industrial Development: Farafina.

Syrimis (1989), *A review of vocational training activities in The Gambia key issues and proposals for action*, Hendrikson Associates: Banjul.

TANGO, (1990), 'TANGO talks', *The Quarterly newsletter of the Association of Non- Government Organisations*, TANGO: Serrekunda.

TANGO, (1992), *TANGO's Tenth Anniversary Souvenir Brochure*, TANGO: Serrekunda.

TANGO, (1993), 'TANGO Talks', *The quarterley Newsletter of the Association of Non- Governmental Organisations*, TANGO: Serrekunda

Tansley, R. (1993), [*Unpublished consultancy report ,under assignment of the ODA, on the localisation of Vocational Examinations in The Gambia*], the International Office: Huddersfield.

Tansley, R. (1994), [*Unpublished consultancy report, under assignment of the ODA, on the localisation of Vocational Examinations in The Gambia*], the International Office: Huddersfield.

Theisen, G. and Adams, D.(1990), 'Compartive education research' in Thomas, M. (1990), (ed.).

Things Jamaica Ltd (1991), *Organisational chart showing the operation of Things Jamaica Ltd*, Ministry of Youth and Community Development: Kingston.

Things Jamaica Ltd (1992), *Budget plan of action for Things Jamaica Ltd-April 1991 to March 1992*, Ministry of Youth and Community Development: Kingston.

Thomas, M. (1990) (ed.), *International Comparative Education, Practices, Issues and Prospects*, Pergamen Press: Oxford.

Tomlin, A. (1991), *Overview of Technical and Vocational Training and Education in Jamaica*, USAID: Kingston.

Todaro, M.(1989), *Economic Development in The Third World*, Longmen: Singapore.

Tzannatos, Z. and Johnes, G. (1997), 'Training and skill development in East Asian Newly Industrialised Countries: a comparision and lessons for developing countires', *Journal of Vocational Education and Training*, Vol. 49, No. 3.

UNESCO, (1993), *Education financing in The Gambia; Analysis and Prospects*, MOEYSC: Banjul.

USAID (1987), Module for machine operators course at the Garmex Academy, HEART-Trust: Kingston.

USAID (1989a), *Evaluation summary of the Basic Skills Training Project, Part I*, USAID: Kingston.

USAID (1989b), *Evaluation summary of the Basic Skills Training Project, Part II*, USAID: Kingston.

USAID (1990), *Project report on the state of the Basic Skills Training Project*, USAID: Kingston.

USAID (1991), *Jamaica Project Paper - Basic Skills Training Project*, USAID: Washington D.C.

USAID (1992), *Basic Skills Training Project, project assistance paper (532-0083)*, USAID: Kingston.

Vasquez, O. and Peluffo, W. (1994), *Privatization and Vocational Training in Chile, Training Policy Studies*, International Labour Office: Geneva.

Verspoor, A. (1991), 'More than business-as-usual: reflections on the new modalities of education aid' in Turner, J (1991) (ed.) *The Reform of the Educational Systems to Meet Local and National Needs*, Oxford Conference Papers: Oxford.

Vice Presidents Office (1986), [*Unpublished letter from the Vice PresidentsOffice to the Permanent Secretary of the Ministry of Works and Communication*], Vice Presidents Office: Banjul.

Vulliamy ,G., Lewin, K. and Stephens, D. (1990), *Doing Educational Research in Developing Countries, Qualitative Strategies*, Falmer Press: London, Ch.3.

Wallerstein, I. (1974), *The modern world system*, Academic Press New York.

Warren, B. (1980), *Imperialism, Poineer of Capitalism*, New Left Review: London.

Watson, K. (1973), 'The monastic tradition of education in Thailand', *Paedagogica Historica*, XIII. pp.415-529.

Watson, K. (1994), 'Technical and vocational education in developing countries: western paradigms and comparative methodology', *Comparative Education*, Vol.30, No.2, pp.85-96.

Webster, A. (1989), *Introduction to the Sociology of Development*, Macmillan: London, Ch.2.

Weber, M. (1971), *The Protestant Ethic and the Spirit of Capitalism*, Unwin University Books: London.

West African Examinations Council (1989), *The localisation of Technical Examiniations in The Gambia*, WAEC: Banjul.

WAEC (1991), *Report on the localisation of Technical Examinations in The Gambia*, WAEC: Banjul.

WAEC (1992), *Assessment guidelines for technical education and vocational training in The Gambia*, WAEC: Banjul.

Westlake, M. (1992), 'Donars demand that the Third World should clean-up its Act' in The Guardian, London.

Wilber, K. and Jameson, K. (1992) (eds), *The Political Economy of Development and Underdevelopment*, Mcgraw-Hill Incorporation: NewYork.

Wilson, D. (1993), 'Reforming technical and technological education', *The Vocational Aspects of Education*, Vol. 45, No. 3.

160

Wilson, D. N. (1994), 'Comparative study of reforms in post-compulsory education and training of young adults' *Comparative Education,* Vol.30, No.1, pp31-47.

World Bank (1978), *Report of the External Advisory Panel on Education,* World Bank: Washington DC.

World Bank (1979), *The Education I Sector Project,* Ministry of Education, Youth, Sports and Culture: Banjul.

World Bank (1985), *The World Bank, Country survey of The Gambia,* World Bank: Banjul P.64.

World Bank (1988a), *Policy Study: Education in Sub-Saharan Africa: Policies for Adjustment, Revitalisation and Expansion,* World Bank: Washington DC.

World Bank (1989a), *The Gambia Education II Sector Project - staff appraisal report first draft,* Project Implementation Unit: Banjul.

World Bank (1989b), *Project Performance Audit Report -Third Education Project,* Ministry of Education, Youth, Sports and Culture: Kingston.

World Bank (1989c), *Appendix IV of World Bank Technical Committee,* Ministry of Education: Banjul.

World Bank (1989d), *Sub-Sharan Africa, from crisis to sustainable growth a long term perspective study,* World Bank: Washington DC.

World Bank (1990a), *The Gambia Education II sector project - Annexation,* The Ministry of Education, Youth, Sports and Culture, Banjul.

World Bank (1990b), *Staff Appraisal Report, The Gambia Education Sector Project,* World Bank: Washington DC.

World Bank (1990c), *Project Completion Report Jamaica - Third Education Project,* World Bank: Washington DC, Ch2.

World Bank (1991a), *Third Education Project in Jamaica - Draft Project Programme Audit Report,* World Bank: Washington DC.

World Bank (1991b), *Annual report,* The World Bank: Washington DC, p.56.

World Bank (1991c), *Vocational and Technical Education and Training,* The World Bank: Washington DC.

World Bank (1991d), *Third Education Project in Jamaica - Draft Project Programme Audit Report,* The World Bank: Washington DC, Ch 1.

World Bank (1992a), *[Unpublished letter, from the World Bank to the DTEVT on the subject of consultancies under the Education II project],* MOEYSC, Banjul.

World Bank, (1993), *Annual Report,* The World Bank: Washington DC.

Witter, M. and Claremont, K. (1990), 'The informal economy in Jamaica some empirical exercises', *Institute of Social and Economic Research University of West Indies,* Kingston.

Yee, I. (1991), 'Export opportunities going to waste', *The Sunday Gleaner* Sept. 22nd: Kingston.

Yin, P. Y. (1989), *Case Study research design and methods,* Sage publications: London.

Yin, P Y. (1993), *Applications of case study research,* Sage publications: London.

Index

163